D0429079

Praise for
Why Simple Wins
and Lisa Bodell

"*Why Simple Wins* makes a compelling case against the scourge of complexity. Lisa Bodell shows that simplification can be the competitive advantage of our time, helping us to be more innovative, more adaptable, and better positioned to thrive and truly have an impact."
—Arianna Huffington, author of
Thrive and *The Sleep Revolution*

"Americans work among the longest hours of any advanced economy. We're time starved, busy, burned out, and disengaged at work. But far from throwing up her hands in despair, Lisa Bodell uses compelling real world stories, eye-popping statistics, and practical hands-on tools to show how work itself has become too complex and how simplifying can help reclaim what's gotten lost: time for work that matters. *Why Simple Wins* is a must-read for twenty-first century workplaces."
—Brigid Schulte, award-winning journalist and author of the
New York Times best-seller *Overwhelmed: How to Work,
Love, and Play When No One Has the Time* and
director of the Better Life Lab at New America

Once again, Bodell hits the bullseye; this time with *Why Simple Wins*. She presents a compelling case that complexity is killing organizations— backed up with stone-cold data—and then delivers practical and effective tools to enable leaders to make simplification a habit. True to her message, Bodell conveys it all through the use of storytelling.
—Camille Mirshokrai, Managing Director, Leadership
Development and Succession Planning - Accenture

WHY
simple
WINS

WHY
simple
WINS

Escape the Complexity Trap and
Get to Work That Matters

LISA BODELL

bibliomotion
inc.

First published by Bibliomotion, Inc.
711 Third Avenue, New York, NY 10017, USA
2 Park Square, Milton Park, Abingdon, Oxon OX14 4RN, UK

Bibliomotion is an imprint of the Taylor & Francis Group, an informa business

ISBN 978-1-62956-129-5 (hbk)

CIP data has been applied for.

To **Lindsey,** who fills me with joy.

To **Jack,** who warms my heart.

To **Brian,** who calms my mind.

Thank you for always reminding me that it's the simplest pleasures in life that matter.

I love you all very much.

Contents

Introduction   xi

CHAPTER 1: Creating the Monster   1

CHAPTER 2: The "What" and "Why" of Complexity   19

CHAPTER 3: Gauging Your Complexity Problem   39

CHAPTER 4: Work That Matters   57

CHAPTER 5: The Simplicity Mindset   79

CHAPTER 6: The Simplicity Toolkit   97

CHAPTER 7: Become the Chief Simplification Officer   135

CHAPTER 8: Getting Simplification Right   175

Acknowledgments   191

Appendix: 50 Questions for Simplifying   195

Notes   203

Index   215

About the Author   223

Introduction

It's 8 a.m., and as Mike McCall merges onto a traffic-choked highway heading into work, he thinks about how unsatisfying his job has become. It's not the long hours—as a VP of product management at a global technology company, he expects to work hard. It's how little headway he believes he's making. Every morning, he shows up at work hoping to move the ball forward, yet despite ten hours or more of solid effort, he constantly leaves feeling as though he *got nothing done.*

As an example: for more than a week, Mike has come to work early with a single, critical "must-do" on his agenda: developing a long-term product strategy to meet the revised growth targets set for his business unit. Business hadn't been going as well as expected, and plans had to change. His unit hadn't contributed the sales it had expected, and management had to find new channels for growth immediately. Strategic insight is why Mike was hired and where he knows he can really add value—as the boss tells him, given how increasingly competitive their market is, he needs to "think big and think ahead." But despite his best efforts, Mike continually gets swept up in a tornado of unnecessary or overly complicated tasks. How much strategizing did he get done this week? Zero.

The previous day, much of Mike's time was swallowed up with—wait for it—unproductive meetings. Five minutes into a morning project meeting, it became apparent that he had no reason at all to be there. His colleague had invited a number of people to provide status updates on a project, but the updates easily could have been provided via e-mail, saving everyone's time. Later, in a milestone meeting for a new technology his business unit was implementing, the manager leading the project spent most of the two-hour session bringing people up to speed (the meeting agenda was vague, so her colleagues had come ill prepared). When the meeting started running over time, several people had to leave, and the group wound up adjourning before there was a chance to recap next steps and timelines.

During ten-minute breaks between meetings, Mike tried to cope with the endless flood of e-mails in his inbox. With direct reports spread out across five countries, he'd been receiving e-mails at all hours of the day and night. In fact, this morning he had seventy e-mails in his inbox from the night before. An additional hundred or more e-mails came in during the course of the day: requests from customers and the product support team; updates and requests from sales, marketing, and finance; numerous announcements from human resources and the executive team; and a whole slew of "FYIs."

After scrolling through the list to determine which messages were truly urgent (not just marked that way) and which could wait, he started to tackle the most important ones first. He knew he could get through several that afternoon while on conference calls; multitasking while on mute was the new normal. No wonder half the time people on these calls asked speakers to repeat things they'd said; they weren't really listening because they were trying to keep up with other tasks.

Around lunchtime, Mike's colleague Jim stopped by to tell him that, based on recent lower sales projections, senior management was asking for a reduction in development expenditures for several of the upcoming product releases. New numbers had to be submitted in three days. Mike pulled up the most recent product road map and began e-mailing his direct reports to get input on what to cut. He couldn't compile the numbers himself; he needed to loop in several colleagues in multiple time zones. Those in Europe and the Middle East had already left for the day, so he had to call them at home. The Asian markets would be up soon and would see his e-mail.

Mike compiled what he could, which took nearly two hours. He then called Jonathan, the product development lead on his product, to loop him in. Mike knew Jonathan would resist cutting anything because the new release was already so far along. Mike felt exhausted from constantly being so reactive; he wished he could think about costs more thoroughly—alternative strategies, pricing options—but there wasn't time.

For most of the afternoon, Mike worked to get the new numbers. Toward the end of the day, he saw an e-mail from human resources informing everyone about an updated hiring policy. While Mike had already received approval to hire three new managers for his team, the new policy required him to submit a revised requisition form that included new compliance information before an offer could be made. Just the day before, Mike had finished interviewing a great candidate and planned to make an offer right away, knowing that this candidate had a competing offer. Now, if Mike didn't quickly resubmit the required forms and get approval—again—by the end of the week, his candidate would likely take the other offer and Mike would have to start all over. Mike took an hour to fill out the form and e-mail it to the required people. By that time, it was after 6 p.m., so he said good-bye to his colleagues and headed for home.

But Mike's work wasn't over. Later that night, after his kids were in bed, he responded to several more e-mails, many of them coming from Asia. He stayed up late finalizing the numbers for senior management and handling an important but time-consuming personal task, a mistake on his health insurance bill that required a half-hour live chat with a customer service representative to sort out. Mike also reviewed his latest personal financial statement, which he always found long, confusing, and complicated. It had been a long day, but all too typical.

That was yesterday. Now, as Mike pulls onto the highway on-ramp once again to head into work, he's feeling even more frustrated. He *never* gets time for strategic thinking, not even early in the morning or late at night. He took this job to work on high-profile projects and develop cutting-edge applications. He imagined himself not just framing strategy, but brainstorming with marketing teams and helping R&D create better, more innovative products. In reality, most of his efforts were encumbered by the highly inefficient ways that people in his organization work. Too much structure, too many outdated systems, too many complex forms for human resources, IT, and accounting. Why was it so hard to collaborate? Why did decisions take so long to make? Why couldn't meetings and e-mails be shorter, simpler, and fewer?

Mike sighs—the traffic is now so bad that he feels lucky to ease his car forward at five miles per hour. Staring at the taillights of the car in front of him, he realizes that this is exactly what his job feels like: he yearns to go faster. He yearns to "think big and think ahead," but he is consistently forced to drive slowly and stay in his lane. Just as he thinks his work might accelerate, he has to put on the brake. He is constantly feeling held back.

By whom? By what?

By *everything*.

Why Simple Wins helps leaders and their teams move beyond the feelings of frustration and futility that come with so much unproductive work in today's corporate world. Mike's story will sound vaguely familiar to many, and strongly familiar to some. So many of us yearn to do meaningful work but find ourselves paralyzed when we try to make it happen. We continually pledge to do things differently, to simplify our work, to get unnecessary tasks off our plate, to shorten our "to-do" lists, but still we don't make headway.

In the chapters that follow, I'll provide concepts, exercises, and tools that help you create corporate cultures in which valuable, essential, *meaningful* work is the norm. Complexity is killing companies' ability to innovate and adapt, and simplicity is fast becoming the competitive advantage of our time. By learning how to cut out redundancies, communicate with clarity, and make simplification a habit, individuals and companies can begin to recognize which activities waste our time and which create lasting value. As low-value work disappears, individuals feel less overwhelmed, more empowered, and more able to spend each day doing things that matter.

Ultimately, I hope to convince you that simplicity isn't just a series of actions to take; it's a mindset. All too often, we embrace a mindset of complexity without even realizing it. With the best of intentions, we value addition, not subtraction, more, not less. We think that more—getting more for our products and services, offering more, building more, creating more—is better for ourselves, our colleagues, our customers, and other stakeholders. But often, it's not. More can become overwhelming, paralyzing, dissatisfying. We add more in an attempt to solve problems; instead we create a monster. To improve our work, we have to move from a mindset of "more" to a mindset of *meaning*. Eliminating elements of our work can enable us to focus and achieve our goals more quickly and effectively.

You might counter that the complexity you and your colleagues grapple with is systemic, out of your control. But is that really true? Some complexity does occur because of external factors such as regulatory requirements or corporate policy. But a great deal of it—maybe even most of it—is created unintentionally by us. We can eliminate complexity and create space for more meaningful pursuits by starting with the parts of our work we can control and expanding from there. And we can perform this simplification on our own, in a relatively straightforward way, and at relatively low cost.

Most people fail to simplify their own work because they don't know where to start. What should you simplify first? How exactly do you do it? It's not surprising that people have trouble: when we first started researching complexity, we were stunned to find that there was precious little out there on simplification, and more importantly, on how to do it. Of course, we knew about many existing processes that have helped companies eliminate waste. There's Lean Six Sigma, for instance, a methodology that many organizations—especially manufacturers—have used to improve collaboration and organizational performance by systematically removing waste. Another option is Agile, a methodology used frequently in software development that emphasizes rapid, incremental, iterative improvements contained in "sprints." In Agile, short daily meetings known as "scrums" are used to improve engagement and help the team manage the change.

If you're seeking to simplify vast, wide-ranging, overly complex processes, then approaches such as these are good options. But what about areas of work that aren't so large? What if you don't have big budgets to roll out established change methodologies and train teams on their implementation? What if you need an ongoing way to improve general work issues or habits?

As useful as they are, Lean Six Sigma and the like proceed from the notion that a formal process is always the most efficient way to get something done. Yet some very basic but important areas of simplification— meetings, e-mail, reports, conference calls—don't need very formal, multistep processes to manage them. In fact, applying a stringent process when trying to simplify these areas can often make things *more* complicated, not less. To make headway, companies and individuals need simple tools to quickly eradicate the mundane, unnecessary, or redundant work that stymies us— tools that don't require a twelve-step program or weeks to roll out, and that don't involve a complicated training manual or certification course.

Looking around for these tools, we found that they didn't exist. So we created them. These tools will do a number of things: they'll help you become aware that you have a complexity problem, identify areas to simplify, prioritize the items to work on, execute on the simplification, and make simplicity a habit. Ultimately, they'll help you escape the complexity trap and get to work that matters.

I'll begin the book by reviewing the problem of complexity, explaining where it comes from and casting light on what is all too frequently lost: work that matters. In the book's second half, I offer tools as well as advice for both senior leaders and more junior people in organizations who wish to simplify. I conclude the book with the inspiring and instructive story of an unlikely, regulated organization that embarked on a simplification journey and, after some twists and turns, wound up reaping significant benefits.

Simplification is one of the most underutilized skills out there, but it's also a skill that any of us can cultivate and deploy. And we *must* cultivate it. In our age of complexity, simplicity is one of the most powerful ways to add value and stand above all the mediocrity and complacency. By simplifying, we can make our organizations more dynamic, innovative, and profitable, transforming them into places where people feel more fulfilled and productive. We can redefine work, departing from traditional norms and processes that at one time might have helped but today only hold us back. And we can make our workplaces more civil, respecting the time and effort people contribute by wasting less of them.

On so many levels, simplification is the *right* thing to do—for our customers, for our colleagues, for ourselves. Complexity, in other words, is a losing proposition—it's simplicity that wins. This book will show you how to make simplicity win for you.

CHAPTER ONE

Creating the Monster

"Life is really simple, but we insist on making it complicated."
—Confucius[1]

It's our most precious resource. More precious than anything else. I'm talking about time. When you've lost an hour, it's gone forever.

Given how precious time is, you would think we would be more deliberate, both as individuals and as organizations, about how we use it. But we're not.

Step back for a second, and set aside all the things you "need" to do today—all the meetings, all the e-mails, all the phone calls, all the bureaucratic forms and processes that require your attention. Imagine for a moment that you could spend the day investing your work time in anything you wanted. What would you do? You would probably choose to work on things that really matter. You would solve big problems, think strategically about how to get ahead of the competition, help brainstorm your company's next innovation.

Imagine what that would feel like—how satisfying it would be to know, when your head hit the pillow, that you had maximized the opportunities you had to learn something new and make a real, discernible contribution at your job. Compare that satisfaction to what you *actually* experience at the end of each day. The sense that, for too much of the day, you're just spinning your wheels. That you're deluged with work, but constantly struggling to get important things done. That you're juggling a hundred balls but still failing to make the meaningful impact you *could* make if the (busy? mundane? meaningless?) work that eats up so much of your day could magically vanish.

Busy, Busy, Busy

Not long ago, if you asked people how they were doing, they'd say, "Good!" A few years later the standard answer became, "Okay." Today, a new answer is the norm: "BUSY." We've made a sport of talking about how busy we are. We compete to be the busiest person in any conversation. "I'm so busy!" is always met with "Tell me about it. My day was crazy. All I did was sit in meetings and put out fires." "That's nothing! I had a conference call that started at 7 a.m. and then..."

We're consumed with what we call "busywork," all the tedious, thankless, but sometimes quite urgent things we have to get done before we can call it quits for the day. These tasks frustrate us, stress us out, exhaust us, and eat up our valuable time, getting in the way of work that matters. A 2013 Gallup global survey found that thousands of employees were so busy they found no time for meaningful activities such as creative thinking, had little chance to do work they actually enjoyed, and didn't realize "a level of meaning and significance" in their work.[2]

Why do we do so much busywork? One cause looms larger than the others: complexity. Wherever you look, work has become more complicated. To get even the smallest thing done, we must navigate through a thicket of *stuff*. We can't help but sit through endless meetings, respond to bottomless scheduling requests, attend to overflowing e-mail inboxes, rush to complete an endless checklist of regulatory mandates—all because rules, processes, and procedures are too complex. Our teams and organizations become bogged down, rendered less productive, less creative, less innovative, less competitive, less successful. Meanwhile, as individuals we feel guilty that we're not giving each challenge the attention it deserves and resentful that our potential to make a bigger contribution is being squandered each and every day.

Technology: A Mixed Blessing

One source of complexity these days seems obvious: technology. Recent advances were supposed to make us more efficient, and in some ways they do, but there's a price for this advancement. Without noticing, we've become e-mail *machines*. We feel obligated to respond immediately to the person who posted his reaction to the latest numbers coming in from China or Europe. As a result, we wind up writing more e-mails that generate more responses that necessitate still more messages from us. It's not that electronic communications are inherently bad, but because we can cheaply and easily convey even the most trivial or unnecessary ideas via e-mail, we decide: why not?

As a result, we now find ourselves spending a good part of our time using e-mail for anything and everything—even if we shouldn't. Its immediacy creates a vicious cycle of "off my plate and back on to yours." And the fact that we *can* share more information on a group e-mail means we *do* share that information, even if most people on the receiving end find the information useless. The McKinsey Global Institute found that people typically devote over a quarter of their time—thirteen hours each week—to dealing with e-mails.[3] In the case of John and Bert Jacobs, who cofounded the apparel company Life is Good, the time spent on e-mails may have been even higher. As they have explained, once their company grew to 250 employees, they were utterly inundated with e-mail. "The time we spent daily just shoveling out our e-mail inboxes was daunting. And we were going to bed at night feeling guilty and inadequate because we couldn't get ahead. The more e-mails we sent out, the more flowed back in."[4]

It isn't just e-mails. The fact that we *can* have a videoconference means that we *do* have a videoconference, even if it's overkill. The fact that we *can* talk and text and walk and eat simultaneously means that we *do* talk on our headsets while texting our children while walking to a meeting while scarfing down our lunch (and maybe even checking Facebook along the way). Bob Moore, director of a software engineering subsidiary of Emerson Electric Company, once noted that when he visited regularly scheduled meetings, 80 percent of attendees had their heads buried in their phones for at least some portion of the two-hour gathering.[5] Researchers at Bain & Company found that when you combine all the ways that

executives can receive communication—phone calls, e-mails, IMs, etc.—
the number of incoming messages the average executive gets has grown
from a thousand each year in the 1970s to more than thirty thousand per
year today.[6]

Multitasking lets us feel like we're getting a lot done—or at least like
we're getting more done than we would have if we had performed those
tasks in succession. But at the end of the day, you have to ask yourself
whether your frantic efforts to fit everything in prevented you from div-
ing deeper into what's *really* important. Evidence now confirms that we're
less effective when multitasking than we would be if we simply focused on
each task one after the other.[7]

The complexities created by technology go further than lack of focus.
Because of our mobile devices, we're always on, everywhere we go. It used
to be that when you turned the light out in your office and headed home
for the evening—or even if you just went out for a quick bite at lunch—
you could leave your office worries behind. With iPhones, tablets, and
Bluetooth, work is always accessible to us, and we're always accessible to
work. The clear boundaries that once made even tedious jobs more palatable have been breached by the fact that the boss can send us a quick
question—and expect a quick response—even when we're having a nice
meal on a Saturday night or watching a new show on Amazon after we've
put the kids down.

Technology has invaded our downtime, and no place is safe. A recent
survey by Accenture found that 87 percent of people who watched long-
form television or movies did so while simultaneously looking at another
device.[8] The time that we once devoted to things that actually matter—
at home, that means helping your kids with their homework or having
dinner together; at work, it means thinking about how to take advantage
of the next big strategic opportunity—is constantly being interrupted by
minutiae, like whether we can pull a few more numbers for a report due
tomorrow "just in case we need them" or whether you can change a morning staff meeting to the afternoon because Julian decided *not* to take the
red-eye back from the West Coast and won't get in until lunchtime. No
barrier allows us to escape the constant churn. The benefits of technology fade away; instead of eliminating tedious tasks, technology winds up
eliminating time to do important things. Everything in our lives seems to
mush together into a stress-inducing stew of complexity.

Calendar Requests Galore

Technology's effects are an instance of what we might call *unintentional complexity*. We don't intend for technology to bog us down, but it does as a secondary effect. Unintentional complexity extends beyond technology. For instance, we spend *way* too much time in meetings that are the calendar equivalents of empty calories. We agree to these meetings over and over and even organize them ourselves, sacrificing time we might otherwise invest in more worthwhile activities. As Elizabeth Grace Saunders, author of *How to Invest Your Time Like Money,* has written: "'Let's schedule a meeting' has become the universal default response to most business issues. Not sure what to do on a project? Let's schedule a meeting. Have a few ideas to share? Let's schedule a meeting. Struggling with taking action? Let's schedule a meeting."[9]

In 2013, organizational analytics company VoloMetrix studied how 7,600 of Seagate's employees were spending their time. What the researchers found was frightening: some of Seagate's employees were losing twenty hours of each workweek to meetings.[10] And Seagate wasn't unique. In a collaborative study of seventeen companies conducted by VoloMetrix and Bain, one stressed-out middle manager learned he was wasting roughly eight hours each week by attending unnecessary meetings and four hours each week to the hassle of reading and responding to e-mails that were, in the end, entirely superfluous to his role in the company. Given all the other time-consuming things he had to do, he could only devote eleven hours per week to working alone on his primary responsibilities.[11]

Researchers at Bain found that of the forty-seven hours the average mid-level manager or frontline employee works each week, twenty-one hours are spent in meetings with four or more people, and eleven hours are spent on e-mails and other electronic communication. Do the math: that leaves less than fifteen hours to get everything else done! Now subtract the unproductive time in between meetings and other obligations and you come to a startling conclusion: "The average manager has less than 6½ hours per week of uninterrupted time to get work done."[12] That's less than *one day* per week.

You might argue that we've always sacrificed valuable time to useless meetings. Maybe, but evidence suggests that the problem is getting worse. A survey performed collaboratively by Clarizen and Harris discerned that average American workers lose as many as nine hours every week to "project update meetings," whether it's preparing for them or actually sitting in the room. That was up 14 percent from what the figure had been four years earlier.[13] Researchers at Wharton and the University of Virginia found that "over the past two decades, the time spent by managers and employees in collaborative activities has ballooned by 50% or more."[14]

Big firms may have it worst of all. Bain & Company has been keeping track of the way managers spend their time since 2008, and their research reveals that the proportion of each manager's day spent in meetings has grown every year—to a whopping 15 percent. The more senior you are, the more that meetings consume your time. The same survey found that leaders of many organizations spend 40 percent of their time in meetings with three or more of their colleagues.[15]

To understand the impact of numbers like these, it's helpful to take a closer look at what happens in specific organizations when meetings are scheduled. Bain studied one large company and computed the number of hours lost to the effects of a single, regularly scheduled executive committee status meeting of eleven unit heads. Because the unit heads who gathered in that one meeting prepared by gathering their own senior advisors, and because those senior advisors prepared for their meetings with their unit heads by gathering their subordinates, the weekly status report meeting of the executive committee actually spurred more than 130 meetings throughout the rest of the company. This cost the company's workforce 300,000 hours annually, the equivalent of $15 million.[16]

It's not that companies shouldn't have meetings, or that strategic planning meetings in particular don't have merit. Employees need to share ideas, electronically *and* in person. And studies have shown that executives want to spend roughly a third of their time plotting out their corporate strategies, or roughly 80 of 240 working days per year.[17] But if those meetings and e-mails and phone calls and conversations are spent trying to untangle knots of complication rather than focusing on the challenges ahead, they aren't effective, and they won't help steer a company in the right direction. Dr. Bill Starbuck, an organizational scientist who spent parts of his career studying organizational planning, found that companies that engage in a lot of long-term planning do no better than those that do less. The difference isn't how much planning you do—it's how well you do it.[18]

Death by Accounting

Besides technology and meetings, another source of unintentional complexity is actually our well-founded desire to solve problems at work. We seek to avoid a danger, minimize a risk, or address a challenge, and so we add a process or a layer of bureaucracy that seems reasonable at first blush. But then another danger, risk, or problem crops up, and we introduce another process to solve it. And another. And another. Before we realize it, our impulse to improve something has left us with a monster of our own inadvertent creation.

One of my clients told me a story he called "The Laundry Decree." Executives at a big financial services firm discovered that some of their consultants were bringing their families' dirty laundry with them on business trips. This handful of consultants had discovered that they could have the hotels wash it for them, on the company's dime.

Executives couldn't tell how many consultants were abusing the company's good will, but no one suspected it was more than 2 or 3 percent. Nevertheless, executives came down hard. They instituted a new cap on the number of shirts employees and consultants could have laundered, and they restricted the privilege to senior managers embarking on long trips. Makes sense, right?

This regulation reduced the fees charged to the company for hotel laundry services, but it produced some unanticipated problems. Consultants and employees traveling long distances—some were traveling to Asia for weeks at a time—now had to wear dirty shirts close to the end of each trip or pay for laundry service themselves. The 95 percent or more of consultants and employees who hadn't done anything wrong had to pay closer attention when they packed, wasting time counting their shirts and worrying that they'd be caught with one starched collar too many. Their lives suddenly became more complex, all because of the sins of a few.

This story is typical in much of the corporate world. The wonder isn't why the company's executives had issued The Laundry Decree—they were responding to a legitimate concern. Rather, we should ask why they laid down the law when so few people were committing the offense. In this case and likely others, the unintended costs of a solution far outweighed its benefits. Very few employees were abusing the privilege, but taking the privilege away made everyone else's lives more difficult. A well-intentioned but needless complication victimized the people who played by the rules.

Performance Evaluations That *Don't* Perform

A classic example of the way organizations inadvertently make life complex in the process of trying to solve a legitimate problem is performance evaluations. Initially, performance evaluations served their purpose rather well—certainly well enough for companies in every industry to deploy them. But as human resource departments have become more data oriented, what once were fairly simple systems for evaluating an employee's contribution have become incredibly complex, capturing a mix of hard and soft skills that are both qualitative and quantitative: sales and profits and kindness and team orientation and attitude and inclusiveness and on and on and on.

For managers, all of this represents more data points to plot, more questions to ask and answer, and more paperwork to complete and submit to HR for review. Meanwhile, the average employee finds it impossible to actually use her boss's evaluation to improve her job performance moving forward. What should Maria do if she wants to improve the rating that emerged from the appointed algorithm? Be more of a team player? Assert herself more in meetings? Follow directions better? Take her own initiative? All these directives cut across one another, leaving the average employee confused, frustrated, and demoralized.

Research has shown that nine out of ten companies do employment evaluations, but fewer than half actually believe that they're effective. As UCLA management professor Samuel Culbert has concluded, "[Performance reviews are] fraudulent, bogus and dishonest. And second, they're indicative of and they support bad management."[19] Indeed, an analysis of

607 separate studies of the impact of performance reviews found that at least three in ten actually diminish employee performance.[20]

Even when performance evaluations don't do harm, they usually waste our time. Aubrey Daniels, a legendary clinical psychologist and an expert in performance management, highlights a study by the Society for Human Resource Management that reveals just what a disaster the system has become. The headline? A full 90 percent of performance reviews are unsuccessful.[21] Worse still, by rewarding workers who are, above all, good at following the rules, performance evaluations discourage employees from harnessing their passion for improving performance. John Hagel III, who cochairs a research arm of Deloitte, argues that passion is a rare and valuable commodity within any workforce, possessed by fewer than 12 percent of United States employees. But "passionate workers often don't play by the rules."[22] Here again you can see how *unintentional* complexity gets in the way of meaningful work.

The Iron Curtain

As the example of performance evaluations suggests, a great deal of complexity arises because it's easier to build on top of the things that we've already established than to blow up what exists and replace it with something simple. In this way, we don't *choose* complexity. We don't ask ourselves if we *want* complexity. Rather, we ask ourselves: What's the easiest way to accomplish the task at hand? What's the most expedient way to get what we need done right now? Our failure to take time *in the moment* to get down to what really matters sets us on the path to complication. When we opt time and again to add more to what exists, we wind up with a web of complexity we can't even begin to fathom.

> Our failure to take time *in the moment* to get down to what really matters sets us on the path to complication.

Decades ago, when change wasn't so constant, the costs of complexity weren't so great. You weren't always looking for a new market to conquer. You weren't always afraid that a competitor would introduce a disruptive technology. So you weren't constantly called upon to modify everything you do on account of change in the marketplace. Today, we *are* subject to perpetual disruption. And in a world with so much change, it's become much more tempting and destructive to add more and more and more without sweeping away what's no longer useful. Who has the time up front to think aggressively about how to simplify? We're all just trying to keep pace.

Drowning in Red Tape

We've been talking about sources of complexity that we create ourselves, but complexity is also frequently imposed on us by outside forces. We've all been sitting in the waiting room at a doctor's office, flipping through old magazines because the doctor is running way behind. Why? Well, maybe it's because the doctor is taking a little extra time with the old man who had the appointment before ours. More likely it's because she's been stuck standing at a counter in the back hallway filling out some useless piece of paper mandated either by government regulations or the insurance industry's red tape.

Regulation is at the root of so much complication—from health care to finance to manufacturing and beyond. A few years ago, Deloitte Australia found that one of every eleven workers in the country's mining industry was working in a compliance role. Separately, a bank reported that compliance costs were skyrocketing—tripling over the course of three years—because regulators were demanding all sorts of new reports. Indeed, during the course of a single year, the bank was required to file more than three thousand reports running to eighty thousand pages.[23]

Regulation has hit banking especially hard over the last several years, but in truth red tape has mushroomed across all sectors of the business world. The National Association of Manufacturers (NAM) studied the costs of federal regulations in the U.S. and found staggering figures: each year, bureaucracy costs businesses more than $2 trillion, the equivalent of $20,000 for each worker and $233,000 for the average American company. Tax compliance alone costs nearly $160 billion.[24] "This...is very alarming, because it shows that more than one-third of businesses' income is tied up in compliance costs," explained NAM president and CEO Jay Timmons upon release of the data.[25] A Vanderbilt University study found that colleges and universities spent roughly $27 billion combined per year on federal compliance, eating up as much as 11 percent of expenditures.[26]

You might think technology would help reduce the burdens created by new, more extensive regulations. Maybe algorithms or databases could automatically produce the information that managers required so that businesses would have the green light to carry on. But as evidenced by the amount of time and money businesses have spent on compliance, regulations are making life more complicated, not less, even with the technological tools we now possess. The burden of proving your compliance has become indisputably heavier.

If compliance staffers alone could handle this burden, that might be one thing. Companies would have to invest a bit more in the size of their compliance departments, and ordinary workers would remain untouched. But that's not what has happened. Regulations reach down like tree roots into every department and process. Everyone needs to be made aware of the regulations, what to watch out for, what they can and can't do, which records need to be preserved and for how long, how the regulations have shifted over the last year, how the bureaucrats want the reports written, when they need them to be submitted, who needs to sign off on them before they're submitted, and how those being regulated will learn about required improvements.

Let's face it: people don't get excited about crossing t's and dotting i's. They don't come to work because it's somehow engaging to file paperwork or report a possible violation. They come to work because they want to contribute to the underlying mission or purpose. They focus because they want to add value. They want to know that the effort they expend and the time they invest are moving the ball in the right direction. To most people, the complexity created by regulations is at best a hindrance, at worst a reason to give up and go home.

Globalized Drift

If all these sources of complexity weren't bad enough, the global nature of business adds to the problem in unavoidable ways. One client explained to me how the team he managed was spread throughout seven different time zones across the world. How could he possibly keep all those people aligned, even in the best of circumstances? People in different countries were going to get on conference calls at odd hours. Memos and directives were going to have to be more comprehensive, since information couldn't be individually tailored and shared in person.

As companies and product lines have become more global, the reporting structures that support them have become that much more convoluted. Today, marketing and sales and IT and customer service and finance and human resources all have overlapping responsibilities and mandates. It's often unclear who should assume the lead on a given project and who should take credit for successes. It's equally unclear who possesses authority to make final decisions. If a whole cross-section of folks has worked collaboratively on a new product, who signs off? Only one department head? Two? What if two department heads can't agree?

All too often, the absence of a clear reporting structure leads not merely to confusion, but to something worse: a consensus-driven culture. No one can move unless *everyone* has signed off, which means few things get done quickly, and many things don't get done at all. People grow fearful, unsure what will happen if everyone isn't looped in and anxious that someone will strip them of whatever small fiefdom they still control. So they schedule more meetings and more calls. They e-mail more colleagues, cc'ing people who need not be included. They seek sign-offs before doing anything adventuresome. They get wrapped up ever more deeply in the web of complication, and they ensnare others around them as well.

Bad and Getting Worse

Given all the forces contributing to complexity, we might wonder how bad the problem has really gotten. The answer has moved beyond pretty bad. It's dire.

Each day, more than one hundred billion e-mails are sent and received, but fewer than a seventh of them are actually important.[27] Furthermore, a study found that four out of every five business interactions either require no follow-up action or will not result in any serious consequences if parties to the interaction do nothing.[28] That's telling: if any real wisdom had bubbled up, you'd expect someone to have made a decision as a result. A McKinsey Global Institute study likewise found that managers at some companies were spending 40 percent of their time writing reports.[29] Say what you will about the value of communicating and coordinating with others, but if you don't have any time to act on new insights or develop good ideas, what's the value of reports?

The Boston Consulting Group has established an initiative to track complexity, building an index based on their surveys of more than one hundred companies on both sides of the Atlantic. What they've found is both eye-opening and terrifying. Over the last decade and a half, "the amount of procedures, vertical layers, interface structures, coordination bodies, and decision approvals needed in each of those firms has increased by anywhere from 50% to 350%. According to the analysis over a longer time horizon, complicatedness increased by 6.7% a year, on average, over the past five decades."[30]

All this complexity is damaging companies' performance. SAP's Global Simplicity Index found in 2013 that complexity destroys a full tenth of company profits every year—or a combined $237 billion for the top two hundred firms around the world.[31] Much of that loss amounts to opportunity costs. The time we waste individually is time that isn't spent growing our businesses or improving our products. The hours we spend in quiet frustration are hours lost to our colleagues and our customers. Our frustrations prevent us from harnessing our creativity and beating the competition. They also cause us to leave our jobs more quickly, costing millions in added recruitment costs. Study after study has found that professionals today are frustrated and miserable. They're also less engaged, and on this count, less productive and innovative. A 2013 Gallup poll found that only 13 percent of employees were actively engaged in their jobs, and 87 percent of professionals did not find sufficient satisfaction at work or weren't focused on creating value for their employer.[32] Gallup has also found that one in five people hate their jobs, and that lack of engagement costs companies $550 billion a year.[33]

It's easy to understand how complexity can cause good, talented people to head out the door. One of my clients related a sad pattern she had noticed in the organizations where she'd worked. At the start of nearly any job, people enter with high hopes. They're inspired, excited, engaged, and energized. For those first six months, they're eager to participate and willing to buck the system in the name of progress. They're motivated to fight for the cause. But then they see what they're up against; they feel the inertia wrought by excessive complication. During the first and second years after they've been hired, they become increasingly frustrated and constrained. They get how the game is played, and they're not impressed. They begin searching for work-arounds to get things done. The bloom is off the rose.

Two years in, these employees are resigned to the reality of excess complication. They say things to new hires like, "This is just how it's done," almost as if they've given up. They don't have the time or energy to fight the system or to try something new. And in any case, why bother? They remember what happened the last time someone tried to change the way work gets done: absolutely nothing. So they carry on in a state of quiet desperation until they just can't take any more. Finally, to save themselves, they leave.

The Simplicity Imperative

The costs of complexity are not news to many executives. More than 70 percent of organizations in a recent study ranked simplification as an important challenge, and more than a quarter cited it as "very important."[34] But too few companies are actually working to address the issue on the ground. A 2014 Future of Work study by SAP highlighted three statistics that, when taken together, convey the scope of the problem: more than half of business leaders believe business simplification is of significant strategic importance to their senior leaders; two-thirds believe that the issue would be even *more* important three years down the line; but barely more than a quarter believe their top management is "strongly aligned" to address the challenge.[35] That's a problem.

> More than 70 percent of organizations in a recent study ranked simplification as an important challenge, and more than a quarter cited it as "very important."

It's not that every company is content with business as usual. Some companies have taken steps to counter the scourge of complexity,

simplifying processes or experimenting with measures to reduce the burden of technology. The Italian company Gabel, for instance, has experi-
mented with banning e-mail for a week.[36] The software firms Intuit and
Atlassian have set aside a certain amount of "clutter-free time" for employees. Volkswagen and Boston Consulting Group have each reworked their
internal policies so that employees can go "offline" during non-work hours,
saving them from being tethered to their smartphones every minute of
every day.[37] Companies like Bloomberg and Google have created spaces
where employees can escape to re-center themselves. While all of these
examples represent some progress, the truth is that the vast majority of
firms still have essentially dodged the problem, taking little or no action.
As of 2015, only one in ten corporations had a major work simplification
program on tap, and fewer than half were working on one.[38]

What many companies have done is up their performance expectations. Regarding time as the employer's most precious resource, they've
tried to squeeze as much productivity out of employees as possible, and
they've implemented metrics to help ensure that people do perform better.
Such measures have only made things worse. Increasing expectations only
pile more stress on the backs of already overtaxed workers, while the pro-
liferation of metrics makes life at work even more complicated. Research
has shown that companies now measure themselves against *six times as
many metrics* as their counterparts did in the mid-1950s.[39] Six times! We
tend to regard data as the answer, yet left unchecked data can also prove
our undoing. Just because we *can* delve more deeply into the data doesn't
mean we *should*. More isn't always more. In a world where it's become
increasingly difficult to sort the signal from the noise, more is actually *less*.

But something else is true: in such a world, eliminating complexity is nothing less than a strategic imperative. We've hit a tipping point.
Although no single shift has produced the complication that inundates
us, complexity in the aggregate has emerged as the single greatest barrier to organizational success. In today's hypercompetitive markets, only
the agile survive, and complexity makes it difficult to keep up. You don't
have time to think—in fact, thinking becomes a daring act. Yet this in
turn spells an opportunity for companies that can somehow wriggle free
of complexity's grasp and achieve more simplicity.

There's no way to strip *every* complication out of each employee's routine. In fact, the value of a given employee hinges largely on how well he

can navigate a complex environment as a member of a productive team. Yet, as we'll see later in this book, companies that manage to simplify at least some part of the way their work is done usually see a sustained competitive advantage. This is why, for example, GE and its competitor Siemens have been racing to combat the scourge of complexity within their organizations. GE's CEO, Jeffrey Immelt, has championed a movement to embrace a corporate "culture of simplification" while Siemens has eliminated an entire level of middle management.[40]

Bain did a study of a manufacturer that instituted a simple rule, halving the default length of meetings to a half hour and mandating that no more than seven employees attend any company discussion. The results were powerful: employees who were left alone to attend to their own responsibilities were much more productive. In the end, Bain calculated that the productivity savings garnered from their new rules had the same impact on the company's bottom line as cutting two hundred jobs from the payroll. For executives, that should be plenty of inducement to simplify![41]

In fact, companies that simplify will see all kinds of benefits. They'll bring new products and services to market more quickly. They'll amp up customer satisfaction, and with it, employee engagement and satisfaction. They'll achieve more efficiency in their operations. They'll be more profitable. Overall, they'll be better companies, more focused, more purposeful—places where work actually gets done.

That Was Easy

If you were selling office supplies to the legions of people around the world who work in small businesses, how would you approach them? Would you focus on keeping prices low? Stocking a broader inventory? Adding more retail locations? Offering better customer service?

Staples, the office-supply superstore, was founded as part of an attempt to solve this very problem. During July 4th weekend of 1985, Tom Stemberg discovered that the ribbon had snapped on his typewriter, making it impossible to work on a draft of a business proposal he was writing. No problem, he thought—he'd just go out and buy another. To his chagrin, the local stores that kept stock were closed for the holiday weekend. Even if the stores had been open, they probably wouldn't have had the specific brand of ribbon he needed for his particular typewriter. What a pain! So Stemberg, who had previously worked as an executive in a supermarket chain, decided to fill a market niche, creating an office supply store that was both accessible and affordable.[42]

More than a decade after the first Staples opened in Brighton, Massachusetts, the company's marketers came up with a slogan that tapped right into Stemberg's vision of what the store meant to the average customer. We've all seen and heard about the "That Was Easy" campaign—it has become almost synonymous with the Staples brand, and a marketing gold standard. Why? Because it took the essence of Staples's value proposition and brought it to a new place. Looking beneath customers' more obvious concerns for expense, choice, and proximity, "That Was Easy" addressed an even more basic desire: simplification.

Small-business owners were starting to see benefits to simplification. Recent research found that, for small businesses, "simplifying the decision-making process made consumers 86 percent more likely to purchase a brand and 115 percent more likely to recommend it to others."[43] Yet small-business owners themselves were drowning in complexity. With limited funds, resources, and time, they had a million better ways to spend their time than on low-value tasks like ordering office supplies. The time they wasted re-upping their stock of toner or buying more printer paper weighed heavily in their minds. Small-business owners were willing to pay a premium for their time. They wanted simplicity. In the end, Staples sold more than a million "That Was Easy" buttons, giving a portion of the proceeds to charity.[44] In time, 96 percent of customers would associate the phrase with the Staples brand, contributing to the company's dramatic growth.[45]

We're clearly at an impasse with complexity. It is overwhelming individuals and bogging down organizations. This scourge needs to end— and it will take more than pressing an "easy" button. We must learn to spot complexity in our organizations and understand better what work that matters really is. We must then take a new approach toward work, embracing a framework for cutting out what we don't need from our workplaces so that work becomes simpler. "That Was Easy" shouldn't just be what you think about when buying more pens—it should be what you think about throughout most of your day, your week, your year, your life. To the extent we can, let's break free of the complexity that traps us. Let's pare nonessentials from our workplaces. Let's reclaim our time and the meaningfulness of what we do. Let's make simplicity the new way to work.

CHAPTER TWO

The "What" and "Why" of Complexity

> "If you had to identify, in one word, the reason why the human race has not achieved, and never will achieve, its full potential, that word would be meetings."
>
> —Dave Barry[1]

It was just a monthly e-newsletter. Nothing complicated. A large bank had hired my company to improve the e-mails it sent periodically to a group of current and potential customers. The marketing team wanted to learn how to engage new clients and assure the loyalty of those already banking with them. My New York–based firm had developed innovative ideas for making e-newsletters much more engaging. Both sides figured it would be a nice collaboration.

This wasn't a big project—a four-week assignment at best. And that's one of the reasons protracted negotiations weren't necessary. We would provide a fresh new approach and receive a modest fee in return. Simple, right?

It didn't turn out that way. To do business with this big corporation, each prospective consultant first needed to become an approved vendor. So once the banking executives expressed interest in hiring us, we began the process of getting vendor approval. What did that entail? A better question: What *didn't* it entail? There's a famous scene from an old Steve Martin movie, *L.A. Story*. In order to get a reservation at a restaurant, prospective diners have to let the restaurant do a complete financial history.[2] Mr. Perdue, the maître d', asks one customer: "You think with a financial statement like this you can have the duck?"[3] Obviously, the joke was that the background check was completely unnecessary. Diners were forced to jump through absurd hoops for no particular reason, save exclusivity. My experience becoming an approved vendor was like life imitating art. Hoop after hoop, for no reason except that the bureaucracy demanded it.

The process began with a few forms: we shared information about our company, acknowledged that we understood the imperative of confidentiality, and so on. Nothing out of the ordinary. But then we got a second packet, and this one wasn't so ordinary. It was massive. Pages and pages of fine print. Pages and pages of places where we needed to sign and initial and date. This second packet was longer than all of the e-newsletters we were contracted to produce—combined! It just went on and on. For a larger project, the forms might have been appropriate; the company had an interest in assuring that its vendors met its standards. For our project, this seemed like complete overkill.

And that wasn't the half of it. Even though our project was small, with a fee less than $10,000, the big bank's bureaucracy required that we show proof of having $5 million worth of general liability insurance. At the time, I had the standard $2 million worth of coverage—I had never needed more. But now I was required to get 150 percent more, eating the cost of a premium that would claim half the revenue I expected from the project. When I inquired about this requirement, the bank's bureaucrats explained that they were protecting the bank against the risk of having someone slip and fall while working on the project on-site. I explained that this was a *virtual* project, all done via e-mail. No one would be on-site. There was no need to hedge the risk because there was no risk. Could I skip the extra insurance? No, the bureaucrats answered. A rule's a rule.

While we were negotiating over liability insurance, the bank's employees let me know that we would need an "on-site" security audit for our technology. The bank wanted to send someone over to our office to walk through all of our equipment, since people at the bank would be e-mailing us information. I didn't understand. It's not as if we were going to weave our technology into the bank's or even work within their databases. In fact, we were creating everything from scratch, using mostly Microsoft Word, on our own premises. We would originate the work and send it to *them*. We had signed a nondisclosure agreement, but that wasn't sufficient. The bureaucrats needed to audit us anyway, to make sure we met their security standards on the off chance that one of their employees might e-mail us proprietary business information.

No one doubted that the bureaucrats were following the bank's rules. No one doubted that they'd been told to dot every "i" and cross every "t." We even suspected that the bureaucrats themselves sensed on some level how absurd their vetting process was. But there was no getting around the rules. As a result, we pulled the plug on the whole thing. We lost a nice project, and the bank lost a chance to harness our expertise. The complexity of the vetting process got the better of what could have been a fruitful collaboration. Left unaddressed and unacknowledged, a complexity problem on an institutional scale had reared its ugly head.

Shake It Off

Those of you who lived through the 1970s probably remember the story of Patty Hearst, the young heiress who was kidnapped by a group of radicals and then purportedly brainwashed by her captors. As the story goes, shortly after being snatched she joined the movement and participated in a bank robbery. When she was rescued by the police, people across the country began to debate whether she really bore responsibility for the crime. Some psychologists claimed that she'd become a victim of Stockholm syndrome, whereby victims come to sympathize and collaborate with the people who have taken them hostage.

Complexity is not remotely as serious as a real-life kidnapping, but I do believe that something similar to the Stockholm syndrome is touching many who inhabit the professional world. We've become captives to complexity, and like the bureaucrats at the bank who weren't willing to bend the rules for my e-newsletter project, we're now unwitting participants in our own victimization. Employees from the C-suite on down go through the motions every day, almost like Patty Hearst did (she actually claimed to be something of a zombie during her captivity). On some level it occurs to us that we're wasting our time on meaningless nonsense. Certainly, we're frustrated that we're not getting the return we expect from all the elbow grease we put in. But even amid all that frustration, we don't quite know how to, as Taylor Swift likes to say, shake it off.

As we saw in the last chapter, complexity often crops up indirectly and undetected, as an unintended side effect in the course of problem solving. But it turns out that the problem runs deeper than this. Complexity is firmly entrenched because, to some extent, it originates inside us. As we'll see in this chapter, cognitive biases such as the tendency to focus too narrowly on certain parts of our business blind us to complexity we create inadvertently. Meanwhile, powerful and primal emotional needs compel us to embrace complexity and ignore the extent to which it has taken hold of our lives at work. I'm talking about the universal human needs for security, constancy, control, and power. We're often unaware of these needs and how they're shaping our behavior, and we feel uncomfortable acknowledging that we have such needs. But we do, and the first step to snapping out of it—or shaking it off—is to recognize the truth.

> Complexity often crops up indirectly and undetected, as an unintended side effect in the course of problem solving.

Simple Definitions

In identifying and naming your complexity problem, it's helpful first to understand more clearly what simplicity is. So often in business, we get tripped up because we don't bother to define foundational terms. At some point in your career, for instance, someone has no doubt told you to "go and be innovative." And that's *all* you're told. So you wonder: Innovate to do what? Innovate to go where? There's a reason people often joke that when you ask two executives to articulate their definition of innovation, you often get three different answers. Innovation is an inherently vague term.

On the surface, the meaning of simplicity seems obvious: it's the situation that arises when you pare back anything unnecessary. But how simple are things supposed to be? Can you go too far in simplifying a specific area? When looking at an entire organization, how broadly do you extend the imperative to simplify? To every process or just the most important ones?

To understand how complicated defining simplicity can be, check out the chart below. It represents an attempt by one division of a Fortune 500 company to list all the different places where the company could *try* to simplify things.

Documentation Simplifications	Manufacturing Simplifications
Design Simplifications	Process Simplifications
General Simplifications	Program Simplifications
Systems Simplifications	Procedural Simplifications
Travel Simplifications	Platform Simplifications
Initiative Simplifications	Product Development Simplifications
Reporting Simplifications	Packaging Simplifications
Financial Management Simplifications	Training Simplifications
Workplace Simplifications	Work Simplifications

What, might I ask, is the difference between "work simplifications" and "workplace simplifications"? And how do "process simplifications" and "procedural simplifications" differ? Whoever came up with this chart meant well, but this taxonomy of simplification is enough to make your head spin. Even when we sense we have a complexity problem, as this company did, we can't readily scope out the problem because we don't know exactly what simplicity is.

Minimal, Understandable, Repeatable, Accessible

It's time to make simplicity clearer, and complexity too. Something that's properly simplified is:

• As **minimal** as possible: Simple things reduce the number of steps, pages, features, functions, sign-offs, requirements, and other hurdles required to get something accomplished. There's nothing extra, but at the same time, there's enough to get the job done. Why has Uber become so successful? In large part, it's because—rather than calling a car service (or just waiting for a cab, and good luck if you need one at rush hour, when it's raining, or during a shift change) and seeing if they've got a driver available, explaining where you are, telling them where you want to go, and haggling over the price—you can get your ride with a few swipes of the Uber app. It's *much* less work for the consumer.

• As **understandable** as possible: Simple things are defined by clear, straightforward language. They are comprehensible to someone who doesn't already have expertise in the subject at hand. Simple things could easily be replicated by a novice—even if they often require some common sense. Brad Katsuyama, the subject of Michael Lewis's book *Flash Boys*, differentiated his firm from other financial services companies by making things easy for people to comprehend: "People trust things they understand; they don't trust things they don't understand. We spend our time making complex concepts easy to understand."[4]

• As **repeatable** as possible: Simple things can be scaled or replicated. They aren't one-offs. They aren't customized. It should be easy for someone to do them over and over again. Think of a pilot entering a cockpit. Does she have to figure out what each and every button and gauge means each time she transfers from one plane to another? No. With slight modifications, the various pieces of equipment are placed in the same places, for *simple* ease of use.

• As **accessible** as possible: Simple things are made available and transparent to as many audiences as possible. Outsiders can make use of them with as few gatekeepers as possible. Why does Progressive Insurance allow you to see their competitors' prices when you search online for a new policy? It's not because they want you to take out a policy with someone else. Quite the opposite, they're betting that you'll choose them because they've made the information more accessible to you, saving you the trouble of obtaining information on your own.

Complexity, then, is the lack of these four elements. It's a process, product, communication, or procedure that *isn't* as minimal, understandable, repeatable, and accessible as possible.

The Simplicity Sweet Spot

Note the qualifier "as possible." While complexity is bad, it *is* possible to oversimplify. Organizations can make their products so simple that they're no longer useful to consumers. They can make workplace processes so simple (largely by stripping away requirements, checks, etc.) that quality suffers. There is a "simplicity sweet spot" in which products and processes are neither too complex nor too basic. If you doubt this, do something for me. Go out and purchase a really nice piece of furniture at IKEA. And then lock yourself in a room with some tools and try to put it together.

Now, look, I love IKEA. There's no secret to why a Scandinavian company that sells items with unpronounceable names has become a staple brand in countries around the world: it offers great value. IKEA's furniture is simple, functional, and affordable. If you're furnishing an apartment on a budget, you can do very well on a single trip to an IKEA outlet. But I'll be damned if everyone who excitedly opens a box when he gets home doesn't end up cursing the place while trying to put together his new dresser, table, or cabinet. One of my friends recently joked that every IKEA purchase should come with a coupon for marriage counseling.

Why is putting together IKEA furniture an experience that makes you want to pull your hair out? The problem isn't that the directions are too complicated. It's the opposite: they're too simple. The pictures aren't detailed enough. The steps aren't delineated in any clear way. You have to squint just to figure out which screws go in which holes—and frequently, after you're done accidentally putting the shorter screws into the deeper holes, you realize (upon finding that the longer screws don't fit in the shallower holes) that you have to take the whole thing apart and start over. Your afternoon just got more complicated—because the instructions were too simple.

Albert Einstein is famous for having argued that "everything should be made as simple as possible, but no simpler."[5] And that's exactly what some companies have failed to realize: if you remove too much information, the remaining information becomes useless. Some pursuits truly are complicated—by necessity. You want your surgeon to understand the whole anatomical picture before your operation, even if the procedure he plans to perform only requires a little bit of that knowledge for a good outcome. You want a pilot to understand the physics of flying, even if her job is nothing more than shifting the plane into autopilot.

The trick is striking an appropriate balance between detail and nuance on the one hand, and the imperative to simplify on the other. If you reduce a one-hundred-page document down to a single page, that's great. But if doing so means that you then need to continually explain the terms on the page, you've actually made things more complicated. A ten-page document might work better—shorter than the hundred-page tome, but more complex than the one-page summary.

Intentional Complexity

Now that we understand what complexity and simplicity are, let's examine in more detail why you might be aiding and abetting the scourge of complication. At one extreme, some companies and individuals *purposely* and *consciously* pursue complexity because they see it as a means of reaping more profits or gaining some other advantage. This type of behavior has been noted in several industries, and quite visibly within financial trading firms.

IEX was founded in 2012 in response to questionable trading practices "that had become widely used across traditional public Wall Street exchanges as well as dark pools and other alternative trading systems."[6] As Michael Lewis recounts in *Flash Boys*, IEX's group of traders and tech experts noticed that traders were "pinging" various exchanges to electronically "front-run" ordinary investors.[7] In other words, they were using sophisticated algorithms to discern when someone was purchasing a certain security. With that information in hand, they'd buy the security microseconds before the actual buyer's order had arrived, inflate the price, and then sell the security to the buyer without anyone being the wiser.

For instance, at any given moment, shares of the same company are bought and sold on different exchanges, including the NASDAQ, the New York Stock Exchange, Direct Edge, and BATS. When a broker submitted an order to buy shares on several exchanges at the same price at one time—say ten thousand shares on the NASDAQ, twenty thousand on Direct Edge, and five thousand on BATS—the orders should theoretically arrive at the exchanges simultaneously. In fact, because the electronic signals had to travel across various cables, nodes, and geographical distances, the moment of arrival varied from exchange to exchange by a matter of milliseconds, or even microseconds. Traders took advantage of this by building algorithms that automatically bought up the shares on *other* exchanges when the first purchase had been completed. In those fractions of a second, they would raise the price of their newly purchased shares and then sell them to the original purchaser, who was almost never aware of what had happened. Blind to the complexities of stock trading, and trusting the traders to handle the complexity for them, the original investor ended up paying a premium to an unknown front-runner.[8]

But that wasn't all. In some cases, the traders were getting early word that an investor was making a purchase or sale from the exchanges purporting to serve the general public (exchanges were selling the "first look" to them for a piece of the action). Few investors noted the difference between the original price they intended to pay and the inflated alternative—they tended to chalk it up to some technological glitch. But over time, those small discrepancies added up. By Lewis's telling, the traders, exchanges, and banks were making billions off the scheme. Complication was mobilized purposefully to facilitate high-class thievery.[9] Financial institutions profited by recognizing and exploiting a lack of transparency.

Not all companies are quite so unscrupulous, but in subtler ways many use complication to hide the truth from stakeholders, to the benefit of the company. Think of how difficult it is to unsubscribe from most e-newsletters. In many cases, companies trick you into signing up by pre-checking the boxes you would have to uncheck if you wanted to avoid any future spam. And then, when you want to opt out, you find there's no obvious button to select. You have to click through, type in your e-mail address, and explain *why* you're opting out. Even then, you often discover later that you've only opted out of some subset of the company's newsletters, and you will continue to receive the rest.

Another, even more common example is the fine print that's so ubiquitous in everyday life. With respect to privacy policies, one recent study found that it would take roughly a month of every year for you to read the fine print associated with all the products and services you encounter every day. If you read every word of every privacy policy, you'd spend roughly 244 hours reading or 154 hours skimming.[10] Some, or even much, of the legalese may be necessary, but most of it has the obvious effect of confusing customers.

If you buy an airline ticket, take out a mortgage, or sign up for a credit card, you'll find that the fine print is so frighteningly long that you're dissuaded from reading *any* of it. As a result, you don't know what you're signing up for, and you may get more (or less) out of the deal than you expected. As Roland Vogl, the executive director of the Stanford Program

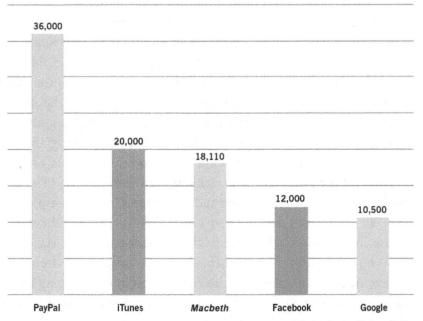

Approximate word count of terms & conditions for well-known companies (some are longer than a Shakespeare play)[11]

36,000 — PayPal
20,000 — iTunes
18,110 — *Macbeth*
12,000 — Facebook
10,500 — Google

Source: Business Insider

in Law, Science & Technology, has argued: "Some companies make things complex to justify themselves. . . . It's complexity by design. Designed to be painful."[12] Even if we give companies the benefit of the doubt and assume they're not purposefully *trying* to cheat consumers, they're not in much of a hurry to simplify their terms and conditions. I wonder why.

The Endless Look Inside

Intentional complexity is maddening, but it probably accounts for a relatively small proportion of the complexity that weighs down our organizations. Most people and organizations contribute to complexity unwittingly and unconsciously, and they do so in part because of various cognitive biases that affect them. Two biases in particular are worth mentioning here: our "insider mindset" and our quest for "more."

Let's first examine the insider mindset bias. Ours is an age that celebrates personal authenticity. Musical acts explain their success by claiming that they've "stayed true to who they really are." Graduation speakers tell kids to "be true to themselves" in order to succeed. Over and over, we hear that we can best answer the "big questions" if we look deep within ourselves. All of this inward searching may be helpful and good and right. But in the world of business, looking inside has an important consequence: it leads us to avoid looking outside. "Don't take your eye off the ball," we're told. Stay focused on your "core business." Pay attention to the "basics." Master what's happening internally, we think, and we'll control the future.

Some of that is true, of course. There's only so much you can control, and most of it *is* internal: the people you hire, the raw materials you purchase, the shape of the products you manufacture, the quality of the services you provide. But our unending focus on what's happening inside frequently distracts us from something that's even more important: the customer experience. And all too often, this results in a tide of unintended complexity unleashed upon the people who buy our products and services.

Here's an example. A few months ago, I tried to book flights for my family vacation. I wanted to use my reward miles, so I called the toll-free number the airline had designated specifically for redemptions. After discussing the options with the airline representative, I chose our family's itinerary and had the requisite number of miles deducted from my account. Easy enough. But when I was through making the reservation, I asked that same representative to help me select my seats. My husband and I have kids, and we never like to show up at the airport to discover that we've been seated separately. The representative who had just booked our tickets explained that her department did not handle seating—I would have to call a different toll-free number, wait on hold once again, and then discuss with that separate department *of the same airline* whether we could all sit together or not on an hours-long flight.

So I called. And I waited on hold. I tried to respond to a few e-mails while listening to the repetitive hold music. I was tricked time and again into thinking a real person had come on the line when, in fact, I had to endure yet another advertisement for a new direct route to Asia that the airline would be introducing the following fall. Finally, a representative came on the line. And do you know what she told me? The seating assignments for the flights we had booked would not be handled until closer to the date of departure because the flight was actually on a partner airline. I would need to call back.

Infuriating? Absolutely. Typical? Without a doubt. But why? Why would an airline separate the tasks of booking award travel and doling out seat assignments? Because it's more efficient and effective for the *airline*. They don't have to train employees who book the flights to use the system that assigns seats. They don't have to train seat assigners to use the system that books award travel. By separating the tasks, airline managers can make sure that the departments are performing the individual tasks as efficiently as possible. What suffers is the customer experience. We want to be able to interact quickly with a single representative and get everything we need done. We don't want to have to call multiple numbers. We don't want to hear conflicting advice. We want the companies we support to invest in *our* experience by eliminating the elements that are complicating *our* lives.

Insider bias doesn't just operate on the enterprise level to make life more complicated for customers. It exists inside companies to make life more complicated for internal "customers." An accounting department has a system in place to process expense reports. Is the system set up to simplify the experience of those submitting their expenses, or is it set up so that the accounting department can process the reports most efficiently? You know the answer. All too often, we design our processes with *our* needs in mind rather than the needs of those we're trying to serve. This happens at every layer of organizations, in every function, and in every industry.

The Pursuit of More

A second cognitive bias that all too often leads us unwittingly to make life more complex has to do with our demand for reporting and accountability. Companies want to measure where they are. They want to keep track of what's happening. They want to reward those who perform and punish those who slack. They want to track (in real time, if possible) all the work being undertaken inside, and everything that's happening as a result. And those efforts don't reward simplicity. Rather, they reward the pursuit of *more.*

Driving the demand for reporting and accountability is a familiar culprit: executive disconnect. Those sitting atop big organizations feel pressure from board members worried about the quarterly numbers. To tighten up the company's performance, executives demand more data as well as more real time tracking of operations. They're not just interested in monitoring revenue generation and costs, but also compliance, quality, and safety—any area where an operational lapse might result in a lawsuit. Affinion's chief human resource officer Jim Daly has argued that "Most organizations continue to add on to what's already being done rather than replacing or upgrading processes or activities. If five data points on a report are good, seven would be better; nine must be better still. As the ease of capturing and storing information continues to improve, it becomes seductive to ask for and receive more."[13]

As a result, frontline employees—those actually interacting with customers, providing services, manufacturing products, purchasing materials, marketing the company—must spend more time feeding the beast of accountability. That leaves them with less time to get their real work done, and also to unwind unnecessary complication. It can also drive them toward what some psychologists have termed "decision fatigue." When facing an important choice, their internal reservoirs of focus and energy can be so drained that they haphazardly come to the wrong conclusion, or fail to come to any conclusion at all.[14]

Reporting itself can often become so complicated that it's nearly useless. Reporting occurs more frequently these days, and it cuts against more complex sets of metrics. From brand to brand, from country to country, from region to region, from channel to channel, this data is processed and compared and laid out, all of which takes time. Eventually there are so many conflicting indicators that no one receiving the report can derive anything actionable from it. A manager might see, for instance, that sales were up on certain brands but not others; in certain locations but not others; online but not in stores; with one promised rebate but not with another; on weekdays but not weekends; in locations where certain advertisements were in place but also in locations where they were not. By the time this manager deciphers what's really going on from a report, a whole new tranche of statistics is coming in for analysis.

Often, this whole process of reporting and accountability becomes the force that drives a company forward. Employees are rewarded if they're producing more, more, more. They're given warnings if they're producing less. Everyone *thinks* that the report she produces contributes significantly to the company's overall mission, although in many cases it really doesn't. "More" takes on a value of its own. Employees know that they'll be promoted and rewarded for generating more revenue, managing more people, controlling more business units, inventing more products, offering more services, producing more reports. No competing incentives exist to encourage them to cull waste or redundancy, or to focus on work that *really* matters. Invariably, complication piles on without addressing the natural impulse toward more, more, more.

The Enemy Is Us

In addition to the cognitive biases so visible in companies, a great deal of complexity is driven by something even more basic: our emotional needs. Take those useless meetings. We all hate them, so why do we continue to schedule them? If we're planning a course of action, we may feel that it's better to involve all the possible stakeholders; that way, we can make sure they're okay with our plan before we act. To avoid the consequences of making a mistake, we err on the side of caution, inviting *everyone* to the meeting, even those who probably will add little to the conversation. We act out of fear, a desire to "cover our behinds," to be sure "just in case." We also may invite those stakeholders out of an unconscious desire to maintain

> A great deal of complexity is driven by something even more basic: our emotional needs.

control over an initiative, or out of an unconscious (or conscious) desire to display to others the power we wield in the organization. Our emotional needs do us in, without us even knowing it.

We also *attend* unnecessary meetings to satisfy emotions like fear. We don't want a colleague attending the meeting to make a decision that bears on our department. To protect our turf, we end up spending our time jumping from one conference room to the next, trying to get real work done in the brief moments in between.

In any number of ways, people make things more complex, consciously or not, as a way of protecting themselves from perceived threats. You *want* your peers to believe you have invaluable expertise—to think that they couldn't possibly perform your job responsibilities—for fear that otherwise you'll be seen as expendable. And so you create PowerPoint presentations with forty slides when ten would have sufficed. Or you use needlessly complex jargon to communicate simple ideas. Academics are notorious for doing the latter, using overly complicated language as a way of telling people outside their discipline to mind their own business. As Victoria Clayton has written in the *Atlantic,* many frustrated readers of academic literature believe that, "academics play an elitist game with their words: They want to exclude interlopers."[15]

Or consider why it often takes managers so long to make decisions. Quite often, they're afraid. They don't want to look bad. And so they ask perpetually for more information, more data, and more reports. Should we invest more of product A in Asia or Africa? "Give me the specs on each country in each market. How have those changed over the last twenty-four months? What about the last ten years? How have our products done in each market? How has that been evolving? Do we know where each market is headed, and how the next set of elections will affect the growth of each sector of each economy? Are there demographic trends that bear on the decision, and how do those vary between the various submarkets?" Fear of taking a wrong turn spurs managers to complicate the lives of those beneath them, and the deluge of information can prevent them from divining intuitively the best choice from among those at hand.

If emotions like fear generate complexity on the individual level, systemic complexity can emerge when many people interact fearfully or defensively with one another over time. I mentioned earlier how complicated reporting can become. Consider a story from one of my clients, an employee at a manufacturing company. Margins were thin, and the pressure to produce was high. The company's leadership needed a way to assess performance in real time. Leaders came up with a simple tool: a dashboard of key performance indicators (KPIs). It seemed like a great idea; the dashboard contained no more than a half dozen figures, color coded to make it easy for anyone to understand at a glance.

It wasn't long before complexity began rearing its ugly head, largely because of fear. Some people started to worry that the numbers chosen for the dashboard weren't capturing important dimensions of the company's operations. "Are we missing something?" they asked anxiously. Others worried that the dashboard metrics didn't cast them in the best light, so they requested that leadership add figures that might "balance out" the group's understanding. Senior members of the leadership team began asking for additional figures to be included so they could dig down a level deeper. Fearing for their jobs, or that they would be passed over for promotion, they sought to look smart and impress their peers.

The whole exercise began to change. More information got crammed into the chart. More colors. More data. More complication. After about a year, the tool became so unwieldy that it was essentially useless. In fact, the guys running the dashboard actually had to *reduce the font size* so that all the numbers being tracked could still fit on one page. No one could read it anymore, let alone get a sense of the company's big-picture performance. It was a nightmare of the company's own making.

Emotions like fear often lead to what we might call a "mindset of more" that tends toward increased complexity. This mindset is everywhere in the corporate world. More, we assume, is better. We want more power. More glory. More control. More income. More responsibility. You don't rest on your laurels; you try to grab more market share. You don't assume what you have is enough; you try to beat your competition to the punch on the next disruption. Only the hungry survive, so even when we've got a sufficient amount of power or money or glory, we look for more. We attach *value* to more. We envy those who have more. And what we often fail to see is that in opening the door to find more, we let complication slide in as well.[16]

Indeed, we've become so obsessed with the pursuit of more that we're suspicious of anything that seems less complicated than it would ordinarily need to be. If a solution is too quick or too easy, we doubt it'll actually work. Or we assume anyone could do it. Or that it isn't worth as much as we paid to harness it. Jack Welch put it well: "You can't believe how hard it is for people to be simple, how much they fear being simple. They worry that if they're simple, people will think they're simpleminded. In reality, of course, it's just the reverse. Clear, tough-minded people are the most simple."[17]

One locksmith found this issue of "more" being more valuable particularly confounding. All his years of experience fixing locks made him a master at his job—he could fix the toughest locks in mere minutes. But customers weren't always pleased with this—why should they pay him so much money for something that took no time at all? Doesn't that mean that anyone could do this work? So he figured out a way to address the problem. He found it was better to waste a little time, do a little extra handiwork, and give the customer the sense that the job really required a great deal of expertise, even if it was actually fairly simple. Why? The value we attach to *more*—more time, more expertise, more complication—leads us to believe that a job that takes a few extra minutes is one for which we're getting more value.

Bombs Away on Complexity

Complexity, as you can see, is often a scourge of our own making. But left unchecked, it is also insidious, in some cases wreaking havoc for decades on end, wasting untold billions of dollars. A stunning example of how big a problem complexity can become is the U.S. government's fruitless quest to replace the legendary B-52 bomber.

Much as I fondly remember the song "Love Shack," the B-52 isn't just famous because of the new wave band formed using the same name.

The Stratofortress, as the B-52 is officially named, flew its maiden voyage in 1952.[18] Four years later, it became the first model of plane to drop a hydrogen bomb, and fifty years later it was the first aircraft to drop a laser-guided bomb. The youngest B-52 was built during the Kennedy administration. And it is still in service, flying missions on behalf of the U.S. Air Force.

Why has the B-52 lasted so long in the long-range bombing fleet of the greatest military force in the history of the world? Clearly, it's a durable aircraft, but more importantly, the planes designed to replace the B-52 have repeatedly proven too complicated to be pressed into service. As the *New York Times* reported in 2015: "Even as the bombers were being assembled, defense officials were planning their replacement, but each plan was undone by its own complexity. First was a nuclear-powered bomber able to stay aloft for weeks (too radioactive), then the supersonic B-58 with dart-like wings (kept crashing), and then the even faster B-70 (spewed highly toxic exhaust)."[19]

Nevertheless, four years after the last B-52 was constructed, experts expected the plane to be rendered obsolete by 1975. But when 1975 rolled around, the military still hadn't produced a new model of aircraft capable of performing the same types of missions. An early model of the B-1, which was championed by the Reagan administration, wouldn't power up during an inaugural demonstration in 1985 (much to the shock of the thirty thousand people assembled to celebrate the occasion), and no one's been able to get the kinks out of the design in the decades since. The B-2 "stealth" bomber—one of the most sophisticated weapons systems ever built—was constructed with radar-evading skin that, by one account, "cannot handle the heat or the damp or the rain."[20] Celebrated as the $2 billion B-2 bomber was when it was announced, it's too delicate to do what the B-52 has done for more than six decades.

And that's the point: make anything too complicated, and it won't get the job done. A decades-long failure to keep things as minimal, understandable, repeatable, and accessible *as possible* is why the U.S. Air Force plans to keep its B-52s online through 2040.

It's probably not news to anyone that parts of the U.S. government have a complexity problem. But you and your organization have probably got one, too. It might not be costing you billions or have persisted across decades, but it's still costly and is becoming more so with every passing month. As we've seen, you yourself may be helping to sustain the harmful complexity, not merely because of your need to solve pressing problems, but because of your right brain and your left, your cognition and your emotion.

It's time to do something about it. It's time to embrace simplicity. And the first step is to look more closely at *yourself.* Take a deep breath and turn the page, because I've got some hard questions for you to answer.

CHAPTER THREE

Gauging Your Complexity Problem

"Things which matter most must never be at the mercy of things which matter least."

— Johann Wolfgang von Goethe[1]

We've talked about the many reasons we become complicit in complexity. Now let's talk about you. Chances are, you've been thinking, "Yeah, I've seen stuff like this happen at my job." But the question of whether you and your company have a real complexity problem is too important to address through anecdotes alone. I want you to think about your own experience, and to do so honestly and objectively. Ask yourself: Do I have a complexity problem? Does my company suffer from the scourge of unnecessary complexity? In what specific areas does complexity seem the worst?

When contemplating these questions, it pays to stay alert to the warning signs. The prevalence of status quo thinking is one of them. When someone proposes a new idea, do people automatically push back with a litany of reasons why the organization can't implement it? Do they say, "It'll never work" or "We can't—we've always done it a different way"? Do fewer people even bother to propose new ideas, cynical about their chances of getting a fair hearing? Such entrenched traditionalism is not direct evidence of complexity, but let's face it: it's hard to pare back when an organization is firmly wedded to what already exists. An organization resistant to change will often contain many processes and rules that once served a useful purpose but no longer do. This deadwood weighs down daily work, rendering it far more complex. Meaning and purpose recede in turn.

Another warning sign may be the prevalence of initiatives that sound great but deliver paltry results. One large financial institution spent more than $1 million implementing a system to "spur innovation" across the company by breaking down silos and leveraging cross-disciplinary thinking. Only 50 percent of employees queried knew the system existed, and only .1 percent knew how to submit new ideas via the system. Why? Because the company didn't budget for training and marketing to roll out the system. And why was that? Because the system's implementation was overly complex. It required an intense amount of focus and funding, and as a result the organization overlooked key elements that would have actually made the system *usable*. The innovation team touted this initiative as a win, even if it didn't deliver the intended ROI.

Besides status quo thinking and fruitless initiatives, a number of other telltale signs may suggest the presence of a complexity problem:

- **Too Many (or Too Lengthy) Approval Processes:** If it takes weeks or months to receive approval for relatively minor decisions, and if people "don't know who to go to" to secure approval, then your organization likely struggles with complexity. Good ideas should travel from farm to table, so to speak, without delay.
- **Frustrated Customers:** If you receive constant complaints about how hard it is to work with your company *even when the clients like the end product or have been with you for a while*, you're likely subjecting them to needless complexity. And here's a further test: When you tell your colleagues that your team needs to take a more customer-centric approach, do they roll their eyes?
- **Coordination Overload:** Do you find yourself performing tasks in multiple ways because systems in your organization are not compatible? Has someone put a system in place that makes *his* job easier but not yours? Some coordination will always be necessary, but too much time spent coordinating may be a symptom of excessive complexity.

- **Too Many Rule Changes:** How often do your employees receive memos outlining new internal policies? How regularly does legal tweak the way sales or marketing goes about their daily work? Do your people feel overmanaged and treated like children? Every company must update standard operating procedures to adapt to evolving markets. But if policy tweaks come down as frequently as updates to your iPhone apps, watch out.
- **The End of Easy:** How smoothly does your team work? If you have to complete a twenty-page report to request basic office supplies, if everyone talks in self-important jargon, if every legal contract is thirty pages long in extra-small font, then complexity is probably impeding your collective flow.
- **Mystery Rules:** Are people at a loss to explain *why* certain rules, processes, and procedures exist? It may be that your operations are legitimately complex, or that management simply hasn't communicated enough to explain how things work. But it may also be that these rules, processes, and procedures *no longer have a good reason for existing*—in other words, complexity.
- **An Acronym "Zoo":** Does every sentence uttered in your workplace come littered with acronyms? Do you and your colleagues not even know what half of them mean? And while we're at it, what about jargon? Is every other word a piece of clichéd business speak with a meaning that is elusive? If so, there's a good chance that complexity lurks.

If you spot any of these warning signs, you'll want to probe more deeply and methodically. To help you with this task, my team and I have created a diagnostic survey designed to help a leader, business unit, or organization understand how much complexity is present, where it exists, and what can be done to reduce or eliminate some of it. We began crafting the survey by brainstorming a list of questions designed to unveil hidden complications. Soon we understood the importance of distinguishing between two distinct kinds of complexity—organizational complexity and individual complexity.

Organizational complexity afflicts areas of work that are structural and mandated by policy or regulation, or that involve two or more parts of the organization. Individual complexity pertains to complications that a single person generally creates or that may be contained within a single business unit (e.g., the colleague who runs a terrible, five-hour meeting or sends a flurry of unnecessary e-mails). Because people require different strategies to deal with these two kinds of complexity, we resolved to separate the two categories in the course of creating the diagnostic on the following page.

We originally crafted our questions as a series of true–false statements. Then we realized that a binary approach masked important subtleties. We wanted to be able to register whether a certain wrinkle was a persistent frustration or an occasional annoyance. So we created a four-point scale (0 = consistently simple; 1 = sometimes; 2 = rarely; 3 = never), designed so that those taking the diagnostic couldn't choose a nebulous middle ground.

You can use this diagnostic either to get a quick read on where complexity lies or to dive deep into solutions designed to eradicate the issues. Companies of any size can use it, from small start-ups to multinational organizations. We designed the tool to reveal the personal habits and organizational areas that contribute to complexity, and we intend it for use by all levels of staff. It should take you less than three hours, or at most four, to complete the exercise, but we think you'll agree that getting closer to work that matters is well worth the investment.

Here's how the exercise works:

Step 1: Complete Diagnostic.
(20 minutes)

Complete the diagnostic a week prior to your meeting (if this isn't possible, you can do it in the meeting, but it will take up valuable time). The diagnostic subcategories (legal, HR, product development, etc.) are the areas where we typically find complexity lurking in most organizations. Participants should answer each statement according to their own personal opinion or from the perspective of their business unit/team. For example, if RARELY is their honest answer to "Simplification is expected and discussed in our organization," participants should place a 2 in the RARELY category of that statement. If a statement doesn't apply to them or their team, they should mark "N/A" in the NEVER category—but hopefully they will have five or fewer "N/A" answers. Instruct participants to be brutally honest, and to answer from the perspective of the work environment they experience every day.

CATEGORY	DO WE VALUE COMPLEXITY OR SIMPLICITY?	0-Consistently	1-Sometimes	2-Rarely	3-Never	CATEGORY SCORE:
ORGANIZATIONAL:						
Vision/ Communication	1. Simplification is expected and discussed in our organization.					
	2. Employees understand the vision and values of our business.					
	3. I believe the messaging from our leaders is clear and authentic.					
	4. Messaging I receive from managers is consistent with messaging from senior leaders.					
	5. I view simplicity as a core operating principle of our company.					
	6. I encourage my team to operate with simplification in mind.					
Org. Structure	7. Our organizational structure is easy to understand and clearly outlines how my division relates to other functions.					
	8. Our reporting structure enables me/my team to quickly make decisions and gain approvals.					
	9. Productive collaboration occurs between groups in our organization.					
	10. My business unit is free of duplicate functions.					
HR	11. I can explain my and my colleagues' roles in 1-2 jargon-free sentences.					
	12. When I hire/my unit hires a qualified candidate, excessive levels of approval are not required.					
	13. I/we believe that this organization rewards employees' simplification efforts.					
	14. Performance reviews are easy to complete.					
	15. Performance reviews are meaningful and help employees improve their performance.					
Strategy/Planning	16. We finalize our annual strategic plan within a quarter (or less).					
	17. We finalize the budget for the next fiscal year within a quarter (or less).					
	18. We can easily track our costs against our budget in real time (via a report, online system, etc.), so we can re-adjust or course-correct as needed.					

CATEGORY	DO WE VALUE COMPLEXITY OR SIMPLICITY?	HOW OFTEN IS THIS TRUE?				CATEGORY SCORE:
		0-Consistently	1-Sometimes	2-Rarely	3-Never	
ORGANIZATIONAL:						
Strategy/Planning (cont.)	19. We use our strategic plan as a reference point throughout the year, and it directly connects to our operational plan.					
	20. We use a balanced scorecard or similar system to track our actions vs. results throughout the year.					
	21. My/my team's simplification efforts are measured against a clear set of metrics.					
Legal	22. The legal department advances, not hinders, my/my team's work.					
	23. My team and I would agree that contracts and agreements created within this organization are understandable.					
	24. My team and I would agree that contracts and agreements created within this organization are of a reasonable length.					
	25. The legal department provides flexibility to modify documents when necessary.					
	26. The legal department provides clear timelines for review of contracts or other legal documents (NDAs, M&A docs, etc.).					
Operational	27. My ability to perform my job isn't stifled by the day-to-day rules of how things operate in our workplace.					
	28. I'm encouraged/I encourage my team to identify and eliminate redundancies or unnecessary policies and reports wherever possible.					
	29. At our company, expense sign-off levels are reasonable. Managers' time isn't wasted signing off on low-value items.					
	30. Once I have approval for something (new hire, capital expense, etc.), I don't need to ask permission for it again.					
	31. Decision-making processes within the organization are clear, quick, and don't require excessive layers of approval.					

ORGANIZATIONAL:		0-Consistently	1-Sometimes	2-Rarely	3-Never
Operational (cont.)	32. If I don't know how to accomplish a task, I know exactly where to go for information or support.				
	33. I/we find our company's tech support process to be easy, clear, and effective.				
	34. I aim/encourage my team to template or standardize as many reports, contracts, or processes as possible to create efficiency and scale.				
	35. The number of vendors with which my unit works is manageable.				
	36. To my knowledge, client or customer complaints are typically resolved in a reasonable amount of time.				
Product/Service	37. Our product development or R&D departments approach projects with simplicity in mind.				
	38. We keep the customer at the core of our product development process.				
	39. We review our new product or service development pipeline and eliminate projects that aren't showing promise or don't align with business goals.				
	40. I think the number of products and services we offer is easy to manage.				
	41. We review our existing product and service offerings and eliminate those that are not performing well.				
	42. We/our product dev team offers a clear way to give input on new products, services, features.				
	43. We/our product dev clearly articulates how they prioritize/select the products, services, features to be developed.				

CATEGORY	DO WE VALUE COMPLEXITY OR SIMPLICITY?	HOW OFTEN IS THIS TRUE?				CATEGORY SCORE:
		0-Consistently	1-Sometimes	2-Rarely	3-Never	
INDIVIDUAL:						
Meetings	44. I spend 20 percent or less of my time each week in unproductive meetings or calls.					
	45. I operate/encourage my team to operate with simplification in mind.					
	46. The meetings I lead/attend start and end on time.					
	47. Meetings in my group have a clear purpose and agenda.					
	48. Only essential people are invited to the meetings I attend.					
	49. I feel comfortable declining meeting invitations or delegating attendance to someone else.					
Emails	50. I receive a manageable number of work emails and IMs.					
	51. Email correspondence I receive includes only essential recipients.					
	52. Emails sent from my team are concise and clear.					
Reports	53. Every report to which I contribute serves a clear purpose and adds value or insight to the organization.					
	54. My team and I would agree that the number and frequency of reports we're asked to generate is reasonable.					
	55. Data needed for reports in my group is easily accessed and compiled.					
Presentations	56. My team and I would agree that the number of PowerPoints or presentations our group generates is reasonable.					
	57. My/my team's PowerPoints or presentations are understandable and fact-driven with visuals that serve to simplify data or illustrate possibilities.					
	58. The presentations I create/my team creates are short and leave time for discussion and next steps.					
	59. We view our presentations as valuable and worthy of our time.					

INDIVIDUAL:		HOW OFTEN IS THIS TRUE?				SCORE:
		0-Consistently	1-Sometimes	2-Rarely	3-Never	
Value of Staff Time	60. I am encouraged/encourage my team to find smart workarounds and timesavers that solve a problem or address a client need.					
	61. I've observed/bestowed recognition or rewards for smart workarounds and timesavers that solve a problem or address a client need.					
	62. I don't/management doesn't create unnecessary urgency or set false deadlines to speed delivery of work.					
	63. I am never asked to do unnecessary busy work. When I'm busy, it is because I'm doing meaningful work.					
STEP 2: TALLY CATEGORY POINTS + SCORE	**Add up your points for each category section (N/A answers are worth 0 points) in the far right column. Then tally the category sums for your diagnostic score.**					**Overall Score:**
	Compare your total score to the diagnoses on the next page. →					

Step 2: Tally Points/Receive Diagnosis. (10 minutes)

Add up the points for each category *separately,* and then add the category scores together for an overall score (N/A answers are worth 0 points). To determine your organization's diagnosis, use the following legend:

- 0 points = STRONGLY SIMPLIFIED. Congratulations! Your organization is among the healthy few that aren't suffering from complexity. Simplification is encouraged and rewarded across your business, and messaging from leaders is consistent and authentic. Boost your immunity by continuing to focus on valuable work and to question any process without purpose.
- 1–20 points = OPPORTUNITIES FOR SIMPLIFICATION. Your organization is functional but a handful of NEVER or RARELY answers is reducing overall productivity and negatively impacting morale. To prevent further damage, continue to Step 3.
- 21–50 points = COMPLEX. Complexity is bottlenecking one or more areas of your business, and it will spread to others if left unchecked. Operations are likely clogged by policies and processes or a disconnection between senior leaders and the rest of the organization. Pinpoint the exact areas of complexity in Step 3.
- 51–70 points = SERIOUS COMPLEXITY. Complacency has already set in, possibly at the highest levels of leadership, and your organization's core values have been replaced by frustration, fear, and powerlessness. From meetings and messaging to hiring and tech support, nothing is simple or swift in your workplace. Get treatment now in Step 3.
- 71+ points = CRIPPLING COMPLEXITY. Complexity is paralyzing your organization, and every corner of your business has been affected. You're wasting resources on a massive scale, but employees have been trained to shrug and maintain the status quo. Some areas of the organization are barely functioning, which has put your business at risk of a takeover or going under. To start fighting this disease at the source, turn to Step 3 in a hurry.

Obviously, the higher the score, the more complex your business unit or organization is. But scores can be slightly deceiving, if only because the point allotment can tell you a lot about what's *really* at issue. Obviously, it's not ideal to have a high score in one category, driven by several SOME-TIMES and RARELY marks. But that may be better than having a series of NEVER answers that each cripple your business in much more significant ways. For Steps 3 and 4, participants should focus on the categories with the *highest total scores*. But Step 5 focuses on those statements that received NEVER scores because they likely deserve some additional attention down the line.

Step 3: Identify High-Scoring Categories and Discuss. (20 minutes)

Now that you've assessed your organization, list the three highest-scoring categories. Then, assign a team leader to capture the teams' answers to the questions below:

- Did everyone list the same highest-scoring categories? If so, these are your organization's main areas of complexity.
- If not, where are the differences? Continue discussing until you determine the most crucial areas to focus on.

Step 4: Articulate Core Problems and Discuss. (60 to 90 minutes)

For each NEVER or RARELY answer to statements in the three categories from the previous step, specify which statement it was for, and discuss the key issue that's driving the complexity. One category isn't more important than another. You need to tackle simplification across the board; leaving complexity in even one area of a company can prove crippling. Often, the smaller things (e.g., meetings and e-mails) are the problem. Indeed, in many cases the day-to-day encumbrances take up *more* time, becoming the true source of depleted morale.

Step 5: Brainstorm Solutions and Discuss. (60 to 90 minutes)

Now that you've assessed the organization, list your ten highest-scoring statements. What solution would turn a NEVER or RARELY answer into a CONSISTENTLY answer? Use the following prompts to learn how to stop complexity:

- What can we stop doing immediately?
- If we can't eliminate the problem, how can we minimize it or reduce it?
- Does an opportunity exist to outsource this area or to consolidate it with a similar or related activity?
- How could we streamline the problem to reach the end result more quickly?

Into the Field

Once my team and I had crafted the diagnostic's initial draft, we went over it repeatedly and solicited feedback from dozens of clients and experts. Then we went out into the field, hoping that our new tool would indeed help individuals and companies unearth complexity's hidden sources. We were amazed by what we found.

In one instance, we administered the diagnostic to a product team embedded within a large multinational company that operates in a heavily regulated industry. During the process of completing the tool there, we found that this company was burdened with a series of ORGANIZATIONAL complications that spanned from corporate structure to HR to IT and especially to regulatory and compliance issues. Yet strikingly, almost no one thought organizational complexity worth fighting. As the group went through their answers to the questions, we saw employees roll their eyes and sigh, "this is so typical," at each new topic. One person complained: "Legal contracts are over fifty pages long no matter what I'm working on. Why?! The lawyers then always tell me it's their *job* to be thorough, and the contracts are structured like that for a reason. I'll *never* get them to make things simpler."

Participants in this session were sure they'd have to expend a great deal of political capital and energy to make a change, and even then they were fairly confident they wouldn't get anywhere. As one employee said: "Changing something like this would be like rolling a boulder uphill." But it wasn't just that people didn't think they'd succeed; in many cases, they thought they'd be *punished* for trying to simplify. This is all too typical: leaders rarely feel compelled to reduce complexity, and people below them worry about rocking the boat. In this case, people worried that any effort to drive simplicity would be perceived as dereliction of duty.

But organizational complexity wasn't the only problem here. Many of the most significant pain points at this larger corporation stemmed from INDIVIDUAL complexities. These garnered the most visceral response; people often became irate when describing the specifics. For example, many in the group perceived e-mails as a double-edged sword: they knew e-mails were a big problem, sucking up valuable time and energy. They knew that they were generating too many e-mails on their own. But what were they supposed to do about it? They couldn't choose unilaterally to stop responding to incoming messages—then their bosses would perceive them as slackers. They were trapped, perpetuating a cycle they couldn't escape. To really simplify e-mail, *everyone* would have to change his communication habits. Participants believed this was unlikely at best.

In general, the diagnostic established that the greatest source of frustration was *other people's behaviors.* There were too many meetings with too many people; meetings with no decisions or outcomes; urgent requests for redundant reports; mind-numbing presentations delivered via PowerPoint with far too much text; and e-mail chains that never ended. These individual complexities generated the most discussion and annoyance. They were

> In general, the diagnostic established that the great-est source of frustration was *other people's behaviors.*

at heart of the team's diminished morale. All this sharing, collaboration, and technology meant to liberate us was making people miserable.

We wanted to see how the diagnostic might work in a second company—a small business with fewer employees, regulations, facilities, layers of bureaucracy, and legacy systems. We did a second field test and discovered that the small-business employees we queried filled out the diagnostic differently. These employees were more likely to answer "N/A" to questions. Why? Certain questions simply didn't apply: there were fewer legal needs at this organization, and HR was smaller in scale. Still, we found that both individual and organizational complexities were rearing their ugly heads. The culprit: growth. As soon as the company tried to scale, operational processes spiraled out of control and became wildly complicated. Unsure of where things were headed, employees had become fearful and controlling. They sought consensus, communicated more, managed risk, provided guidelines or processes to maximize efficiency, and requested additional reports and data before making decisions. In the process, they scheduled unnecessary meetings and demanded duplicative reports. The diagnostic revealed the degree to which this small business had become infected with a serious case of CYA.

After these two trials, we decided to put our diagnostic to one more test: we filled it out ourselves. Future**think** isn't huge—only seventeen employees—and we consider ourselves far more attuned to complexity than most. So imagine our surprise when we found that we, too, suffered from complexity. Not a lot, but some. A few too many processes. A few too many sign-offs. And yes, a few too many meetings. As a team and as individuals, we hadn't taken enough time to ask whether our own behaviors were burdening our peers. Sometimes a colleague would create a new process and a manager would require others to follow it even if it added unnecessary steps to their work. Other times, a client would require that we follow *their* regulations, even though they were overly complex. When the engagement was over, we'd continue following the client's rules without thinking. The result was entirely predictable, and the ensuing complexity made everyone unhappy.

In general, if you're in a larger organization operating across multiple geographies, you can expect that the diagnostic will uncover more organizational complexity. More people and markets mean more HR policies. They also mean more government regulations to contend with, a more complicated organizational structure, more reports, and more complex day-to-day operations. Yet even smaller companies can experience high amounts of complexity in certain highly regulated industries due to legal requirements.

Individual complexity can exist in both small and large companies, but in larger companies, the diagnostic is likely to uncover even more risk aversion, fear, and CYA behavior. Cultural factors can also affect individual complexity scores for companies of all sizes. For instance, in some cultures, it is disrespectful not to include many people in a meeting, and longer e-mails are expected.

Although these general patterns may prevail, every organization is unique. The only way to truly gauge where you are on complexity is to sit down with the diagnostic and work through its questions.

The Perpetual Diagnosis

How often should you take the diagnostic? As we'll see, no one ever wins the battle against complexity outright—it's an ongoing challenge. So use the diagnostic every twelve months to help weed out complexity progressively and proactively. Your initial simplification efforts might have addressed some areas of complexity but left others untouched. Or maybe new complications have arisen as your business model has evolved. Don't let too much time go by without encouraging everyone to take a fresh look. The pace of business has sped up in recent years. The processes you use to evaluate progress need to speed up as well.

In addition to such regular "simplicity maintenance," certain occasions or episodes in the life of an organization may also require a check-in. Have you seen turnover in the C-suite? Are you now leading a new team? Has the business expanded to offer a new product or service? Have you merged with another division or company? Changing circumstances frequently spur organizations to create new processes, standards, and norms. Once the "new normal" has been established, it's worth revisiting the places where complications tend to lurk, and to begin a discussion about how to get back to simplicity.

You might also want to run the diagnostic if your company has been implementing procedural overhauls lately to improve consistency. I see it all the time: such overhauls often lead to inadvertent complexity. One large management consulting company implemented an organization-wide system for reporting expenses. The benefit for the organization's procurement department: consistency. Yet employees and outside vendors lacked training on the system, and they were now required to enter more data to receive reimbursement. The system became a huge burden for them, impeding their work and prompting many complaints. If your team or organization has rolled out a system such as this, wait a few months and perform the diagnostic, just to make sure you haven't created undue or unintended complexity.

Finally, be sure to use the diagnostic any time you feel the need to start a conversation about complexity. Results from the diagnostic can serve as a valuable "proof point," enabling you to convince management that a complexity problem exists and *where* it exists. Running leaders through the diagnostic exercise can also give them common language and concepts for discussing the problem. During an executive leadership training course I ran at a large global pharmaceuticals company, I asked more than two hundred leaders in the organization across seven markets about their complexity issues. Using this diagnostic as a conversation starter, the group collectively gained a new awareness about the topic of complexity. They had all known that complexity existed, but they had no formal opportunity to talk about it with one another, and no way of organizing their thinking about it. Rather than speaking in vague terms about a "complexity problem," these leaders could now discuss categories of complexity and specific opportunities for improvement.

Face Up to Your Complexity Problem *Now*

This chapter has sought to help you identify complexity in your own organization. To give you a sense of how important this work is, I leave you with a story. Some among the legions of people who have flocked to Silicon Valley over the last several decades may not realize this, but the peninsula running from San Jose to San Francisco wasn't always the center of the tech world. A few decades ago, when companies like DEC and Wang drove technological innovation, people talked about Route 128, the road ringing Boston, as the computer industry's hub. Young engineers were heading to the Bay State rather than the Golden State. Michael Dukakis tried to take credit for "The Massachusetts Miracle" during his 1988 presidential campaign.

AnnaLee Saxenian, now dean of Berkeley's School of Information, asked in the 1990s why, if technology was centered on one coast through the 1980s, the technological world had subsequently chosen to pack up and move out West. She discovered that the issue was largely cultural. The firms along 128 were behemoths. They were bureaucratic. They were suffused with rules and legalese. In a word, they were *complicated*.

Eventually, the talent that once streamed to Route 128 refused to stay there. They opted for the culture of the West Coast. The start-ups popping up along Sand Hill Road celebrated the free flow of ideas. There was no expectation of endless loyalty, no big bureaucracy, no crap work to do simply because the bosses upstairs demanded that everyone do things one certain way. If you had an idea in the emerging Silicon Valley, you pitched a funder and, if they gave you the capital needed to get up and running, you got started. In a word, things were a lot *simpler*.[2]

Complication had become normalized within the community of companies surrounding Route 128. It became part of the air people breathed, and as a result, they barely sensed it—even as the best and brightest began heading west. Complication can become embedded in the culture of individual companies, too, with equally devastating results. It can become so natural and seamless that it feels inevitable to people, even if it weighs heavily on them and makes their life at work less fulfilling. Before you know it, people are shaking their heads at the complexity and saying, "That's just the way things are."

Does your company produce complexity unimpeded? Do the cognitive biases and emotional needs I've described have free rein? Does the impulse to insert complexity into a company's routines become overwhelming? Perhaps your company is allowing some complexity to slip by as a matter of course because it serves its interests? If so, you've got a complexity problem. And the time to end it and embrace simplicity is *now*.

CHAPTER FOUR

Work That Matters

"There is no greatness where there is not simplicity, goodness, and truth."

—Leo Tolstoy[1]

I couldn't have been more excited. It was my first job out of college, and I was on my way in for my first day. The offer had come from Leo Burnett, a Chicago advertising agency. And my new bosses had known just how to pump up my sense of anticipation: in the weeks before my first day, they'd sent me a box of products from their long and illustrious list of clients, including Pepsi, Sony, and Procter & Gamble.

The first day did not disappoint, and neither did the days, weeks, and months after that. Assigned to the Allstate Insurance account, I was immediately immersed in all sorts of interesting work. My bosses asked me to generate new product ideas, attend brainstorming sessions, and even coordinate television production shoots. The team around me was terrific, showing me the ropes each time I encountered a new challenge. The atmosphere was so fluid that I had a chance to jump in and get involved in *everything*.

After a few months on the job, my boss put me in charge of a team working on "Natural Disaster Advertising," the campaigns that let victims of floods and tornados know that Allstate was setting up special facilities to expedite their claims. I would later hear victims describe how much those efforts had meant to legions of people whose lives had been torn apart. I felt great knowing that the work I was doing was making a difference, even if in only a small way.

The job wasn't perfect. No one loves an accounting meeting, and I also had trouble getting excited during the hours we spent reviewing magazines to make sure our ads had been placed in the appropriate sections. But on the whole, I had few complaints. The work was engaging, the people were fun, we were charging ahead, and I could go home each evening feeling fulfilled.

And then, two years into it, things changed.

I was offered an opportunity to jump to one of the agency's largest accounts. My boss said it was an early promotion, but he warned that it carried some risk. The woman running the account was notoriously difficult and had been known to ride employees hard. Did I still want the job? I took the leap.

My new position started off well enough. I dove into the minutiae of production schedules, ad rotations, staff meetings, and budget reports. I didn't mind the eighty-hour weeks because everything was new and I was learning a lot. But as the weeks wore on, my enthusiasm faded. I found that I was handling mostly mindless tasks, and that my boss was excluding me from the bigger, more important work many of my peers were doing. My to-do list never seemed to get shorter, and everything was marked "urgent" for no apparent reason. Meetings felt disorganized and inefficient. We'd make indiscriminate changes to ad campaigns at the eleventh hour, even though everyone had already signed off on the scheduled rotations. We were killing ourselves to create production reports that no one had asked to see, and to provide clients with additional options when a pared-down list would likely have pleased them more.

I felt like I was on a treadmill, day after day. More last-minute ads "just because." More reports "just in case." I started asking myself whether working at Leo Burnett was really worth it. After months of soul-searching, I concluded it wasn't. I was tired of wasting time performing an endless stream of inconsequential tasks. After eight months in my new position, I did what just a short time earlier I could hardly have imagined: I quit.

Meaning Is the New Black

Today more than ever, people don't just want a paycheck. They want meaningful work *and* the chance to make a good living. They want to feel like they count, and they want their *work* to count. Millennials, of course, are helping to drive this trend. As *Fast Company* reported, "More than 50% of millennials say they would take a pay cut to find work that matches their values, while 90% want to use their skills for good."[2] Unfortunately, millennials have been decidedly disappointed by the opportunities on offer. Three in four millennials are convinced that businesses care more about their own agendas than about making the world a better place, and barely more than a quarter of millennials believe their current job is utilizing their job skills to the fullest.[3]

Millennials are notorious for feeling *entitled* to meaningful work, and for quickly giving up on a job if work doesn't somehow connect with a larger mission or purpose. A study by State Street Global Advisors found that between a half and two-thirds of millennials have jumped between jobs one to four times over the last five years. And a full two-thirds *expect* to make a switch at some point over the *next* four years.[4] As more millennials rise up in organizations, we can expect that workers in the years ahead will pay even closer attention to the way they spend their time than they do now. They'll take it personally if it seems like their talents are going to waste.

Now, you might dismiss millennials (not to mention the rest of us who want meaningful work) as idealistic. Not all work can be as richly significant as curing cancer, educating underprivileged children, or reducing a company's carbon footprint. Some people have to perform lower-level, support roles that seem less directly altruistic, don't they?

This is the wrong way of thinking about it. Building a meaningful work environment isn't about promoting everyone to a loftier title. It's about all levels of employees in every area feeling that the hard work they put in—whatever that may be—makes a difference somewhere down the line. Researchers have found, for example, that the people dialing for dollars on behalf of university scholarship funds work harder if they've had an opportunity to meet the people who will be awarded the benefits. Summarizing the researchers' conclusions, reporter Olga Khazan observed that meeting these people "[gave] their work meaning."[5] And meaning is important for nearly everyone. Most of us simply want to understand that the majority of our work contributes *in some way* to the greater good. We want to know that the work we do every day has a purpose.

Get the Work Right, You Get the Culture Right

Organizations and leaders are very good at talking about mission, values, and purpose. They post high-minded statements in the lobby, on their social media pages, on the home page of the company website. Many leaders wouldn't miss a beat if asked precisely how a young accountant's job helps their firm contribute to the social good. But this rings hollow if excessive rules, processes, or bureaucracy get in the way. Nothing separates individuals more from a sense that their work is worthwhile than the curse of complication.

> Nothing separates individuals more from a sense that their work is worthwhile than the curse of complication.

Complexity sucks the life out of your career because it forces you to break a sweat while receiving nothing good in return. Any job worth having comes with a certain amount of pressure and stress. Even the meaningful jobs millennials claim to want—cancer researcher, schoolteacher of underprivileged children, environmental engineer—carry deadlines and accountability. But the stress arising from complexity is entirely different. It's stress without reward.

In this sense, it's not just meaning that is "the new black." It's simplicity. Recalling our definition of simplicity, employees of today and tomorrow want workplaces where the processes and rules that structure work are as *minimal, understandable, repeatable,* and *accessible* as possible. And when they get simplicity handed to them, well...watch out. Simplicity brings with it all kinds of benefits for individual workers. Over time, these

> Employees of today and tomorrow want workplaces where the processes and rules that structure work are as *minimal, understandable, repeatable,* and *accessible* as possible.

cycle upward and spread outward, changing the culture of teams and organizations.

Many people think that culture is paramount. Not true. If you get the work right, you get the culture right.

Let me say it again because it's so important: if you get the work right, you get the culture right. Simplicity is about finally getting the work right—for everyone. The culture follows in due course, naturally, organically, without a lot of extra effort and expense. "Wow," people

> If you get the work right, you get the culture right.

start to say, "things feel different around here. What a great culture we have." And we all know what happens when organizations have dynamic, innovative, high-octane cultures. They win.

A Thought Experiment

Simplicity's impact on individuals isn't especially hard to grasp. A brief thought experiment suffices to make the point. No matter where you reside in your organization's hierarchy, I invite you to take out a piece of paper and draw a line down the center, dividing it into two columns. Consider the specific set of talents and desires you bring to work with you every day. If you could rework your role to make it more effective and meaningful—if you could better leverage your talents in support of the company's goals—what would you spend your day doing that you're not currently doing? In the left-hand column, make a list of these new work activities.

Now ask yourself: "What tasks in my daily work currently occupy most of my time?" Write the answers in the right-hand column.

Compare the two columns. How do they differ?

As a final step, circle the items in the right-hand column (the tasks you do every day) that add value to your work. Looking at the list of the things that you didn't circle, ask yourself: "How can I eliminate, out-source, or streamline those things to make more space for items in the left-hand column?"

I'll tell you what's in my left-hand column. If I had more simplicity in my workday, I'd:

- Spend more time thinking about how to make my team or organization more efficient.
- Spend more time thinking through the strategic threats confronting my team and organization, and how we might handle them.
- Spend more time thinking about hidden marketplace opportunities, and how we might grasp them.
- Spend more time thinking of new products, and new ways of selling those products.
- Spend more time talking to my customers, learning what they think about us, what *they* want.
- Spend more time thinking about what skills my team could develop to help them do their jobs better.

You get the idea. For each of us, simplicity amounts to an enormous, untapped opportunity. The time we currently spend checking Instagram updates while waiting for that unnecessary biweekly conference call to begin could be time spent doing the most daring act of all in the modern workplace: thinking.

But that's only the beginning. The time we waste could also be time spent building our skills, talents, and relationships. It could be time spent exercising more, enjoying family more, pursuing hobbies more. Just imagine how invigorated and eager to contribute you'd be every morning if you had more time for the things you care about, and if you were wasting less time on the things you don't.

Simplicity Is the Solution

Let's turn now to organizations and explore the many benefits simplicity can bring to them. In 2002, trouble was brewing at the drugstore retailer CVS. The market was fiercely competitive; lots of companies had the technology required to fill prescriptions either in-store or through the mail. Unfortunately, surveys revealed that customer satisfaction among CVS's customers was dropping precipitously. If CVS was going to remain competitive, somebody needed to pinpoint the problem and fix it straightaway.

Senior managers dug around and learned that one out of every five prescriptions CVS tried to fill was delayed by the "insurance check"—the moment in the purchasing process when the company confirmed that the customer was covered by the same insurance policy that CVS had in its database. Pharmacists at CVS frequently performed insurance checks *after* customers had left the store, when pharmacists could no longer request the information required to set everything straight. As a result, customers faced long waits for prescriptions, and getting their meds became a huge inconvenience.

Remedying the situation didn't require an expensive fix like investing in new technology, hiring more staff, or retraining pharmacists. Rather, senior managers made a small but significant tweak to pharmacy operations. They moved the insurance check to the *beginning* of the process, right before the pharmacist went through the required safety review with the customer. That way, if the insurance didn't check out, the folks behind the counter could remedy the problem right there by asking a question as simple as: "Have you recently switched jobs?"

CVS spread this process shift to its four thousand–plus pharmacies within twelve months. Customer satisfaction rates jumped from 86 percent to 91 percent—a substantial improvement. As one analysis concluded: "The redesigned protocol helped boost customer satisfaction scores without compromising safety—and not just in one store but in all of them."[6]

And that, in a nutshell, captures the powerful impact of simplicity. As Jack Welch once said, "For a large organization to be effective, it must be simple."[7] Every organization wants better performance. And simplicity is the way to get there.

CVS is hardly the only company to achieve better performance through simplicity. In 2014, the world-renowned Cleveland Clinic employed roughly one hundred analysts and developers to manage its reporting information. The business intelligence group (BI), as it was called, wrote and maintained the analytics that gathered all the little bits of data that made improvement possible, and it also aggregated numbers on everything from visits to appointments to medications to procedures. If incoming data dealt with the operational or clinical sides, it was BI that built the web apps, dashboards, and data marts that allowed front-line caregivers to know exactly what was happening. Because of BI's work, physician leadership could analyze trends in patient care and improve outcomes, ultimately saving lives.

In keeping with Cleveland Clinic's ongoing commitment to continuous improvement, a collaboration between the continuous improvement (CI) group and BI was launched. Chris Kucharik from CI and Patrick Day from BI saw an opportunity to try a new way of producing the information so critical to the clinic's decision-making. They posed a challenging question: What could they simplify about the process of developing software to make it more efficient and effective?

It wasn't an easy question. BI sat at the hub of one of the world's most complex information systems, producing metrics for one of the economy's most heavily regulated sectors. At any given time, the group had thirty to forty projects in process, many of which required hundreds of work hours to complete. Streamlining BI's development processes was akin to changing an engine on a jet airplane in midair. Kucharik and Day had to demonstrate success before wide adoption. "We knew we had to start small and develop tangible proof," Kucharik said. "The first, large hurdle is often, 'That's nice but it doesn't work for us.'"

With support from BI department leadership, the two decided to introduce a different way of thinking on two projects from the existing queue. They knew that if they succeeded in finding a simpler, faster approach to solving problems, they might open the door to a new *culture* of improvement within the department. This, in turn, would allow Cleveland Clinic to harness its data more effectively, and *that* could save even more lives.

BI had planned to enhance the existing scorecard to track what is known as hospital transfers—the process of moving someone into or out of a bed. Data showed that limiting the transition time to fewer than four hours would improve outcomes. Caregivers needed a tool that tracked which patients in the queue were nearing that four-hour mark. Could BI come up with software that the medical staff could use to expedite transfers?

That might sound pretty easy—like an Uber service for gurneys. But this wasn't the kind of software you could craft after attending a couple classes of Coding 101. The systems that track patients were complex, interacting with all sorts of other software, bringing in data points from a whole variety of devices and departments. Business knowledge needed to be combined with technical ability to build the right tools. "With facilities and diverse specialties scattered across northeast Ohio, the transfer team needed to quickly place a patient in the right nursing unit to ensure proper care and positive outcomes," Day said.

Typically, big institutions like Cleveland Clinic had extensive development processes for their software. Software developers and the clients (in this case, those handling the transfers) first met to discuss the underlying challenge they wanted to tackle. The clients, who often possessed only a vague understanding of the technology that made the software work, explained what they wanted in plain language. The technologists explained the limits of what they could do, maybe using terminology the clients didn't entirely comprehend. The two sides went back and forth, each trying to clarify as best they could. And then, after some semblance of a plan had emerged, the software engineers retreated to their offices to build what they *thought* the client wanted.

All too often, multiple gaps in communication—between client and engineers, and between members of the engineering team itself—yielded an end product entirely different from what the client envisioned. Engineers then had to go back and redo the entire software package, sometimes multiple times, until the client was satisfied. The result was wasted time and unnecessary frustration on all sides.

Fixing the traditional waterfall software development process through traditional Lean manufacturing process improvement would have resulted in deeper standardization of the existing process. That wouldn't have been enough. To flip the paradigm, the team started by introducing Lean software design (also known as Agile Scrum) to the pilot development teams. Yet, even this was too cumbersome and complicated, and it didn't fit within the environment at BI. So the team went a step further and adopted an alternate strategy: simplify. They boiled Agile Scrum down to the essential elements and introduced flexibility to the development process.

To develop the new hospital transfer software, the team would apply the basic methodology of Agile Scrum and use rapid cycling to progressively develop and refine small pieces. Rather than disappearing for months on end and then unveiling a new system to their clients, the engineers would stay in close contact with the frontline folks who would eventually use the software. During "sprints," engineers would develop a piece of the overall project and then check in with the people doing hospital transfers to make sure they were producing something useful. Because everyone was working hand in hand to monitor and influence the software's development along the way, the whole process would flow more easily, quickly, and simply. "Through simplified visual management (Post-its and flip charts) we were able to communicate effectively between the development team and frontline to produce exactly what they needed," Day said.

Throughout the process, BI was determined to keep everything it did as simple as possible. Team members made sure never to deviate from the mission of achieving exactly what the clients wanted, avoiding the temptation to build in unnecessary bells and whistles. Meanwhile, as the cycles turned over, it became clear that certain functionalities that the clients had initially requested—elements that would have been built had BI used the traditional software development model—were now obsolete. And so, as Kucharik explained, in the new rapid cycle development process, "We built what they wanted. We didn't build what they didn't need. And we built critical discoveries." Meanwhile, BI's trajectory to the finish line was far more direct and efficient.

If rapid cycling hit the target more adeptly, it did so in significantly less time. BI team members estimated that they had shaved off 20 percent of the time they would otherwise have had to invest in the project. A subsequent project that used the same process to develop software for critical care transport (the movement of patients off ambulances, helicopters, and fixed-wing aircraft) was shortened by 25 percent, allowing BI to finish more than a month early.

After these two initial successes, other members of the BI team were eager to apply the new rapid cycle methodology to other projects. They soon found one: the development of software to manage follow-up medical appointments. In this case, rapid cycling *halved* the time needed for completion—a whole new level of efficiency. Taken together, the three deployments saved BI more than six hundred hours of work, representing more than $100,000 in cost savings. Most importantly, the operational director overseeing the frontline department received a more efficient delivery and a higher-quality software product. "I cannot put into words the excitement and thankfulness of both the crew members and administration...I look forward to 'sprinting' into the future," Kucharik said.

Using rapid cycle software development, Cleveland Clinic improved the delivery of that information with higher quality, in less time, and at a lower cost. It's a prime example of how an organization can put simplicity to work at a grassroots level to drive better performance.

Unlock Creativity and Innovation

Increased productivity would be reason enough for an organization to pursue simplicity. Yet simplicity doesn't just make organizations more efficient; it also helps them become more creative. Scott Barry Kaufman, scientific director of the University of Pennsylvania's Science of Imagination Project at the Positive Psychology Center, has found that 72 percent of us come up with new, creative ideas when we're showering. Why? According to Kaufman, "The relaxing, solitary, and non-judgmental shower environment may afford creative thinking by allowing the mind to wander freely, and causing people to be more open to their inner stream of consciousness and daydreams."[8] In other words, simplifying your environment so that you can be alone with your thoughts makes it more likely that you'll tap into your own creativity.

In a work environment, it isn't just solitude that helps people become more creative; it's also contact with a variety of people and ideas. In a famous study of the defense contractor Raytheon, sociologist Ronald Burt found that those employees who had a hand in more than one department were more likely to innovate. As he put it, the employees who spanned "structural holes" were at "higher risk" for coming up with good ideas.[9] Today, many people don't have the bandwidth to span "structural holes." They're so bogged down in complication that they confine themselves by necessity to their own domains. If they're in sales, they're focused on formatting the numbers properly and filling out three expense reports when one would do; that preoccupation prevents them from following what's going on in engineering, marketing, or operations.

Over the years, I've conducted sessions on change and innovation with tens of thousands of people, from all different countries, cultures, industries, functions, and tenures. I've found that organizations, while well intentioned, tend to approach innovation incorrectly. The very things they put in place to drive innovation—meetings, reports, policies, procedures, task forces, and governing bodies—wind up constricting it. While some structure is important, the best approach to change and innovation usually isn't to do more, but to do less. Get rid of things that aren't working to make space for new things that are.

> Get rid of things that aren't working to make space for new things that are.

It was this revelation that led Julian Richer, the founder of retailer Richer Sounds and one of the U.K.'s leading business executives, to institute a "cut the crap committee" within his company—a team dedicated to "[getting] rid of unnecessary stuff."[10] What happened? In the words of one analyst, "Richer Sounds holds the Guinness Record for the highest sales per square foot of any retail outlet in the world and also gives the biggest percentage of its profits to charity of any company in the UK."[11] Eliminating the complexity allows people to escape their routines and try new things. Although largely unseen and unspoken, simplicity is the most fundamental gateway to innovative thinking and action.

> Although largely unseen and unspoken, simplicity is the most fundamental gateway to innovative thinking and action.

Let's say you already have some good ideas. If complexity plagues your organization, chances are you won't be able to apply them. As we all know, good ideas often come from frontline employees—the people who touch customers and markets. Most organizations today realize the value of insight from frontline employees, and quite a few have introduced technological solutions to crowdsource ideas and solutions. Yet complexity still gums up the flow of good ideas in all sorts of ways. Lower-level employees can't hope to understand the "complicated" processes governed by other departments. Fear of ridicule deters them from proposing new ideas; they don't want to look stupid.

Quite often, good ideas get lost in the system, frustrating grassroots employees and discouraging them from innovating in the future. In simpler work environments, people at every level understand better how things work. They know who holds power, and they know who's for and against a given decision. They're not guaranteed that management will adopt an idea they propose, but when they're denied, they at least know *why* their bosses turned them down, *who* blocked their path, and *if* modifying their idea might make it more palatable.

Complicated companies can't boast the same transparency. It's much easier for bosses to kill off good ideas thoughtlessly or for political reasons, or simply to let them die on the vine because they're too busy or resistant to change. Why didn't an employee's idea get adopted? A boss can always claim that it wasn't she who blocked it, but another leader or department that had to sign off. In simpler environments, greater transparency allows employees to engage in a dialogue with bosses when ideas aren't adopted rather than muddle along feeling frustrated and ignored. Over the long term, more innovation occurs.

More Engagement, Less Stress

Amy Poehler's hit sitcom *Parks and Recreation* chronicles the trials and travails of parks department employees serving the small, fictional city of Pawnee, Indiana. The show's central backdrop is bureaucracy. Its central conceit: Poehler's character, Leslie Knope, refuses to submit to the red tape. Driven by idealism, she fights for the public interest.

As for her colleagues, well, they're a different story. They might be capable, but the complications of government have made them cynical, leading most of them to put in halfhearted efforts, at best. In one episode, a friend ducks in and asks the department's director, Ron Swanson, whether she's interrupting anything important. "Impossible," he responds, "I work for the government."[12] To make it through the day, Ron's subordinates turn to little pleasures and pursuits. For instance, two of Leslie's colleagues, Tom (played by Aziz Ansari) and Donna (played by Retta), decide to make life more pleasant by devoting a day each year to "Treat. Yo. Self." On this day, they indulge themselves in every possible way. Manicures. Cocktails. Fancy restaurants. You name it.

Tom and Donna *need* "Treat. Yo. Self" because their workplace is so disengaging. When I watched that episode, I couldn't help but wonder what life at the parks department might have been like had the bureaucracy not been so stifling.

Granted, a simplified and effective Pawnee Parks Department wouldn't have made such a great television program. But when simplicity takes hold, doors open to a new kind of engagement. People know their sweat equity will result in a real return. They know what to do—and they're more focused on their goals. They have the confidence to take action simply because the path ahead is much clearer. And to top it off, they're healthier. Complexity is *stressful*. It's hard to stay on the treadmill. It's draining.

For all these reasons, eliminating complexity can save an organization real money. Studies have revealed that stress-related health conditions cost businesses between $200 and $300 billion a year in lost productivity.[13] In fact, 5 to 8 percent of national health-care spending is due to workplace stress.[14] As far as engagement goes, one study found that "presenteeism"—the phenomenon of a worker being "present" at work without being engaged—accounts for $150 billion in losses across the corporate world.[15] That figure doesn't reflect all the good ideas and innovations that *don't* emerge because workers aren't mentally and emotionally invested in their employer's broader mission.

One more thing: studies have found that multitasking spurs the body to create more of the hormone cortisol, and that an excess of cortisol can impair your memory. In addition to all the other damage it does, complication actually makes the average employee more forgetful![16] Imagine the toll *that* levies on your average company.

Business Results That Matter

More innovation, more engagement, and more productivity: simplicity packs quite a punch for organizations. But none of this would matter if simplicity didn't ultimately allow organizations to compete better and achieve better financial performance. Evidence shows that it does exactly that.

Simplicity's benefits add up to a competitive edge by making companies nimbler, more efficient, and faster. We all know that markets today are more volatile than ever. The player that can adapt to new conditions more quickly wins. Guess what? It's easier to adapt when your teams don't have as many meetings, e-mails, tests, reports, quality controls, and so on slowing them down. And when you go further and bake simplicity into your operational models and customer interfaces, you've changed the game entirely.

Years ago, Southwest Airlines placed a bet on simplicity. While other airlines flew a variety of aircraft models (American Airlines at one point used fourteen!), Southwest chose to build its fleet around a single model of plane, the Boeing 737.[17] In the event of a storm, when one plane couldn't make it to a destination on time, another plane could take its place seamlessly, helping customers get where they needed to go while saving the company money. As Chris Wahlenmaier, the airline's Vice President of Customer Support and services, has explained, the benefits of one plane are surprisingly far-reaching: "We only need to train our mechanics on one type of airplane. We only need extra parts inventory for that one type of airplane. If we have to swap a plane out at the last minute for maintenance, the fleet is totally interchangeable—all our on-board crews and ground crews are already familiar with it. And there are no challenges in how and where we can park our planes on the ground, since they're all the same shape and size."[18]

In so many ways, simplicity made the airline easier to run, more flexible, and better able to meet the needs of customers. Meanwhile, American Airlines struggled to compete with the mishmash of planes in its fleet. As American's onetime CEO Gerard Arpey once explained: "The cost of complexity isn't offset by what you can charge."[19] It's no coincidence that for years Southwest won the customer satisfaction "Triple Crown," registering the best "on-time performance, baggage handling and low complaint rates."[20] In due course, all those happier customers chose Southwest over the more established players. Advantage Southwest!

Southwest isn't the only transportation company to have used simplicity to its advantage. In 2013, General Motors consolidated and simplified its brand lineup, dropping its Pontiac, Saturn, and Hummer divisions. The CEO at the time, Fritz Henderson, noted that the move was "an intensely personal decision in many ways," especially given Pontiac's long history and heritage (the brand dated from 1926).[21] Yet a little pain brought real benefits, helping the company save as many as 1.2 million jobs.[22] In 2015,

Fast Company cited GM's story as one of "The Biggest Business Comebacks of the Past 20 Years."[23]

Turning to the technology sector, we find that LinkedIn has also made strides thanks to simplicity. For years, the company had barraged its customers with e-mails notifying them that someone wanted to connect, reminding them, and reminding them again. Customers became frustrated and many complained. In 2015, LinkedIn's executives addressed the issue by making some policy changes: users hit with lots of incoming requests to connect would receive a weekly digest rather than singular pings in real time. And users who had joined the site's user groups would be updated in a more streamlined fashion. The company reduced outgoing e-mail by roughly 40 percent, and complaints fell by half.[24] From 2014 to 2015, LinkedIn's revenue grew by 35 percent, and membership grew by 20 percent, from 347 million to 414 million users.[25]

Google offers another example of a technology company that competes better because it integrated simplicity into its business strategy. For years, the firm has ranked near the top of the branding firm Siegel+Gale's Global Brand Simplicity Index. Google's work itself isn't simple; the company's underlying technology is extremely complicated. Yet the customer experience is extremely simple, especially as compared with that of Google's competitors. As chief marketing officer Lorraine Twohill noted: "All the complexity can be behind the scenes, but the user experience should be simple. We need to get people what they're looking for, fast, and simplicity is a core part of our promise." Asked about the business impact of simplifying the customer experience, Twohill replied: "Faster and greater adoption. We've seen it time and time again—if you eliminate friction you get better adoption, and better word of mouth. The product gets used by more people."[26] And that's the point.

While complexity leaves companies vulnerable to market disruptions, simplicity has proven again and again that it helps them *become* disruptors. Look, for example, at what happened to Blockbuster and the mom-and-pop video stores that preceded it. Today, Netflix controls the market those companies once served because Netflix has made it much easier for consumers to rent videos, either through the mail or online. The same is true for Capital One, which has taken the credit card industry by storm by eliminating the frustration wrought by complicated "blackout" dates.[27]

It's hard to imagine, but years ago, wireless carriers trapped their customers by refusing to let them keep their phone number if they jumped to a different carrier. As a result, few customers switched, even if they thought they could get a better deal on a different network. It was just too much of a hassle to tell all your contacts that your number had changed. Realizing that this trap was doing a real disservice to the general public, Britain's Office of Telecommunications mandated that customers be allowed to keep their numbers when they switched plans. Simply by removing that barrier, regulators allowed disruptive companies to enter the marketplace, presenting consumers with new choices while incenting existing companies to provide better service.[28]

Simplicity is compelling all around—and markets reward it. Siegel+Gale has calculated that consumers are often willing to pay a "simplicity premium" of as much as *6 percent* more for a similar product if the product is simpler to use.[29] Indeed, one survey found that nearly two out of every three consumers will pay more for a simpler experience. Moreover, nearly seven in ten will more likely recommend a product or service if the customer experience is less complex than a competitor's.[30] No surprise, then, that publicly traded companies in the top ten of Siegel+Gale's Global Brand Simplicity Index over the last six years have outperformed the average global stock index by 214 percent.[31]

If simplicity boosts companies' competitiveness, the converse is also true: complexity causes customer interest to dry up. I was recently trading stories with a CEO whose large company runs an online business providing licensing tools to third parties. This executive, a client of mine, had become frustrated that his company's offering wasn't growing as quickly as he and his team had expected. The company's customers *needed* the service; in fact, it had the potential to transform their businesses. The service had all kinds of client endorsements and testimonials backing it up, and potential customers had received promotional videos and been offered free trials. My client's team had tried *everything* and just couldn't understand why their licensing tools service was not killing it.

Finally, my client took one of his biggest customers out for lunch and pointedly asked why he wasn't using the new licensing tools. The client's answer surprised him: "You have so many resources!"

"So *many* resources? I don't understand." My client had thought that offering a broad selection of licensing tools was one of his firm's key selling points, as it allowed his firm to be a "one-stop shop" for innovation.

"Yeah," his customer said, "You have so many resources that I'm over-whelmed. I don't know where to start."

Customer overload is hardly limited to the business-to-business (B2B) arena. In 2015, J.D. Power published a study that suggested that of every five people who purchased a new car, at least one never used almost half of the car's newfangled technology features. Some of the vehicles had "concierge" services—but more than 40 percent of people had never used them. Some had automatic parking systems—35 percent had never used them. Some had mobile routers—38 percent had never logged on. All in all, the study found that the billions of dollars automakers had invested in these technologies were largely wasted, given how few drivers were actually using them.[32]

We all experience customer overload in our everyday lives. Yes, it's nice that we don't *all* have to watch *The Ed Sullivan Show* every night; we can choose from a much wider diversity of television programs and movies. But if you subscribe to a cable, streaming, or satellite service, do you really watch more than a handful of the hundreds of channels you pay to receive? Or when you sit down to order at a nice restaurant, do you ever struggle just to get a glass of water? Sparkling or still, with ice or without, lemon or lime: if you weren't thirsty when you *began* ordering your meal, you're thirsty by the end just because you've had to talk about it so much!

We really do live in the age of "busy." Too many choices, decisions, data, and things to figure out. Everybody's pushed to the brink. As Jim Daly, the chief human resource officer at Affinion, once told me, "Option-ality kills!"[33] So how do you differentiate yourself? Cut the complexity. Make it shockingly easy for the people buying your products and services to get what they want with minimum hassle. Let them experience the joy of doing in five minutes what they thought would take an hour. In other words, simplify.

Simplification Emergency

Scripps Health in Southern California is one of the nation's largest and most admired health-care companies. Yet, like everyone else in the industry, Scripps has had to evolve with the market. Health-care costs in the United States have skyrocketed over the last several decades. Why? Like the domestic automobile industry in the 1980s, health-care companies have grown fat and lazy, adding people and processes without much thought about costs or the overall quality of the care they're providing. Yet with the advent of health-care reform, the days of plenty ended. Today, the economy simply can't sustain the sorts of expenditures eaten up by hospitals, nursing homes, doctors, nurses, medicines, therapies, and the like. Health-care organizations must either streamline or go out of business.

Scripps CEO Chris Van Gorder and his leadership team began transforming their organization earlier than most. During the early 2000s, they saw health-care reform coming, but instead of seeing it as a threat to be feared, they embraced it as an opportunity. They saw the potential that existed to do more with less, even a lot less. And for them, simplification became a primary route to cutting costs, improving quality, improving employee satisfaction, and in general making Scripps a far better organization.

In 2007, for instance, the company's executive team realized that their emergency departments alone had twenty-five different functions that all reported up to different people within the hospital bureaucracy. Many people working on the same patients and problems never communicated with one another. In effect, the basic systems that organized work within each facility had remained stagnant for thirty years. Even as radically new diagnostic tools and equipment had come online, the processes used by the personnel inside the emergency departments had failed to evolve.

As a result, patients were having lousy experiences. When they came into the ER, an access representative first typically interviewed them, then a nurse, then another nurse, and then a doctor. The whole process could drag on and on—nonemergency patients could sometimes wait more than eight hours to be served. It got to the point that more than one in eight patients would leave the ER before being seen, simply because they couldn't wait anymore.

What team members discovered, upon studying the problem, was that the patient experience wasn't the central organizing principle at the ER; nothing really was, and as a result, complication had taken hold unchecked. Backroom operating systems and routines were holding health-care providers hostage, stealing their time, attention, and energy. These dedicated professionals were too busy filling out forms, following outdated procedures, and navigating the demands of the bureaucracy upstairs to stay focused on the patients themselves.

Scripps eventually redesigned its ERs to achieve greater simplicity, cost savings, and quality. The triage process was a prime target. Rather than a four-step process, Scripps instituted a new regime: each patient would immediately get an interview with a doctor and a nurse. The two together would determine whether the patient was among the 20 to 30 percent of incoming cases that needed immediate attention. If not, the patient was taken out of the queue and directed to see one of several teams of specialists trained and equipped to deal with *non*emergency issues more expeditiously.

The results were nothing short of transformational. Average wait times in the ER dropped by more than half. Patients no longer left the hospitals without being seen, as they had when wait times were so high. Revenue jumped 20 percent as patients began to come from longer distances, knowing that Scripps would attend to them more quickly than the competition. Both staff and customer satisfaction jumped—and so Scripps began to apply the same model of reorganization to others departments and facilities. As a result of the ER redesign and similar work across the organization, Scripps removed $200 million of annual costs from the system.

Is Scripps still vulnerable to ongoing disruption in the health-care industry? Of course. Yet unlike many of its competitors, Scripps has a huge advantage. The organization is less likely to be caught flat-footed after the emergence of a black swan. And even if they are caught, they've developed the sort of simplified framework that will allow them to adapt and survive.

Unknown Unknowns

Some time ago, one of my friends related an old business fable that made an impression on me. Perhaps you've heard it. A man named John was driving with his son Philip. The two came upon a traffic jam. As they sat in traffic, they could see through the windshield that a large truck with a tall load had become wedged under a railway overpass. Time dragged on, and John became increasingly infuriated. What had the truck driver been thinking? As for Philip, he watched as police vehicles, fire trucks, and construction equipment arrived to figure out some way of getting the truck out from under the bridge.

After a few minutes, Philip shocked John by springing out of the car and running toward the accident. John got out and raced after his son while the boy cried, "I know how to get the truck out!" The workers were concerned for the boy's safety and shooed him away. But Philip persisted until he found someone who would listen. "What do you think we should do?" asked the man.

Philip smiled. "Just let the air out of the tires!"

It was a simple solution—and one that none of the experienced engineers at the scene had thought to do. Phillip wasn't ensnared in the web of complexity that had blinded all the adults on the scene. He wasn't thinking about hydraulics or friction or personal liability. He was blessed with a mindset of clarity and simplicity.

Amazing things happen for companies if they remove complexity and help employees get back to work that matters. Better productivity. More creativity. Better engagement and retention. A healthier workforce. All of which add up to a competitive edge that can help you survive disruption and perhaps even cause it. But the true impact of simplicity doesn't end there. Although we know that simplifying, and getting to work that matters can remake organizations, we don't really know where it can ultimately take us. As this wonderful little story suggests, simplicity opens up whole new worlds to us, yielding insights and solutions that are as yet unimaginable. Most fundamentally, it returns us, in some way, to the time when we were children, when we were in touch with our intuition, when everything seemed fresh, new, and endlessly fascinating—when even the impossible seemed possible.

What new technical solutions will *your* employees generate when they're not as encumbered by bureaucracy? What culture will they help define when you reduce the number of e-mails? What new products will they conceive when the number of meetings shrivels up? What new markets will they conquer when the rules are fewer? What new levels of revenue will they attain when there aren't so many reports to assemble and submit? How much market share will they snare when fewer sign-offs are required on paperwork? What great ills facing humanity will they eliminate when everybody is doing work that matters, and when, as a result, they're every bit as enthusiastic as I was during my first day at my very first job?

We can only imagine.

CHAPTER FIVE

The Simplicity Mindset

"Behind every brand providing simpler experiences is a leader that
understands the true value of them."
—Margaret Molloy, Chief Marketing Officer, Siegel+Gale[1]

Millions of Americans have money invested in mutual funds, but it wasn't
always that way. In 1970, when financial institutions first conceived of
money market funds, everyone saw corporations as the end users. That's
because once you invested your assets in a money market fund, it was
really, really difficult to redeem your investment. Only large companies
with big finance departments had the clerks and accountants required to
figure the whole thing out.[2]

A few years later, leaders at Fidelity Investment started taking another
look at money market funds. If the company could streamline redemp-
tion, money market accounts could serve as a terrific product for an individual or a family. They were (and are) fairly similar to savings accounts,
yet they potentially offered much better returns, at the time as high as 14
percent. Unfortunately, operational and customer service complications
for this type of asset remained a challenge. Cynics argued that individual
investors wouldn't park assets in money market accounts because redeem-
ing their shares would prove such a tedious and cumbersome process.
The consumer would have to draft a letter to the fund managers, get it

notarized, and mail it in. Only then would the company begin processing the request.

Fidelity's leaders continued to study the opportunity. What if the company simplified the system so that individual investors could write checks directly from their accounts? No letters. No notary. Just a check drawn directly from the fund. Could it be done?

"Absolutely not," said many of Fidelity's in-house lawyers. If the company removed the usual procedural safeguards, irresponsible consumers would start writing checks out of their accounts that exceeded what their shares were worth. These checks would bounce—a disaster for the company.

Ned Johnson, the company's CEO, and Bob Gould, the head of operations, weren't willing to give up on the idea. Was it really true that consumers would bounce checks? Couldn't the company at least *try* letting individuals open money market accounts? Searching for other legal opinions, they finally found lawyers willing to acknowledge that there wasn't, strictly speaking, anything in the law that prevented Fidelity from offering money market accounts to individuals. It was a calculated risk, and management would have to decide if it was worth taking.

What happened next is part of Fidelity's—and industry—lore. In 1974, Fidelity rolled out the Fidelity Daily Income Trust (FDIT), the world's first mutual funds targeted to consumers, and found that there was indeed demand among individual investors. *Huge* demand. Within the first six months, Fidelity took in $800 million worth of assets (remember, that's 1974 dollars). Legions of customers who might once have looked past Fidelity became, in the years that followed, some of the company's most loyal investors. When the stock market shot up a few years later, customers started transferring their assets into equity accounts, through Fidelity. It was a huge success.

As this story affirms, simplicity sells itself. The only thing standing between Fidelity and an initial $800 million bonanza had been a big heap of complication that every member of Fidelity's leadership team other than Johnson and Gould—as well as leaders of the mutual fund industry's trade association, the Investment Company Institute—had blindly defended. But there's a more important point here. Fidelity reinvented mutual funds because the leadership team came together, took the reins, accepted the risk, and saw it through. They made simplification happen. And if you're leading an organization or business unit right now, or you hope to be a senior leader one day, then you'll need to make it happen as well. Simplicity won't just well up naturally from lower in the organization (although, as we'll see in the next chapter, everybody at all levels can play a role). You have to make it a strategic priority. You have to give it energy and attention. You have to send the right messages. It's one of the key things leaders do, and it's an essential skill to learn if you want to become a leader.

How Well Do You *Really* Know Your Organization?

In some ways, achieving simplicity is harder for top executives than it is for others in the organization. But it's also more important. As Jack Welch has written: "Insecure managers create complexity. Frightened, nervous managers use thick, convoluted planning books and busy slides filled with everything they've known since childhood. Real leaders don't need clutter."[3] You'll remember from chapter 2 the cognitive and emotional traps that commonly cause people to mire themselves and their colleagues in complexity. Leaders fall prey to these traps as well, but they also face other challenges.

Most notable among these is executive disconnect. Executives are often (rightfully) focused on the bigger picture, and as a result they don't experience firsthand the minutiae of operations—the rules, processes, and practices that employees experience every day. If these become excessively complex and inefficient, leaders often have little clue. Assistants, chiefs of staff, and others around the top executives often serve as a buffer, shielding leaders from the workplace realities that wear down everyone else.

As leaders become more disconnected, they sometimes unintentionally do things that make complexity worse, draining the meaning out of work. For instance, we've all seen or heard about situations in which executives in the C-suite send off missives requiring painstaking work and long hours. As expected, the reports they requested come back incredibly detailed and thoroughly fact-checked. Sometimes the executives requesting the report read it, but in all too many cases, the carefully curated memo simply sits on their desks, lost amid more pressing business. Executives justify their initial request by telling themselves—and anyone who might ask—that they "wanted it just in case." Or that they were sure the information would be useful to someone down the line.

The employees who prepared the report feel like they've spun their wheels for nothing. Their jobs have become more complex and less meaningful. Yet executives never grasp the full consequences of their request. After all, few employees would admit just how taxing it has been to fulfill requests like this, since telling the truth might imply lack of interest or commitment on their part. And executives often feel those employees don't understand the "big picture" of what leaders are trying to achieve.

If anything, executive disconnect has worsened in recent years, rendering it easier for leaders to inadvertently spawn complexity. For decades, we've preached a gospel of "empowering" employees to work as they see fit, chastising leaders for micromanaging when they get too deep in the weeds. A good boss is supposed to set clear standards and then keep his hands off. No one wants to return to the bad old days of unfettered micromanaging; we want individual employees to use their own ingenuity to solve problems, and to feel emotionally invested in getting the job done. The downside is that leaders, with so much of their own work to do, have grown less familiar with the process of how those reporting to them are doing their jobs. It's no longer clear to us, in many cases, if we're asking for work that will take a week's worth of toil, or just a few hours.

Simplicity: An Ethical Imperative

Simplification is extremely difficult—there's no denying that—but it's also critically important. We've already seen that simplicity confers a powerful competitive advantage on enterprises. For the sake of shareholders alone, leaders would be well advised to pursue it. But let me take the case for simplicity just a little bit further. When you think about many of the other stakeholders that leaders serve, you realize pretty quickly that simplification is the *right thing for leaders to do*. In other words, simplification rises to the level of an ethical imperative, not merely a business one.

Simplicity carries real benefits for customers. They're going to get a

How Have You Contributed to Complexity?

1. You often send e-mails that are longer than one paragraph and/or require significant time to read.
2. Emails that you send usually include more than three cc's or bcc's.
3. You expect e-mail replies from staff within twenty-four hours or by the next business day.
4. You often use business jargon and buzzwords in your written and spoken communication.
5. You require your team members to involve you in the decisions they make.
6. Your decisions are always a group effort.
7. You've assigned a project without a clear objective or clear project lead in the past six months.
8. You expect employees to follow formal process steps without exception.
9. You (or your team) consistently add on to project/product/development work, and you rarely eliminate things.
10. You must sign off on all expenses, communications, or contracts within your group.
11. You hold multiple, recurring meetings with your team each week.
12. You have held meetings without agendas.
13. Your presentations are known for being lengthy and containing in-depth information.
14. You don't often provide feedback on reports/presentations that you assign.
15. You require each of your direct reports to create multiple, recurring reports.

If you answered "yes" to any items on this list, it's very likely that you're contributing to complexity.

better product and a better experience if leaders truly enable employees to spend more of their time and attention on "work that matters." Customer service reps will be more focused on customers rather than on needless meetings and e-mails, forms and procedures. And speaking of forms and procedures: if leaders clearly prioritize simplification, the customer herself will encounter fewer of them.

Additionally, a leader's drive to simplify benefits employees. You can empower your people all you want, but this means nothing in an environment that is saturated top to bottom with complication. If your people are so busy completing unnecessary assignments from above that they can't get to higher-level thinking, they're not going to be satisfied. Conversely, think how good it would feel to help make their work richer and more meaningful. You will have increased their happiness and even bettered their health. You will have improved their lives and likely those of their families.

Driving simplicity from the top can also transform your peers. In the course of one of their studies, VoloMetrix uncovered an executive who had consumed hundreds of hours of his colleagues' time by demanding that they read certain e-mails and attend certain meetings. The burden he laid on his peers was "the equivalent of 10 people working full-time every week."[4] Don't be that guy. Be the leader who *saves* the equivalent of ten people working full time. Imagine the impact that even a fraction of that time savings would have on the people around you. Imagine how much less stressed they'd be, how much more they'd accomplish. These are your brothers- and sisters-in-arms. You have the opportunity to make their jobs significantly easier and more fulfilling.

A leader who tackles simplicity can potentially touch *everyone and everything* in the organization. One of my clients explained to me how complex it was to gather data for a single report in his company. There were many different ways to look at the data: across brands and regions. Across lines and products. Across accounts paid and accounts payable. Across strategic opportunities and tactical victories. The tapestry was so complex that departments were perpetually trading e-mails, making demands, setting deadlines, and establishing new reporting requirements. The guy who cut numbers by country was left waiting for numbers from all the different brands so he could arrive at the figures he needed. The woman who looked at the data demographically needed to work from a whole different data set. Everything was a mess and everyone felt as though they were constantly waiting on someone else to hand over the goods.

In the end, the reports generated were often so voluminous that they were difficult to digest. An exercise designed to help bring everyone together—both in collecting the data but also in discerning actionable intelligence (we should invest more in this brand, focus on this market, price our merchandise competitively with this alternative)—became more confusing than helpful.

A problem like this might be handled in part at the middle management level. But for simplification to take hold in earnest, *the directive usually needs to come from the top*. It needs to be woven into the instructions that employees throughout the company receive. Senior leaders should think about the time people invest in each project—not just their own time, but that allocated by those who work below them.

A New Golden Rule

I believe we all have an obligation to make life as simple as possible for colleagues around us, so that they can derive the most meaning possible from their work. We can even speak in terms of a new "Golden Rule": make others' lives as simple as possible, just as you would like them to do for you.

It's easy to think of people who *don't* make life as simple as possible. They're the gossips who draw us into long, meaningless conversations that aren't the least bit productive. Or the blowhards who monopolize meetings by drowning others in unimportant details. Or the busybodies who make it unusually difficult to schedule a conversation, so that you're perpetually running after them. Or the more professorial colleagues who write unnecessarily long memos or who ask unusually arcane questions or who send a barrage of e-mails throughout the day to get things off their plate, and onto yours.

Shouldn't we make an effort to refrain from these kinds of activities? Shouldn't we first put boundaries around our own time, pushing back on complications that affect our own work, and shouldn't we then let others know that we value *their* time as much as we do our own? Shouldn't we do our best to work efficiently and effectively, so that others can work that way as well, and we can create a virtuous cycle of simplicity? As leaders, don't we have a special obligation to adhere to the "Golden Rule" of simplicity?

We have an immense power to set the tone for the entire organization, not just through our policies and strategies or the investments we make, but through our behavior. In embracing simplification, we're duty bound to affirm that the way we invest our time matters as much as the way we invest our money. We're also duty bound to affirm norms of collegiality— the idea that we have no right to waste our fellow employees' time.

What compels leaders to pursue the golden rule of simplification in their organizations? What leads them to take the required risks? In researching this book, I spoke with more than one hundred senior leaders about their thoughts and experiences with simplification. As I quickly discovered, leaders require a broad *mindset* of simplicity: a set of beliefs, traits, and qualities that incline them to embark on simplification initiatives and see them through. As my interviews proceeded, the basic outlines of this mindset became clear. It all came down to six primary leadership characteristics, starting with that most basic one of all, courage.

Leadership Characteristic #1: Courage

In 2014, when Dave Lewis became CEO at European grocery store giant Tesco, the company was struggling. Consumer behavior was changing; people were choosing to go shopping more frequently and to shop each time for fewer items. They liked the convenience of popping in for a couple of ingredients on the way home before throwing dinner together each night. While Tesco operated large supermarkets stocked with a wide diversity of items, consumers were looking for smaller, low-cost shopping alternatives, and competitors such as Lidl and Aldi were offering them. It wasn't just that. Many other aspects of Tesco's marketing were too complicated. As one retail consultant put it: "One criticism that has certainly been levelled at Tesco in the past has been its inability to simply and effectively communicate value, befuddling customers with straplines, slogans, couponing and promotional tools."[5] To make matters worse, Tesco was still recovering from a massive public accounting scandal. The company, which had long dominated the British grocery industry (it was the country's largest retailer), had overstated its quarterly profits. Two government agencies were investigating.[6]

Lewis immediately recognized a crucial aspect of the company's challenge in the market. Shopping at Tesco had come to feel like a chore. Customers looking to buy a single product—ketchup, for example—were faced with dozens of brands and flavors and textures and sizes. The contrast between big, hulking Tesco and its wily little competitors was staggering. Tesco had twenty-eight different ketchups—Aldi only one. Tesco had 224 types of air freshener—Aldi only twelve. Tesco had eleven different varieties of aluminum foil—Aldi a single type of roll. Tesco suffered from too much complexity in its merchandising. It was shouldering the expense of stocking so many products, while alienating the very shoppers it sought to please.

What did Lewis do? He quickly hired Boston Consulting Group to help the company identify which products it should eliminate. He gave them a wide mandate: cut the variety of products on offer at stores by as much as 30 percent, from more than ninety thousand unique items to as few as sixty-five thousand.

Lewis knew he was going to receive blowback from customers. They might say, "You're going to quit stocking *my* brand of coffee? Don't do it!" (Tesco had 283 different coffee beans on offer—Aldi twenty) or, "You can't give up on this certain brand of rice (Tesco had ninety-eight) because it's a favorite among some of my branch's customers!" And what about the suppliers? Those whose products Tesco would eliminate were sure to howl, and maybe even charge more for the remaining brands they delivered to Tesco's shelves.[7]

It took great courage for Lewis to stay true to his mission, but he stuck with it. A year later, the company had not yet entered smooth waters but there were signs of progress. The company's share price remained volatile, and its credit rating below target. There were still scores of issues to sort through: a legacy of broad real estate interests, a wide portfolio of investments in peripheral companies, and more. But sales during the company's first Christmas season under Lewis's watch beat the city of London's expectations.[8] In a complex organization, there are no silver bullets. But moving toward simplicity always adds real value.

Leadership Characteristic #2:
Minimalist Sensibility

After courage, a second characteristic possessed by leaders intent on driving simplicity down into an organization is *an understanding of the value of paring things back.* Effective simplifiers need to have an intuitive appreciation for less. They need to be able to see, in their mind's eye, how a simpler company will be more efficient, more productive, and most importantly, more profitable. They need to embrace the wisdom of minimalism.

> Effective simplifiers need to have an intuitive appreciation for less.

Think what it would mean to your business if you were asked to sacrifice a third of your product offerings. Would you object, as at least some of Lewis's peers and subordinates surely did, that your company would lose many of its customers as a result? Or would you enthusiastically regard this request as an opportunity to totally remake your business and take it to new heights?

To win with simplicity, leaders must believe in the "simplicity premium"—the notion that consumers are willing to sacrifice other benefits for the sake of ease or convenience. We've seen that shoppers will often pay more for the same product if the process of acquiring the product is easier. As the Tesco story suggests, they're also willing to sacrifice variety. And surely they'll sacrifice some part of your company's leading product attributes—quality, say, or durability, or comfort—if they can get something that is much easier to acquire or use.

Leaders should also strongly believe in the benefits of simplicity *inside* the organization. You may remember John and Bert Jacobs, the brothers who founded the Life is Good apparel company and then complained of being inundated by e-mail. The brothers came up with a radical solution: they stopped using e-mail altogether. Despite running a $100 million company, they decided to make themselves available *only* over the phone or in person, receiving instead a summary of important incoming communications from their staff every two weeks. As John explained it, this new way of working, "allows us to spend more time on high level questions, puzzles, or projects and to be more creative." It's not that everyone at Life is Good has abandoned e-mail, but the brothers' decision has sent a powerful message about minimalism to the staff. John concluded, "We find that people are a little more hesitant to pull you into minor matters on cell phones as opposed to e-mail."[9]

It's easy to demand more, more, more. We rarely see the harm in adding new functionality to a website, a new option to a service plan, or a new series of internal meetings. But those sorts of additions *do* have a cost, even if it's not readily apparent on a balance sheet. Leaders who are going to lead an effort to simplify need to understand these costs and the benefits of simplicity *in their bones.*

Leadership Characteristic #3: Results Orientation

If anything will kill a simplification initiative, it's a leader who views simplicity primarily as a way to reduce costs. Smart leaders know that successful simplification isn't just about making do with less, or making people do more with less. It's about enabling people in the organization to do more of the work they are excited to complete (not just *more work*). Leaders with a simplicity mindset champion simplification efforts as a means of making the organization and the people who work for it more effective.

A couple of years ago, Jeff Spencer, then executive director of strategy for Merck Canada, created a long-term strategy for cultivating a culture of simplicity. A survey of roughly 15 percent of the company's employees, representing a cross section of levels and functions, revealed that people felt hampered by too many meetings, too many e-mails, diffuse decision-making, and, most of all, by processes and systems over which they had little control. That was a problem, as it caused them to focus inwardly, rather than on the company's customers and competitors. New products were making their way through the company's pipeline—promising new medications that everyone was excited about. But pharmaceuticals is a highly regulated industry, so each new product launch requires the company to jump through several hoops. With so much work and so little time, many employees were becoming increasingly frustrated by the complexity.

At first, efforts to streamline the company's operations fell short of the success Spencer envisioned. These efforts had focused on fixing many of the systems-related issues that bothered employees, as these were the ones over which individuals had little control. However, even when fixes succeeded in addressing employees' concerns, they did little to create a culture of simplicity.

So Spencer took a different tack, looking for ways to engage employees in simplifying the work around them rather than focusing on "the system." A few months into the effort, the organization had its first breakthrough as a team came together to fix an age-old problem. Traditionally, the organization had lacked a clear, efficient system by which field-based representatives could provide feedback to the marketing department. A team collaborated to create a simple, e-mail-based "fast response system" by which the representatives could provide the office with customer feedback and other observations. These were compiled, reviewed by marketing, and acted upon. Since these insights sprang directly from customer feedback, marketing was able to develop responses that more closely addressed customers' specific needs. And, because marketing got the feedback sooner, it created a much better customer (and representative) experience. [10]

For the first time, employees were working directly to help build the broader simplicity culture. They were becoming aware of and engaged in the many straightforward ways they could act on their own to make meaningful strides toward simplicity. And they were becoming alert to the many subtle but insidious ways that each employee can layer on additional complexity.

Spencer acknowledges that simplification isn't always so easy. Highly regulated environments can be inordinately complex, and noncompliance is not an option. In this case, Spencer suggests looking for ways to "contain the complexity" within specific roles rather than allowing it to run amok within the broader organization. He points to a recent example in which Merck Canada removed some of the reporting requirements from representatives and set up a Center of Excellence (COE) to do that work instead. Not only has this freed up the representatives to do their "day job," the COE does the work more efficiently, saving money in the process.

Leadership Characteristic #4: Focus

Do you think simplification was the *only* thing on Dave Lewis's plate when he took his seat as Tesco's CEO? Of course not. Senior leaders generally begin their days like everyone else does: with a barrage of e-mails, a slew of meetings, and a pile of reports. Still, leaders with a simplicity mindset keep the eradication of complexity at the top of their agendas, refusing to get bogged down in the inevitable distractions. They also don't let the doubters get in the way of their plans. Any initiative that shakes things up will trigger resistance in an organization, and simplicity is no exception. In theory, everyone likes simplicity, but for many of the reasons we've discussed, we all reflexively latch on to the devil we know. Further, while simplicity is great for the company as a whole, it directly challenges certain individuals and groups whose authority is rooted in the outdated, inefficient, overly complex rules, processes, and systems that need to go.

Focus is especially important for leaders of young companies, since these organizations tend to take on layers of complication as they grow. When Mike Dubin and Mark Levine started Dollar Shave Club in early 2012, they intended it largely as a response to complication. Recognizing that consumers were sick of paying a lot for razors at their local drugstore, Dubin and Levine offered an easier alternative: for less than $10 a month, they would send you fresh blades through the mail. No frills, no complicated decisions. Give them your address and credit card number, and your razors would be on the way. Immediately, thousands of customers climbed aboard. For less hassle—and, in many cases, for less money—shavers were guaranteed a high-quality product.

As their company caught hold, Dubin and Levine might have been tempted to expand their offerings. Maybe they could have become a home delivery service for all sorts of toiletries. Or maybe they could have offered their customers different kinds of razors, with fancier blades or brighter colors or more comfortable grips. The two passed up strategic moves such as these, choosing instead to focus on the connections they were building with each customer—relationships built on simplicity. Dubin and Levine continued to offer customers three options, and only three (with a few upsells like shave butter if someone wanted to splurge). Their focus burnished their reputation for simplicity among a growing customer base.[11] By the end of their first year, the "club" had two hundred thousand subscribers. A year and a half later, their original marketing video, used to launch the product through social media, had been shared fifteen million times on YouTube.

In more established companies, resistance to simplification can take many familiar forms: "We can't get rid of that process because…"; "We need to make sure we get it right by…"; "I won't be able to get the job done right unless we…" Leaders need to stay focused and push through such resistance. And they need to keep the pressure on over time. When a leader imposes a simplification initiative on a skeptical staff, it's unlikely to stick at first. Someone will fail to come through on an assignment, purportedly because the "simpler" new process "just doesn't work." Leaders must have the fortitude and determination to celebrate the benefits of simplification, even while acknowledging that change is hard. They have to keep pounding in the message that workers' lives will improve if things are streamlined, not just the bottom line. *They'll* feel more productive. *They'll* share in the benefits. Leaders who stick with the simplicity imperative in this way have the strongest chance of success. They're the ones with a simplicity mindset.

Leadership Characteristic #5: Personal Engagement

A few years ago, my team took on a client in the publishing industry. The leader was a nice guy, had a senior role in the HR department, and wanted our help building new innovation skills and improving the team's morale. Yet there was a problem: while he talked a good game, my client wasn't walking the walk. He was all too eager to tell me how *other* departments around the company were demanding reports that had no real value. But he wouldn't acknowledge that he himself was assigning busywork to his own people, too.

There was one particularly egregious example: the monthly operating report (MOR). No one in the HR department understood its value, and it took staff hours and hours to complete. So they developed a little test designed to tease out the truth. One of my client's direct reports had taken to pulling together all the data for the MOR—but then neglecting to pass it along. Instead, for three consecutive months, after completing each report, he would just stuff it in his desk drawer. From his perspective, the test of the MOR's value was in discovering whether anyone actually asked to see it. And when no one did, it was clear to him that he and his peers had been wasting their time.

Do you think this employee felt inspired upon hearing that his boss was simplifying? Of course not. To his mind, simplification was just lipstick on a pig. It was a talking point, not a real directive. His colleagues agreed. They became even more resentful, spiteful, and frustrated, convinced that the organization had no respect for work that mattered.

If you're a leader hoping to instill an ethos of simplification, you need to exemplify, empower, and reinforce the behaviors associated with simplification. If you're not prepared to simplify your own work environment, don't direct those who work for you to strip things down.

Leadership Characteristic #6: Decisiveness

As Steve Jobs's right-hand man and Apple's chief design officer, Jony Ive is credited with some of Apple's most iconic creations, including the iPod, the iPad, and the Apple Watch. Jobs himself once called Ive his "spiritual partner." It's no exaggeration to say that Ive knows a thing or two about simplicity. If anyone is the living, breathing personification of design with simplicity, Ive is it.

Years after Jobs's death, Ive attributed a measure of his former boss's success to his uncanny ability to get to the meat of every challenge. Jobs had managed to stay fixed on the most important issues, even when other concerns were buzzing around him. But it wasn't just that. In order to get the people working for him to set aside any distractions, Jobs would ask deputies like Ive a simple question: "How many times did you say no today?"[12]

Jobs was sending Ive and his colleagues a message: take control. Jobs didn't want Ive coming to him for sign-offs on every marginally significant decision. He didn't want Ive to be scared to take action. Rather, Jobs was giving Ive authority, and he expected him to use it. For Ive to say no each day meant that he was making real decisions of his own volition.

In addition, Jobs wanted Ive and others working for him to feel comfortable throwing a wrench in the works. Jobs knew that a consensus-driven culture inside Apple would be the company's undoing. If people felt too frightened to cut against the grain, Apple would lose its edge. Jobs was right. Leaders who are going to drive simplification campaigns through to the end must depart from the need to seek consensus. Complicated organizations tend to be overloaded with people who claim they can't get things done because some other department hasn't signed off, or who say they can't move forward because some other team hasn't sent them the specs. Leaders operating under a simplicity mindset short-circuit those complaints. They make decisions quickly and cleanly, and they inspire those they work with to do the same.

Six Characteristics of a Simplifier— Do You Have Them?

1. **Courage**: You are not afraid to challenge the status quo. You are comfortable with change and the unknown. You call people out who are being needlessly complex.

2. **Minimalist Sensibility**: You know the value of less. You seek to eliminate tasks or barriers that hold you back from doing more valuable work. You approach everything you do by asking, "Is this the simplest way to do this and still reach our goal?"

3. **Results Orientation**: Simplicity isn't just about cutting costs for you. You do it because you want to get things done. You like clear outcomes and accountability.

4. **Focus**: You don't give up. You stick with an effort that will help you reach your goals despite resistance. You see pushback as a way to get information and make your case stronger. You don't let business as usual get in the way of simplifying things over the long term.

5. **Personal Engagement**: You "walk the walk." You actively seek ways to simplify and you do it, while empowering others to do the same.

6. **Decisiveness**: You like to move things forward quickly. You don't let a consensus-driven culture slow things down unnecessarily.

A Cautionary Tale

A few years ago, I led a workshop at a large American insurance company. I lead these sessions all the time, providing teams at big companies with both inspiration and tools to embrace the simplicity imperative. On this day, I was happy to be meeting with one of the company's best divisions. The folks in the audience understood instinctively what I was talking about, and they were thrilled to have an opportunity to address the very issues that frustrated them. When you're in my business, you know when you've connected with an audience—this was one of those days.

We were in the middle of one of my exercises, and I was walking around the room, observing the action and taking notice of the way the groups were handling the various hurdles I had assigned to them. I got thirsty, so I wandered to the back of the room for a glass of water. Standing at the table, I was within earshot of several of the more senior executives who had organized the workshop and invited me to come. Rather than participating, they were observing their subordinates from the sidelines.

What struck me was their attitude. These executives were believers; they knew that simplicity was key to their collective success. But they also perceived that *their* bosses weren't entirely bought in. The C-suite had proven adept at talking the talk; they claimed that the company was pre-pared to embrace simplicity. But the folks in the room thought it unlikely that top leadership would implement or support whatever solutions the group in the room had recommended that day. Complexity, they felt, was the status quo. And the status quo was there to stay.

There was no possible way that the engaged employees working through my exercise in the middle of the room weren't eventually going to figure out the real deal. No matter how much they wanted to weave simplification into the company's modus operandi, these junior staffers were destined to discover that they didn't have buy-in from the top. Sadly, this is typical. Why do employees feel so trapped in complexity? In large part it's because the people in charge don't take the problem seriously. In the Fidelity example that opened this chapter, leaders pushed through to greater simplicity despite the naysayers. Here the leaders *were* the naysayers.

If executives in your organization are not bought in, then your organization will not make as much progress simplifying as it might. You won't maximize the opportunity that exists to make simplicity a competitive advantage. Originating at the top, simplification requires a leadership quality that's often in short supply: courage. It requires a leap of faith, the belief that freeing people to do higher-level thinking will pay back dividends. And it requires a mindset—the will, foresight, and fortitude to push simplicity through. Do you as a leader have these things? If not, why not?

Of course, the degree of complexity in an organization isn't determined exclusively by those at the top. No matter where in the hierarchy you reside, you, too, have the power to pursue simplification. Like senior leaders, you also have an ethical duty to refrain from burdening those around you with undue complexity, and to actively simplify what you do. In the next two chapters, I'll give you powerful tools that you and your teams can put to use right now to identify where to simplify, how to simplify, and how to embed simplicity over time into the culture of your organization.

CHAPTER SIX

The Simplicity Toolkit

"The sculptor produces the beautiful statue by chipping away such parts of the marble block as are not needed—it is a process of elimination."

—Elbert Hubbard[1]

If you're a fan of vintage cartoons, you might remember that the cartoon series *G.I. Joe* featured a public service announcement (PSA) at the end of each episode, helping kids handle dangers such as downed electrical wires or strangers offering them a ride home. At the end of the PSA, a kid exclaimed, "Now I know!" and the narrator responded, "And knowing is half the battle."

With complexity as well, realizing it's a problem is half the battle. But it's not the *whole* battle; you also need to take action. Most simplification initiatives go awry because well-intentioned employees and managers, aware that complexity exists, don't know how to tackle it. Their efforts have lacked many critical components (executive support, time commitment, and focus, to name a few), but most importantly, they've lacked the tools and frameworks to guide the initiative from intention to action; as a result, they become bogged down in ambiguity.

A client of mine, one of the world's most recognizable consumer goods companies, is a case in point. In the summer of 2014, a division of the organization, which was in charge of many of the company's top brands, caught the simplicity bug. Senior managers were acutely aware that complexity was dragging the business down. This particular division was among the company's most regulated (due to the brands it managed), and its leaders recognized that no internal reform initiative would diminish the government's oversight. But everyone agreed that streamlining work internally—from the production process to innovation to everyday work—could give the business a substantial competitive advantage.

The senior team gathered twelve people from across the division: engineers, sales executives, marketers, finance folks, etc. Every role had a seat at the table—a crucial ingredient for the initiative to succeed. Importantly, all twelve participants volunteered to participate and were true believers who understood what simplification could do for the division. They discussed how simplicity would spur innovation, drive employee engagement, and enhance professional development.

The group began by surveying the larger division to get a better sense of the way their peers perceived simplification. How did people define the term? Did they know what it could do for the business? Respondents provided feedback on their definition of simplification and why it was important. Employees agreed that simplification would remove barriers to doing more critical, meaningful work, and that it would subtract many unnecessary tasks. If all went as planned, simplification would create a culture that embraced creative thinking. With a definition and purpose in place, the core group methodically identified areas of complexity within the business and asked colleagues for suggestions on what could be simplified and how.

Despite this promising start, the initiative failed to gain traction; a year later it had all but died. Why? First, the team never properly defined and prioritized areas for simplification. The core group identified twenty areas to tackle, but these areas were ill defined. As a result, people spent critical time clarifying concepts instead of taking real action. "What is the difference," people asked, "between an 'initiative simplification' and a 'project simplification?'" and "How does a 'document simplification' compare with a 'report simplification?'" Simplification became a sterile exercise in philosophizing and semantics.

When the group finally prioritized which areas to simplify first, they conducted brainstorming sessions to generate solutions. But the brainstorms were too general and lacked provocative questions. As a result, the solutions weren't specific enough, and many were even off topic. Rather than eliminating steps in particular tasks or processes, the group's solutions detoured from addressing collective work processes to focusing on individual motivation. Team members proposed raises, performance incentives, praise from their superiors, and even nicer platters of catered food at meetings. What did this have to do with streamlining reports or any other area of meaningful simplification?

Teams divided up the potential ideas and agreed to come up with a plan in a few weeks. When they met again, few had made any progress. They'd been distracted by urgent requests. Business as usual got in the way. Since the effort wasn't really well thought out, and because progress seemed to require a lot of energy, participants lost momentum. As one manager put it, "The effort became the flavor of the month."

This group, like so many others, didn't grasp the importance of simplifying. They didn't understand a core theme of this book: *if you get the work right, you get the culture right*. If team members had understood this, they would have quickly delved into the *details* of work, the minutiae— the stuff that frustrates us every day, that wastes our valuable time, that creates unnecessary stress no matter how many raises we're given or snacks we're provided in meetings. Simplifying effectively requires first that we determine which discrete tasks and actions aren't adding value and second that we decide to eliminate the offenders. Once people start spending their time on valuable tasks—things that feel worthy of their time and are in support of a purpose—the culture will follow.

How many times do you hear people say, "Yes, my old company's culture was fine, but I left because I hated the work I was doing?"

All the time.

Simplification: Some Common Misconceptions

To get you and your team focused on the *real* work of simplifying, you need the right tools. This chapter offers a number of powerful exercises that we've tested and perfected at some of the largest, most innovative companies on the planet. I began developing these tools for our clients after a prolonged period of research into complexity. Our team had collected reams of published material on complexity—notes, papers, ideas, statistics. But as I've related, we were stunned to find a lack of tools designed to help teams and individuals simplify general work issues or habits in a straightforward way and without a large budget.

We set out to create these tools, and—full disclosure—it wasn't easy. In fact, it often felt excruciatingly complicated to understand what simplifying entailed and how to attack it. First, we listed the barriers we found that prevented an individual, team, or organization from paring back their work. We asked ourselves: Why was simplification so hard to start? What tripped people up along the way? What could we do to help people eliminate these barriers more quickly and make simplification happen more often?

Pondering these questions, we uncovered a few misconceptions informing prevailing approaches. First, people seeking to simplify often don't realize that their colleagues must recognize they have a problem in order to solve it. (If your team includes people who don't think there's a complexity problem, you're never, ever going to solve it. In fact, you're just going to beat your head against a wall.) Second, would-be simplifiers typically try to first tackle things that are too big. Any simplification effort must break tasks down into the smallest parts possible; only then can people understand them and feel they can take action.

Third, there's a big difference between organizing and simplifying. Just because something is organized does not at all mean it is simple.

> Just because something is organized does not at all mean it is simple.

In fact, many complicated things are quite organized, but that doesn't make them any more valuable or less annoying. Let me give you an example. I am a working mother with two active kids, and I am constantly involved in carpools. The vast majority of them don't work. Why? Not because they weren't organized. Oh, there are online schedules and calendar apps, reminder systems, group text lists set up for alerts, and address and contact information exchanged well in advance. But then two more people join the group ("Hey! That will be less driving for everyone!"), and now the five kids in the car live at locations all over town, so by the time we drop everyone home after practice, it's an hour later than if we had just done it ourselves. Group texts fly constantly with schedule updates, and there's the triple confirmation e-mail of who's driving each day, at what time, and the order of who will be picked up first, then next. Organized, yes. Complicated, most definitely.

Fourth, people confuse improvement with simplification. Simplification is the act of subtraction. Improvement can involve subtraction, but also addition. I'd rather see people discuss eliminating or streamlining instead of improving, because the mindset is different. I don't want to "improve" a crappy meeting by adding more e-mails to clarify things; I'd like first to see how to streamline or eliminate the parts of the meeting that are causing the problem. As we've seen, improvements are sometimes the way we create the monster: good intentions, wrong outcomes.

Finally, simplifying isn't a project, it's an operating principle; it's the *way you work*. Too many people treat it like spring cleaning a house or weeding a garden. Just because you do it once doesn't mean the clutter or the weeds won't return. Habits are hard to break, and simplification needs to be top of mind for it to work.

Five Steps to Simplicity

With these insights in mind, we identified five discrete steps for making simplification happen:

1. **Awareness:** We all begin our journey to simplification by recognizing the toll taken by complexity, not just on our organizations but on us personally. Further, we acknowledge the degree to which we're dependent on or have added to existing complexity, perpetuating the status quo without even realizing it.

2. **Identification:** Once we're aware of complexity, we then uncover areas of our work or specific tasks that create frustrating obstacles for us (e.g., by not adding value or by wasting our time unnecessarily) and we decide which simplification opportunities are worth pursuing. During this stage, we also begin to understand why it's so hard to abandon the systems already in place, and the organizational and human behaviors that

create these complexities. We gain a sense of how much time and energy simplification will require, and the value we might create by simplifying.

3. **Prioritization:** After identifying opportunities for simplification, the next step is to prioritize them. We must evaluate the opportunities using a "time versus value" equation. We assess which complications impede us the most, which problems will be hardest to eradicate, and where we can get the most bang for our simplification buck.

4. **Execution:** Once we identify the opportunities, we must execute, piloting new ways of getting things done and making adjustments in real time. All of this demands both effort and courage, as well as a simplification mindset and commitment among the rank and file.

5. **Habit Formation:** Simplification isn't a "one and done" proposition. It has to become part of the way you operate, part of how you approach everything you do. To make it part of the culture, you must take time to explain simplification's purpose and benefits, and you must take steps to ensure that simplicity becomes ingrained as a habit. I'll address this final step in the next chapter, presenting tools that can help you deepen your team or organization's commitment to simplicity.

As these steps emerged, we realized we needed to create separate tools to overcome each barrier and move people along the steps as easily as possible. We surveyed more than three hundred clients, colleagues, and friends to understand how *they* tackled complexity, asking them simplification-oriented questions (e.g., "If you could ask any question to create more simplicity or eliminate complexity within your company, what would you ask?") and asking them to identify simplification "quick wins" (examples of how they or their company actually simplified something and thereby made life easier, quickly).

The responses we got were incredible, and we were overwhelmed by the number of people who were eager to tackle the challenge of complexity. Our clients wound up passing our survey on to *their* friends and colleagues, who in turn responded to us. Beyond that, we tweeted our two questions to thousands of followers and to more than twenty thousand people who receive our e-newsletter, inviting them to submit simplification tactics of their own. With the resulting trove of information, we began zeroing in on the places where complexity commonly hides within organizations.

Crafting Simplification Tools

Once we had finished analyzing and organizing the insights we gathered, we drafted our tools. To enhance each tool's relevance, drive accountability, and spur immediate action, we decided not to focus at the enterprise level but to design exercises for business units, teams, or individuals to use. We took everything we had learned and began crafting exercises that would help people at every step. We tested each one over and over, making changes each time. Finally, we felt we'd crafted a toolkit that could supplement Lean and the other methodologies, helping those who want to take action around simplification.

Use the tools that follow to focus in on the details and specifics of your work. Choose the ones that conform best to your organization's needs. Some of these tools will take less than half an hour to complete, without training. Many are modular, allowing you to perform the first two steps to get things started or spend more time and see them all the way through.

Simplification isn't easy, but we strongly believe it shouldn't be complicated, onerous, or exhausting either. In particular, there's no need to wait for a lengthy, formal review process. You can make progress *now:* just sit down with your colleagues and get started with our tools. Here they are, ordered in accordance with our five simplification steps.

TOOL: 50 Questions for Simplifying

Once you complete the diagnostic in chapter 3 and are aware of your complexity problem, what then? How can you identify specific instances of unnecessary complication? How do you begin to root them out? Our first exercise here, "50 Questions for Simplifying," helps you with Step 2 of the simplification process—"Identification."

Whether you're seeking a starting point for simplification, solving an ongoing issue, or considering a new process or procedure, these questions serve as a litmus test for simplification. This exercise can either follow the "Complexity Diagnostic," which reveals specific areas of complexity within your organization, or it can be used as a stand-alone tool for problem solving. As your organization embraces simplification, "50 Questions for Simplifying" can become part of the decision-making process in every corner of your business, from meetings to outsourcing to messaging.

We've organized the questions in "50 Questions for Simplifying" around my four-pronged definition of simplification. We also added a fifth category designed to help you determine whether an element of your business deserves additional focus. You'll need all five considerations to get to work that matters, since something can be simple by my definition and yet not be meaningful or useful to your particular organization, given its mission and purpose.

Here are the basic categories, phrased as questions:

- Is it **Valuable?**
  These questions help you decide if something is necessary or worth your time.

- Is it **Minimal?**
  These questions help you decide if something is streamlined or reduced to its simplest possible form.

- Is it **Understandable?**
  These questions determine if communication on a topic is as clear as possible.

- Is it **Repeatable?**
  These questions help you decide if something is as automated, templated, or scalable as possible.

- Is it **Accessible?**
  These questions help you determine if an information source is as readily available to its audience as possible.

You can use these provocative questions alongside other tools here, or you can use them on their own to help people better brainstorm solutions around simplicity. To use these questions to their greatest effect, pick from among the following options:

Variation #1: Do the exercise individually.
Variation #2: Do the exercise as a group. Break into teams and assign each team an area of complexity.
Variation #3: A leader chooses five questions in the relevant areas of complexity and then sends them to the participants for completion in advance of meeting. The group then discusses the proposed solutions.

Here's how it works:

Step 1: Define Simplification Challenge. (5 Minutes)

Articulate the goal of this simplification session using terms that are as specific as possible. Examples could be: "Increase productivity by granting X department access to Y data," or "Improve exchange of real time information between marketing and sales." If your organization's complexity seems too overwhelming to specify, create a general challenge like, "Simplify the daily and monthly processes used in our department."

Steps 2 and 3: Choose One to Three Areas of Complexity and Answer Five Questions Within Each Area. (40 minutes)

Use your simplification challenge to determine which areas of complexity most demand your focus. For example, if your challenge is to "Increase productivity by granting X department access to Y database," choose five questions in the "Repeatable" and "Accessible" areas of complexity. If you created a general challenge, focus on the "Minimal" and "Valuable" areas. When conducting this exercise as a group, break into teams and assign each group a specific area of complexity.

Review all the questions in your chosen area of complexity and choose five that speak to the root cause of your challenge. (Or write your own brilliant simplification questions.) In Step 4, you will build your answers into solutions.

Step 4: Generate Three to Five Solutions for Simplifying. (30–60 minutes)

Would outsourcing solve your issue? What about outright elimination of the troublesome process or task? What aspects or steps could you remove to streamline the overall process? Generate solutions either individually or as a group using a whiteboard or flip chart.

If you identify solutions that can be implemented immediately, these are the quick wins that should top your agenda. If you identify solutions that would have high impact but that require further research, assign responsibility to teams/team members with clear deadlines and schedule a follow-up meeting before ending the session.

For considerations of space, I've included only some of the questions here. At the end of this book, you'll find the full list of "50 Questions for Simplifying."

Is it **Valuable?**
- If the company burned down overnight and we had to start from scratch tomorrow, what's the most crucial item of business that staff would pitch in to accomplish?
- I just won a trip that departs in twenty-four hours: What are the most important things I need to get done before I leave?

Is it **Minimal?**
- If a new CEO started at our company tomorrow, what processes would s/he immediately observe as the biggest time wasters?
- For every new thing we add to our product pipeline, what could be eliminated? (Which process? Meeting? Standing call?)

Is it **Understandable?**
- Could I clearly explain this to anyone outside my business group?
- What jargon could I eliminate from this document or message?

Is it **Repeatable?**
- If we automated some or all of this task/process, who would benefit?
- Can this process be easily replicated for other teams/markets?

Is it **Accessible?**
- How could customers more easily do business with us?
- Would other departments or divisions benefit from access to our systems or data?
- Would we benefit by empowering them to do more of the work themselves?

These questions are meant as a resource or guide to spur thinking. You should use them as circumstances warrant, either by yourself or with a group, picking the most relevant questions for the task at hand. Here's how it works:

Completing the "50 Questions for Simplifying" tool alone won't by itself make simplicity happen. But it will give you a more expansive and thoughtful view of where complication lurks within your own business.

TOOL: Simplification Worksheet

Suppose you don't have a specific task you're looking to improve, or you only have a moment at the end of a meeting to get people thinking about the topic. In that case, try the Simplification Worksheet. Don't let its brevity deceive you; it can be very effective.

The story of this tool's birth began in June 2015. Creating a simplification toolkit had been on my company's to-do list for weeks. While I had sketched out in detail the tools that would support each step of our simplification process, I was stalled. I feared that if I proceeded too far with our tool development and then got feedback beyond what I'd already received, I'd have to redo the entire exercise. Not fun.

I announced to my team that from that day on, we'd create one new tool a week for the foreseeable future, and we'd try it ourselves for an hour every Monday morning. I went first, creating a worksheet designed to help people identify where complexity exists in their organizations. Because a big problem many people face with simplification is that they don't know where to start, I believed people needed a quick, easy way to dive in. I named the tool the Simplicity Worksheet. It had just six questions, no more, no less. Boom—finished.

The next morning, I gave my team ten minutes to brainstorm answers to the questions. The room got *very* quiet. People started writing and writing and writing. Amazingly, one employee had no problem listing complexity he had experienced in his role despite the fact that he had only been working with us for two weeks! My god, what kind of complex organization was I running? After ten minutes I stopped everyone. Time to share. And share they did. I was thrilled to discover that such a simple technique could help a team uncover dozens of ways to make their work better, and in almost no time at all.

My staff had great insights on what made their own jobs complex— from their own behaviors ("I chase clients for little bits of information with ten e-mails when I could send one e-mail a week later when they have more details, and just get all the info at once") to things that I as their boss unknowingly did that wasted their time ("Why does marketing have to stay and listen for thirty minutes to the new business pipeline review at the end of our weekly status meeting?") to things their teammates did and didn't need to do (Trevor suggested that Katherine stop inputting sales data into two different systems—it was unnecessary and redundant; Katherine suggested Trevor increase the productivity of his prospecting calls by using a shorter list of "must ask" questions).

Within an hour, we had changed seventeen work tasks for the better— seventeen! We were all pumped and thought, *Why didn't we do this sooner? When can we do this again?* Some tasks were eliminated, some were outsourced to a vendor, some were streamlined. More than that, we found several ways to improve the worksheet itself.

The magic of the Simplification Worksheet is that it identifies quick wins for simplification. Distribute it to a small group. Use it in a staff meeting. Each participant should spend five minutes identifying the most time-consuming, redundant, or complex tasks, and then five more minutes describing them.

STEP 1: WHAT IS COMPLEX, REDUNDANT, OR TIME-CONSUMING?	STEP 2: WHY?	STEP 3: HOW TO CHANGE IT? (Specify tactics for simplifying each task, such as streamlining, outsourcing, or eliminating.)
Example: What task is most time-consuming for you? *Quarterly proposals for clients outlining recommended events, marketing, & PR programs.*	*Each proposal involves many images, tons of formatting, and I have to chase content from other offices in different time zones. Multiple authors & versions make it hard to track most up-to-date file. I end up pulling content from 5 different versions into one master deck.*	• *Reduce images to 1 per page* • *Only use basic formatting* • *Use Google docs/collaboration tool so there's 1 version & each department is responsible for adding its content*
1. What task is most time-consuming for you?		
2. What task is most time-consuming for your colleagues?		
3. What is the most complex aspect of your job?		
4. What redundant task would you like to remove from your job description?		
5. What small task is your biggest time-suck?		
6. What task do you wish you could eliminate from your responsibilities today?		

Once participants have had time to craft their answers, discuss the following with the goal of identifying tasks that add the least value. Each team should strive to eliminate or suspend at least as many tasks as there are members of the team.

1. What exceptional, time-saving solutions did team members offer for their most consuming tasks?
2. Can any of these solutions be applied to other team members' tasks?
3. Is there any duplication of tasks between team members? If so, can just one person complete this task?
4. Of the tasks that employees wish they could eliminate, which can you get rid of right now? Or suspend for thirty days? A month from now, reexamine the value of those tasks as a group or in one-on-one meetings.

Be warned: once you've identified the key sources of complexity in your work, you're going to be shocked at how obvious they were. Chances are you've known what was wrong, but you'd never really faced up to the reality. You've rolled your eyes and gnashed your teeth but never thought thoroughly about whether there was a way to fix the tasks that were keeping you from doing the work you actually *wanted* to do. These last two tools are designed explicitly to bring more of this to light in your own mind. Once you see the barriers, you can grapple with the challenges of clearing them.

TOOL: Killing Complexity

We've focused so far on tools designed to complete the first two steps of the simplification journey—becoming aware of complexity in general, and identifying the various elements that plague your own routines and businesses. The next tool, called "Killing Complexity," will again help you identify the complications in your midst, but it will also nudge you toward taking the next step of prioritizing which complications to target.

"Killing Complexity" identifies which elements of your own experience claim your time. Then it forces you to decide which of these time-intensive tasks are actually valuable. When using this tool with a business unit or team, be sure to include at least one senior leader with authority to eliminate low-value tasks on the spot whenever possible. All participants should come away from this tool with a feeling that they've been heard; moreover, they should receive a pledge from the leader that he will take action down the line. Ideally, leaders should allot ninety minutes for completion.

Step 1: Complete the Task Worksheet. (10 minutes)

A week before the group is scheduled to meet, send the Task Worksheet to everyone planning to attend and ask them to complete it. Analyzing the key tasks (or time sucks) involved in their work will get participants in the right

TASKS			
Daily	Weekly	Monthly/Quarterly	Annually
1.	1.	1.	1.
2.	2.	2.	2.
3.	3.	3.	3.
4.	4.	4.	4.
5.	5.	5.	5.

mindset when the exercise actually begins, and it will let them think more critically about the most time-consuming tasks they do every day, week, month, quarter, and year. Importantly, keep to the following guidelines:

- Tasks must be related to your business unit (not corporate).
- Include only work-related tasks (not personal).
- Split larger tasks into smaller ones (i.e., certain meetings, specific presentations, different types of e-mails).

Step 2: Identify the Top Five Time-Consuming Tasks. (15 minutes)

The day of the meeting, the group should convene in a room with enough wall space to accommodate two flip charts or whiteboards, and someone should handle the task of capturing answers given by group members. After everyone has convened, group members should take ten minutes to review their Task Worksheets and write their five most time-consuming tasks on separate sticky notes. Then, the group should engage in a discussion around the following five questions:

1. What are our most time-consuming tasks?
2. What makes these tasks so time consuming?
3. Are the majority of these tasks daily, monthly, etc.?
4. Could we alter the timing of these tasks to ease the time crunch (i.e., from daily to monthly)?
5. Is there any duplication of tasks between team members? If so, can one person complete this task?

Step 3: Evaluate the Top Five Time-Consuming Tasks. (15 minutes)

Next, each group member should review the scale definitions below and assign the number that best describes the level of complexity for each of

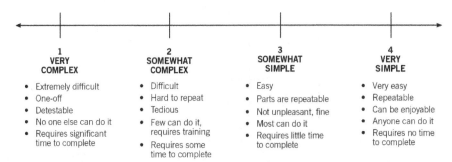

their top five tasks (on average), writing the corresponding complexity number down on each sticky note.

After numbering the sticky notes of each task, the group should spend a few minutes discussing answers to the following questions:

1. Was it a struggle to assign a level of complexity or simplicity to any particular task? Which one(s)?
2. Did any identical tasks receive varying levels of complexity from different team members? Why?
3. Are most of your tasks categorized in one area of the continuum?
4. What about the group at large?
5. Are certain categories of tasks consistently on the same part of the continuum?
6. If most of our tasks are categorized as Complex or Very Complex, what is the cause for so much complexity?

Step 4: Plot Two Tasks on the Simplicity Versus Value Matrix. (25 minutes)

Next, each participant should pick two tasks from the top five to analyze—the two tasks she would most like to modify. For each of these tasks, and in the context of each organization, evaluate how *valuable* each task is. Have each group member consider the following questions:

1. Does the task solve a problem?
2. Does it fulfill an essential client/customer need?
3. Does it provide insight and help leadership make decisions?

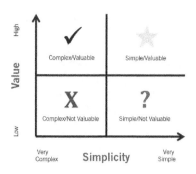

Based on the answers to these questions, each individual should now be able to determine whether each task is high value, low value, or somewhere in between. Each person should then use this knowledge to plot his two tasks on the large matrix in the room according to how valuable and complex (or simple) they are. For example, if one person's task is very complex but low value, it should be placed in Quadrant one (lower left). If it's simple but valuable, plot it in Quadrant four (top right).

You now have a road map to help focus your attention. How you handle or improve each of the tasks that claims your time and attention will be determined by where each task has been plotted on this chart. Start with the best quadrant—the upper right, corresponding to tasks that are both simple and valuable. Perfect. Leave those alone! Next, shift your gaze to the lower left—the complex tasks that are low in value. These are the clear losers: you're getting very little bang for a whole lot of buck. Kill those tasks!

The upper left and the lower right quadrants are the tricky ones. The lower right corresponds to simple tasks that aren't that valuable. If you can kill them, great—but it's not as though they're huge burdens. The upper left is populated by tasks that are complex but valuable. Here's where you really need to think: Is there a simpler way to accomplish those tasks? What can you do to streamline the process? You can't kill these tasks altogether—they are valuable. But these should be your primary targets of opportunity. The group should then discuss answers to the following questions:

1. What kinds of tasks are represented in each quadrant (e.g., reporting, presentations)?
2. Did any identical tasks receive varying levels of value from different team members?
3. Is the majority of our time being spent on tasks that are valuable?

4. Based on what's shown here, do we have a culture of simplicity or complexity? What do we think is driving this?
5. Is complexity or simplicity rewarded in our group/organization?
6. What could leadership do to reward simplification in the workplace?

Step 5: Brainstorm Solutions. (25 minutes)

Finally, the group should tackle the tasks themselves to decide which ones they should eliminate, outsource, or simplify. The quadrant where each individual placed his two tasks should inform the way the tasks can be simplified. After this discussion, members of the group should pair off, each writing down on the form below the two tasks that they had plotted on the matrix. Considering the quadrant placement of the tasks, the pairs should brainstorm solutions for each respective task by either eliminating the task, outsourcing it, or making it simpler (less redundant, more repeatable, more efficient, etc.).

Each solution and approach should be captured in the table below:

LIST YOUR TASKS	APPROACH Check applicable box	SOLUTION Brainstorm + circle top solution	NEXT STEPS (Pilot test, get an outsourcing quote, etc.)
1.	☐ Eliminate. ☐ Outsource to... ☐ Streamline by...	• • •	
2.	☐ Eliminate. ☐ Outsource to... ☐ Streamline by...	• • •	

The discussions should center on the following questions:

1. Did most team solutions fall in just one category (eliminations, outsourcing, or streamlining)? Why?
2. What will it take to implement these solutions?
3. Is anything stopping you from making these solutions happen?
4. Recommended: What three changes are we committing to **right now**?

What I love about this tool is that it prevents us from thinking of our daily routines as a mere "to-do" list. We all have things we need to accomplish. Other people are constantly making claims on our time. But rarely do we ever step back and think: Which of the items on this list is *really* worth my time? Which should I make sure to do—and which do I dread? Figuring out which tasks are actually valuable and which are useless gives you an opportunity to reclaim your time. From now on, you'll be able to devote even more of yourself to achieving your goals.

TOOL: Kill a Stupid Rule

The "Killing Complexity" tool works well when a group has adequate time and bandwidth. If you need a quicker fix, here's an alternative that will still help you identify, prioritize, and execute the path to simplicity by focusing on rules. Everyone loves it because it's simple. It's called "Kill a Stupid Rule."

Like "Killing Complexity," this exercise is relevant for all levels of staff and senior leadership. But here's a big advantage: people can do it themselves or with a colleague, and they can complete it in less than an hour. All that's required is the worksheet on the following page, a whiteboard (if the exercise is being done in a group), colored markers, pens or pencils, and Post-it Notes.

Here's how it works:

Step 1: Identify Stupid Rules. (15 minutes)

Using the worksheets, list three or more rules that frustrate you or slow down your productivity. Then decide whether those rules should be killed or modified. Feel free to focus only on internal rules instead of customer/client rules (or vice versa). As you're considering which rules to choose, keep the following in mind:

- *Red rules versus green rules:* Red rules are government regulated and illegal to change, so they're off limits. Everything else is a green rule and fair game.

- *Focus on your business unit or function:* By concentrating on the rules that affect the area you operate within, you're in a better position to make the case for killing or modifying a rule.
- *Not a gripe session:* This exercise is an ideal opportunity for a productive discussion about what doesn't work, but keep it centered on solutions, not cross talk or complaining.
- *Rewrite the rule:* If you can't kill a rule for some reason, provide specific suggestions on how to modify and make it less frustrating.

Internal Rules

Consider:
- Which systems or protocols frustrate you at work?
- Which processes/reports/forms would you eliminate or simplify to make your job easier?
- What rules slow you down or prevent you from doing your best work?

Rule #1. _____
Kill it? _____
Or modify it? How? _____
_____

Rule #2. _____
Kill it? _____
Or modify it? How? _____
_____

Rule #3. _____
Kill it? _____
Or modify it? How? _____
_____

Customer/Client Rules

Consider:
- What regularly frustrates our clients/customers about us?
- What makes it difficult to do business with us?
- Why do customers/clients choose our competition over us?
- What 1 thing would you immediately change for our clients/customers if you could?

Rule #1. _____
Kill it? _____
Or modify it? How? _____
_____

Rule #2. _____
Kill it? _____
Or modify it? How? _____
_____

Rule #3. _____
Kill it? _____
Or modify it? How? _____
_____

Tip for Success

- Leaders should respond objectively and not defensively when members of the group share their lists of stupid rules.

Discuss as a group:

- How many people were able to come up with at least three rules? How about five? Ten? Share them now.
- Was it easy to come up with rules to kill or change? Why/why not?
- Was it easier to brainstorm internal or customer/client rules? Why?
- How many of our suggestions are actual corporate rules (versus assumptions about how things "should" be done)?

Step 2: Plot Two Stupid Rules on Matrix. (10 minutes)

From your worksheets, choose the two rules you most want to kill or change and write them on separate sticky notes. Ask yourself the following questions:

- In your opinion, would it be easy or hard to kill the rule?
- In your opinion, would killing this rule have a high impact on your business unit?

Based on your answers to those questions, you should now be able to determine whether killing each rule would have a high impact on the business, low impact, or somewhere in between. Use this knowledge to

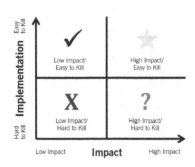

plot your two rules on the large matrix in the room according to how easy to kill and how much its death will impact the business. For example, if you believe your rule is low impact and hard to kill, place it in quadrant one (lower left). If it's high impact and easy to kill, plot it in quadrant four (top right). There's no right or wrong placement because you define what goes where according to your own perspective.

Tips for Success

- Leaders should take note of any rule that appears more than once; this indicates a problem area in the business.
- Participants typically place rules in the top half of the grid, with the majority in the top right box. Conversely, the lower right quadrant might be full. Very few rules will be placed in the lower left quadrant, so it's important to lead an objective discussion about the true impact or ease of implementation.
- Look for rules that appear in the matrix's upper right quadrant. These are easy to change with a high business impact, and killing them will give your team a quick win.

Step 3: Evaluate and Discuss As a Group. (20 minutes)

Team members should now share which two rules they plotted and why they believe each one should be killed or modified. Use the questions below to guide the discussion:

- In which quadrant were most of the rules placed?
- Are there similarities in the types of rules on the matrix? (Mostly related to reports? To HR processes? Etc.?)
- If most of our rules fall in the top right quadrant (easy to implement and high impact), why haven't we discussed eliminating them before now?
- Which rule(s) should we kill immediately?
- Which rule(s) should we modify immediately?

Step 4: Kill Stupid Rule(s). (10 minutes)

Now it's time for the moment of truth—and action. Among these "rules," take an employee vote on which one should be killed. Then do it, right on the spot. If possible, kill a few more. (Or do the next best thing: kill a rule for a few months and promise that if no one misses it, the change will be permanent.)[2]

Discuss as a group:

• Is anything preventing us from killing more rules?
• If so, what can we do to change that?
• Should we do this exercise a few times a year?
• Do stupid rules tend to originate from a specific business unit or division? What if we invited them to a rule-killing session to jointly explore solutions?

The value of "Kill a Stupid Rule" became apparent to me after working with Liz Tinkham, senior managing director at Accenture. Tinkham was continually looking for ways to drive more innovation and value for her largest client, a global high-tech giant. To do this, she wanted new tools that her leadership team could use to further challenge assumptions around how work gets done, as well as drive new efficiencies both internally and at the client. She knew there must be rules, processes, and other barriers that existed within her team, ones she wasn't aware of, that were getting in the way of more great work happening.

Tinkham asked us to facilitate an innovation-focused session for approximately forty of her top reports, including both seasoned leaders on the account and newer team members from across the world. The group covered a range of disciplines, including technology, sales, marketing, strategy, and delivery. This was all done by design; Tinkham wanted to ensure that everyone in a position of responsibility had an opportunity to contribute and drive change.

After learning several techniques in the morning, the group was introduced to "Kill a Stupid Rule" in the afternoon session. The group broke into pairs, and after only fifteen minutes of highly engaged discussion using the tool, Tinkham's colleagues generated a list of forty-one rules to kill or change, each written on a Post-it Note. Tinkham went through *every single Post-it Note* with the team, killing many rules right on the spot, explaining some, and agreeing to take up others. Remarkably, it turned out that many of the "rules" weren't rules at all, but rather misunderstandings that no one had thought to examine.

For example, many of the rules killed were related to meetings that people wrongly assumed they were required to attend but in reality didn't have to; Tinkham corrected those perceptions, specifying the three meetings a month that her leadership team actually needed to attend. As another example of a "perceived" rule, some people thought that specific forms and financial data were required before they could present new sales ideas for approval, which again was not the case. Understanding the source of the misperception and explaining her thinking was great for Tinkham because it also empowered everyone in the room to take action on the misperception.

At the end of the exercise, only a handful of rules hadn't been either killed or ruled out as misperceptions. Some of these rules were corporate-level mandates that the group agreed needed to be changed, but which were more challenging to actually kill. But as good stewards of Accenture, Tinkham asked the team to attack those rules as well, since it was likely that someone in corporate, who was just doing his job, made up the rule without fully understanding the downstream impact. The remaining rules were then assigned to leaders in the room. They committed to follow through on them and report back to the team.

"We had lots of lively debate on a few of these types of perceived rules," Tinkham told me. "I need my leaders to always be removing obstacles for our teams and our clients. This exercise was a very easy way to do it." Tinkham concluded the exercise by encouraging her leadership team to continually question anything that appeared to be an obstacle.[3]

TOOL: Simplification Tactics

Now that you've prioritized which complications to address first, it's time to execute. By some measures, this should be the easiest step: when you uncover elements of your life that are unnecessarily complex, simpler alternatives usually scream for adoption. If that isn't happening, examining how other people have tackled the challenge of complexity can point the way forward.

My team and I have collected and curated a long list of proven tactics, organizing them into a number of categories that tie into our "Complexity Diagnostic" from chapter 3. With more than seventy simplification tactics in hand (from Google's Bureaucracy-Busting Sessions to Airbnb's Meeting-Free Wednesdays), your team will be well armed to attack complexity and improve the way work gets done.

This tool is relevant for all levels of staff, and it can be done individually (just skip Step 4, the group discussion) or as a group, with various teams assigned the challenge of choosing tactics for specific areas of the business. The whole exercise should take as little as thirty-five minutes (if done individually) or as long as ninety-five minutes (if done in a group).

Step 1: Choose at Least Three Business Areas. (5 minutes)

Refer to your completed "Complexity Diagnostic" for easy identification of which business areas to focus on. If you haven't yet used the diagnostic tool, review the eleven business areas below and circle at least three that cause the most complexity in your daily work.

ORGANIZATIONAL		INDIVIDUAL	
• Vision/Communication	• Strategy/Planning	• Meetings	• Presentations
• Org. Structure	• Operational	• Emails/Calls/Voicemail	• Value of Staff Time
• HR	• Products/Services	• Reports	

Steps 2 and 3: Review Tactics Within Business Areas (10 minutes), and Choose at Least Two Tactics Per Area. (20 to 40 minutes)

Read every tactic in your areas of complexity, and check the box beside all the simplification tactics that would be most effective for your organization. Keep big-picture goals in mind as you choose individual tactics. For example, if Strategic Planning is an area of complexity, and your goal is to finalize your annual strategic plan more quickly, choose a tactic that supports this goal.

ORGANIZATIONAL AREA: VISION/COMMUNICATION

☐ **Change the language, change the mindset.** Communication from senior leadership to employees should be simple and concise. Eliminate jargon and clichés from messaging, and encourage authentic statements that do not need decoding. Simplification—in word and in deed—is key to shifting employees' mindsets from fear to freedom and from dependence to empowerment.

☐ **Give it the kindergarten test.** Can you explain your document/presentation/proposal/contract to a 5-year-old? Keep distilling the work until it's as simplified as possible.

☐ **Stop posting everywhere.** Take a tip from consulting firm Box of Crayons and focus your social media efforts on the 1 or 2 channels that are most relevant to your business.

ORG. STRUCTURE

☐ **1-sheet wonder.** If your organizational structure requires 5 slides and a color-coded legend to understand, simplification is needed. Challenge your team (or invite the entire organization) to submit 1-sheets of a simplified org. structure.

☐ **Align each group's goals with simplification.** To embed simplification throughout your entire organization, establish a set of universal metrics (i.e. reduce meetings by 20%; kill at least 10 stupid rules annually, etc.) that apply to every group within the org. structure and keep everyone accountable for simplifying.

☐ **Empower direct reports with decision-making.** Charge each person on your team to make 2 decisions this week without you. At your next status meeting, discuss which decisions they made on their own. Expand this behavior to 3, 5, and 10+ decisions per week, and tie decision-making to individual performance or to a simplification metric for your department.

HR

☐ **Define roles by outcomes, not tasks.** Task-based job descriptions focus on processes, not results, so redefine the roles in your organization for outcome-focused measures of success. For example, "write 3-5 press releases per month" could become "generate 20+ press mentions per month." This approach shifts the focus from "how" to "what." It flexes employees' creative problem-solving muscles and empowers them to concentrate on what actually matters: results.

☐ **Reduce performance assessment criteria.** Healthcare company Abbott reduced the number of assessment items in performance reviews—with a huge impact on the business.

HR (cont.)

☐ **Eliminate (or rethink) annual performance reviews.** Follow Accenture's lead and do away with paperwork-heavy performance reviews. Instead of reserving feedback for a once-a-year exercise, managers at this professional services company now provide employees with more frequent and less formal reviews for real-time improvement. Pro tip: Link assessment criteria to strategy so employees understand how their performance impacts the business from a strategic viewpoint.

☐ **Use tweet-sized feedback loops.** After completing a benchmark event or milestone, send a mini-review to participants requesting Twitter-length answers (140 characters or less) about team or initiative performance, critical skills, and advice on what should be improved next time around.

☐ **Re-examine transfer policy.** Make the transfer policy work for employees, like the Cosmopolitan of Las Vegas did. Staff challenged its rule that employees can't be transferred to another area of the business prior to 6 months from hire date. Now staff can transfer whenever a talent fit arises.

☐ **Shorten employee onboarding.** Kill long-winded orientations by offering on-demand learning during an employee's tenure. Focus orientation on just the basics with a brief Q&A meeting 2-4 weeks after start date, when employees have a better grasp on their responsibilities.

☐ **Establish flex/unlimited vacation.** Reduce HR and senior staff hours spent managing vacation days by eliminating the need to manage it like delivery service Deliv did. If time off affects an employee's performance or work quality, empower managers to adjust policy for that individual.

☐ **Limit hotel rate, not hotel choices.** To give its business-traveling employees more flexibility on hotel price and location, pharmaceutical company Novartis added 40 hotel chains to its travel policy.

☐ **Host a Simplification Jam.** Like IBM's Idea Jam, which engages more than 300,000 employees around the world in far-reaching exploration and problem solving, invite your organization (and external stakeholders like customers or clients) to propose ideas for simplifying complex areas of your business.

☐ **Reward + recognize simplifiers.** Publicly reward employees who make a successful case for killing a project, task, or policy. Positive reinforcement isn't a new concept, but it has the proven power to spread the value of simplification throughout your business.

STRATEGY/PLANNING

☐ **Make simplification a mandatory element of strategic planning.** For every new strategy that's added to the annual plan, remove an initiative that rolled over from last year. Identifying what teams should *stop* doing in the coming year is just as essential as outlining what they need to start doing.

☐ **Finalize annual strategic plan within a quarter (or less).** Filing away your strategic plan until next year is just as ineffective as failing to make a plan at all. Put it into action within 90 days to ensure that your company meets its strategic goals.

☐ **Keep score.** Track your organization's strategic performance throughout the year with a balanced scorecard or similar system.

☐ **Eliminate approval committees** by empowering a single expert with the authority to make and move decisions forward according to a set timeframe.

OPERATIONAL

Kill stupid rules like HBO did. When the cable network conducted this exercise for the first time, more than 100 stupid rules were identified and eliminated to free up time and reduce bottlenecking. Through a Google Doc, the group continued suggesting more stupid rules to kill and other parts of the organization adopted the practice. Rule-killing spread organically throughout the company and has become a best practice.

Cut the contract clutter. Reduce the length of your contracts from 100 pages to 20, like one of GE's groups did. Invite legal and business units to a joint session with the goal of reducing the contract length or finding ways to template or streamline the contracts that are most frequently used.

Open an express lane. Stop bottlenecking in your business by announcing that all actionable items meeting established criteria should be given a green light. The only items that do *not* belong in the express lane are those requiring additional review or approvals.

Stop demanding receipts for items on expense reports that cost less than $75 (or specify the amount that's right for your business).

Increase discretionary spend limits to minimize forms and constant approvals. Monitor and adjust policy only if necessary.

Set contract pricing minimums/ maximums to speed deals. German pharmaceutical company Boehringer-Ingelheim established proposal-pricing minimums and eliminated the need for sign-offs on every proposal. As long as pricing minimums are met, no manager sign-offs are needed so deals move forward faster.

☐ **Get outside-in solutions.** Pair people together from different areas of your organization to brainstorm solutions to each other's operational challenges. Fresh eyes and ears can offer a new perspective (instead of 1000 reasons why X doesn't work or why Z is impossible).

☐ **Track down duplicate work.** Dialog with other divisions to determine whether any redundant work is being conducted in a silo. If so, decide if that work should be eliminated in one group, centralized, or shared.

☐ **Conduct a vendor audit.** Review all your current vendor relationships to assess if a decrease in vendors and consolidation of services could reduce your paperwork and/or ensure lower prices.

☐ **Channel similar tasks to 1 source.** European franchise PizzaExpress shifted the task of slicing cocktail lemons from wait staff to the kitchen, which is more experienced with the duty and completes it more efficiently. By simply changing who sliced lemons, the company saved significant hours, which translated into significant financial savings.

☐ **Implement the 1-over-1 rule.** Reduce approval layers to 2 signatures—your boss and their boss—like GE did.

PRODUCT/SERVICE

☐ **Eliminate or divest** like Sprint does. When the telecommunications company recognized that the "Welcome Call" in its marketing program wasn't adding value to the business, the service was eliminated. With this single decision, Sprint cut $22MM from its operating budget. Review your own offerings regularly (and objectively), and phase out products, services, or projects that waste valuable resources so you can make space for innovation. To incentivize this behavior enterprise-wide, reward people for identifying portfolio areas without strong ROI.

PRODUCT/SERVICE (cont.)

☐ **Want breakthrough ideas? Stop asking for them.** Trade yawn-inducing prompts like "Who has a big idea for our next new product?" for provocative thought-starters that seem outrageous in theory but are potentially transformative in action. For example, "start a business that competes with my current employer" is an idea that could certainly get you fired. But in the context of this tactic, it can start a valuable conversation about crisis aversion. A competing venture would likely exploit your company's biggest weakness, opening up discussion about what can be done now to transform flaws into strengths. Review the list below for thought-starters.
  - If you were guaranteed immunity, what are some ideas that would get you fired?
  - Name 3 free solutions to this problem.
  - Name 3 solutions that wouldn't require any time investment.
  - What ideas do you have that would give the CEO a panic attack?
  - What would our competitors *never* expect us to do?
  - Name 3 small changes that you would love to implement today.
  - What 1 thing would you change to solve this problem?

☐ **Keep it simple** like Google does. Ranked one of the top companies in the world on the Global Brand Simplicity Index, Google intentionally keeps the features of its search engine–and every other offering–as minimal as possible for its users.

INDIVIDUAL AREA: MEETINGS

☐ **Kill stupid meetings** like Sprint did. Upon review of every meeting held in 1 year— from standing and weekly status meetings to events, off-sites, and team gatherings— Sprint eliminated 30% of them. Conduct your own meeting audit and do away with meetings that don't add value or have outlived their original objective.

☐ **Just say no.** After performing a meeting audit to determine the cost of time and resources for all of its meetings, professional services company Accenture empowered its managers to decline meetings without guilt or fear.

☐ **Institute Meeting-Free Wednesdays** like Airbnb did to encourage uninterrupted time for valuable work.

☐ **On your feet.** Stand-up meetings are less comfortable for attendees, which typically reduces the meeting's length.

☐ **Set a timer.** Place a cap on meetings like HBO's division for Domestic Network Distribution did. A designated timekeeper limits meetings to 1 hour, which keeps sessions focused and mindful of attendees' time.

☐ **Rethink default modes.** Adjust your Outlook or iCal default settings from 1 hour to 30 mins. for new events. Manually adjust only if a meeting will require more than 30 mins. to achieve its goal.

☐ **Start meetings with goals...and end with action items.** Require that every meeting agenda includes the meeting's goal *and* is sent to invitees in advance. Similarly, require that next steps be defined at the meeting's conclusion.

☐ **Establish meeting etiquette** and post it on your intranet and in conference rooms to encourage efficiency, punctuality, and preparedness among attendees.

☐ **Simplify meeting materials.** By limiting preparation for quarterly financial meetings to 1 – 2 PPT slides, Novartis shortened both the length of these meetings and advance prep time for every level of staff.

EETINGS (cont.)

☐ **End meetings 15 minutes before the hour.** Standardize the 45-min. meeting, enabling employees to make their next meeting or call in a timely manner.

MAIL/CALLS/VOICEMAIL

☐ **Institute email-free time zones.** UK-based multimedia production company Ten Alps banned morning emails so employees could allocate time for ideating and imagining instead of inboxing.

☐ **Unsubscribe** to every e-letter that adds zero value to your life.

☐ **Enact email quotas.** In organizations where email is overwhelming, an employee may receive more than 200 emails in a single day. Extreme simplification measures call for a daily email quota–starting with yourself—that limits sending or replying to a maximum of 20-30 emails per day. Once that quota is met, your inbox is closed for the day. From this level of simplification, an organization-wide awareness of what's being sent and received is gained, and over time, excessive emailing habits are curbed.

☐ **Limit cc recipients** to 3 people inside your company, which is how Ferrari got its employees to "talk more, write less."

☐ **Use Slack or WhatsApp messaging** to decrease the volume of internal emails.

☐ **Utilize NNTR.** For email topics that are FYI and don't require a response, type NNTR (No Need To Respond) in the subject line. By utilizing this tactic, a business unit at Merck reduced email volume within its group by 20%.

☐ **Reply to non-urgent emails at a slow or set time** of day.

☐ **Distill your message into the subject line** and leave the email body blank.

☐ **Pick up the phone** to resolve any topic that isn't decided after 3 emails.

☐ **No-scroll emails.** Summarize key points or action items for recipients in the body of your email. Lengthy or dense information should be relegated to attachments only.

☐ **Eliminate voicemail** like Coca-Cola and JPMorgan Chase did. By cutting an outmoded means of communication for the majority of its staff— client-facing teams chose to retain it—JPMorgan Chase saved more than $8MM.

☐ **Limit internal calls to 12 mins., 25 mins., or 50 mins.** Benefits of untraditional end times include more time awareness and fewer tangents. Calls of these lengths are designed to provide buffer time afterward to handle any action items requested during the calls.

☐ **Embrace airplane mode.** To focus on valuable work, place your smartphone in airplane mode, move it into a drawer, and check your messages only once per hour.

☐ **Shift weekly calls to bimonthly.** HBO's division for Domestic Network Distribution modified the frequency of its weekly touch point calls for senior leadership to bimonthly, saving time and increasing the quality of information exchanged.

REPORTS

☐ **Crowd-source the complexity.** Are reports your No. 1 cause for complexity? Crowd-source solutions to the issue and implement these ideas. Publicly recognize and reward employees with winning ideas to incentivize more simplification.

REPORTS (cont.)

☐ **Audit your reports.** Is your department contributing to valuable reports or have some of them outlived their usefulness? Is duplicate information already compiled by another division? Analyze all the reports to which your team contributes for opportunities to streamline or eliminate.

PRESENTATIONS

☐ **3 core ideas only.** Research suggests that audiences only remembers 3 points from any presentation they encounter, so save time by distilling your work into 3 core ideas and building your narrative or CTA around them.

☐ **No PPT meetings.** By allowing only 1-page executive summaries, individuals are pushed to provide only the most essential information.

☐ **Utilize Google Docs** for finalizing presentations and proposals among multiple authors/stakeholders.

☐ **Use simple formatting and fewer graphics.** Reduce time investment—and staff headaches—for presentations by limiting graphics to 1 per page and avoiding custom colors and fonts.

VALUE OF STAFF TIME

☐ **Hold simplifying sessions.** Host a formal exercise (like Killing Complexity) where team members are invited to identify tasks that are complex or don't add value to the business. Along with participants, leaders help brainstorm ideas on how to eliminate, outsource, or simplify these tasks in the session.

☐ **Equip managers with outcome-focused solutions.** Train managers to resolve gripe sessions by asking "What do you hope to achieve through this dialog?" This tactic redirects a conversation from "My colleague always gets first choice when choosing holidays" to "I want to pin down my summer holidays, and I need you to review my request this week so I can plan my vacation." By encouraging employees to phrase their complaints as wishes, an issue like "I hate the new hire process" becomes "I wish the new hire process included only 1 level of approval and could be done in 3 days or less."

☐ **Morning priorities = better choices all day.** When you make a conscious effort each morning to focus on specific goals, your afternoon is less likely to be derailed by distractions or unplanned matters.

☐ **Put valuable work on the calendar.** Reserve 2-3 hours each day for work that is most valuable to your stakeholders.

☐ **Eliminate 1 current activity before adding a new one.** This golden rule of simplification emphasizes respect of employees' time and thoughtful examination of existing responsibilities.

☐ **Cut the crap by committee.** U.K.-based audio retailer Richer Sounds founded a Cut-the-Crap Committee, where managers reduce bureaucracy by limiting unproductive systems and paperwork.

☐ **Turn Fridays into Finishdays.** Designate Friday afternoons for wrapping up the week's unfinished business.

VALUE OF STAFF TIME (cont.)

☐ **Introduce blackout periods.** To encourage employees to spend time thinking and ideating instead of attending meetings or answering emails, a department at Fidelity wraps CAUTION tape around their cubicles at designated times each week, and Intel implements dark periods from 1– 5pm on Fridays.

☐ **Hold Bureaucracy Buster sessions** like Google does. Participants are given the freedom to identify and eradicate barriers to productivity and efficiency.

☐ **Who benefits from this process?** Before simplifying a process or procedure, break it down into steps and identify who benefits from the information. If the answer is consistently "no one," eliminate it altogether.

☐ **Replace a main process with its workaround.** If staff has created a workaround to speed a certain process, consider making it the new protocol. Define your criteria for what constitutes a better solution—*X* amount of time saved? *Y* amount of money saved?—and implore employees to find workarounds for other complex processes.

Step 4: Propose Tactics and Discuss As a Group. (20 to 40 minutes)

As a group, discuss the following:

1. Which tactics did everyone select? Do we agree on which tactics should be implemented?
2. Will each of our tactics have a high impact on our areas of complexity?
3. Do our tactics connect directly to our goals? If so, write the tactics for each area. If not, keep discussing until tactics are aligned with goals.

Smelling the Roses

In 2015, one of our international clients invited my team to share our expertise with a cross-section of his colleagues—roughly two dozen employees ranging from engineers and designers to salespeople and customer service coordinators. Immediately upon our arrival, our team could sense that this was going to be a great group. Nearly everyone was energetic, talkative, and enthusiastic.

Our first mandate was to help the group become "less obedient" and more alert to new ways of working with their clients. We started with an interactive exercise called "Aircraft." Each participant was asked to fashion an aircraft out of paper and tape in just sixty seconds. Participants worked furtively on their designs, racing against the clock. They folded the paper and tested wing design, using massive amounts of tape. When time was up, each participant threw his or her aircraft. The most successful flew no more than seven feet across the room.

The group's lead facilitator then asked if participants thought they had accomplished the task. They all nodded. He told them that he had an alternative design in mind—one that might go even further—and wondered if they wanted to see it. They were curious and said yes. That's when the aha moment happened. The facilitator crumpled up his piece of paper into a ball and threw it the entire length of the room. Participants watched it soar. The facilitator reminded the group of the instructions: he said air*craft*, not air*plane*. The participants had jumped to conclusions, spending their bits of time creating wings, playing with tail design, etc. They had neglected to consider alternative (and obvious) ways of accomplishing the goal.

Participants' assumptions held them back from creating a wider range of ideas and better solutions. And it was in that moment that people became aware of how complication thwarts well-meaning professionals. "Some things we *make* more complicated when a simple solution exists," one participant said.

Once we'd completed the first step of the simplification process ("awareness"), we moved on to the next three—"identification," "prioritization," and "execution." Our client had allowed us enough time to take a deep dive, so we began one of the most comprehensive exercises in the set: "Killing Complexity." The group sat back at their tables, ready to eliminate complexity and simplify their own work. But they needed help gaining insight into the core of the problem.

We handed out the worksheet designed to help participants identify where they spent their time. We had participants write down all their tasks, breaking their work down based on time (frequency or duration): daily, weekly, monthly, and annually. The room became quiet. We gave them just ten minutes, but a couple of people asked for more time. Auditing the way you spend your time is not as easy as you might imagine.

Rarely are we compelled to think through all the tasks that define our days. Yet doing so is almost always illuminating.

In this instance, the exercise proved so cathartic that one member of the group asked whether participants could include tasks from their personal life—a reasonable request as technology so often blurs the boundaries between work and home. But to keep the exercise on track, we asked group members to limit themselves to tasks related to the group's own work.

When everyone was ready, group members gathered in a circle to share their lists. They discovered that they were spending most of their time on general work tasks. That's right, most of the big complexity barriers weren't the result of company-wide processes or industry-wide regulations. The big drivers were small tasks—areas in which individuals actually had the power to influence change. What were they?

- **Internal Meetings:** Many group members spent full half-days in meetings. And while these meetings were meaningful and productive on occasion, often they were not.
- **Checking and Answering E-mail:** There were too many e-mails—about a hundred per day—and no system for organizing them.
- **Submissions (Reports):** Every two days, group members were required to submit data on a new product. Each report consumed a lot of time, but there was no way around it. Everyone thought the system was terrible and duplicative. There was no consensus about whether it was meaningful or not.
- **Presentations:** These included both customer reports and internal presentations. They were done on a weekly basis and they certainly added value, but they consumed a lot of time.

Having all their work laid out in front of them really changed the group's perspective. "I cannot believe how much time I spend doing these things," one participant said. But while understanding where they spent their time was important, even more critical was uncovering whether they were spending it on work that mattered. And that brought them to the next challenge: prioritizing and then either eliminating or streamlining those tasks to make their work more meaningful.

At this point, we asked participants to consider the ten tasks on which they spent the most time, assigning each a specific level of complexity. We used a scale of 1 to 5 but prohibited them from assigning any task the number "3"; this would help us avoid middle-of-the-road answers. Participants wrote each of their tasks on a Post-it Note, along with their complexity number.

As a penultimate step, we asked participants to consider the underlying value of each task. To help them think about whether a task was high or low value, we had everyone ask herself: "Does this task solve a problem? Does it fulfill an essential client or customer need? Does it provide insight and help leadership make decisions?" We then showed participants the two-by-two matrix provided on page 113, comparing "simplicity" to "value." This enabled participants to think more deeply about whether they were spending their time on valuable work.

Finally, we began crafting solutions. We asked each person to pick a task from his worksheet that was either complex (and therefore in need of simplification) or low value (and therefore in need of elimination or improvement). We asked participants to brainstorm solutions. So, for example, if the task was "internal meetings," a question could be, "How might I make internal meetings more valuable? In what ways can I make internal meetings more time-efficient? How will I know if I should attend a meeting or not?" We partnered participants, and when the group came back together, several participants shared their ideas and simplification tactics. Here are a few of the insights:

- "Lucky for me, my partner for this exercise works in finance. I explained the very complex and time-consuming process of reviewing the monthly forecast. My partner explained the process to me and now I understand how it works. Having an understanding of it saves me a lot of time and complexity."

- "Meetings are unproductive throughout the month. They last all day long. The most important thing we identified is that we're not prepared so we're not running successful and productive meetings. We need to have some learning around what it means to lead and host a meeting. One solution from a client is that they hang six or seven guidelines for successful meetings in their meeting rooms."

As an important part of the wrap-up, we asked the group to commit to some tactics for simplification, and we shared a few of ours. Below are some of the participants' tactics for simplification:

- Set up rules and processes for successful meetings. Be punctual with the start of meetings. Have tasks and a plan before you get started.
- Celebrate specificity and don't be vague.
- To make leadership less complex, team members should be engaged and the team should be held accountable.
- Carve out some "do not disturb" time in the calendar.
- Focus on more important things first so that the urgent/small things won't steal your time.
- Talk more face to face and send fewer e-mails.
- Empower the team to solve problems if members can find a solution.
- Write shorter e-mails with bullet points. For very large e-mails with a great deal of information, include at the top of the e-mail two sentences in bold that capture the key takeaways (our agreement and actions).

The whole day was a remarkable success. We hadn't solved every problem or reengineered the way our client did business. But we did help the team get control over one of the most frustrating elements of modern professional life: the sense that our efforts amount, in too many cases, to much less than they might.

Use the tools in this chapter. Experiment with them. We all have it in our power to make meaningful improvements in our work—without a lengthy, formal, Six Sigma–type process. Working together with our colleagues, we can delve into the nuances and details of our work, cutting away what doesn't add value and getting closer to the work that *really* matters.

CHAPTER SEVEN

Become the Chief Simplification Officer

> "The ability to simplify means to eliminate the unnecessary so that the necessary may speak."
>
> —Hans Hofmann[1]

We've established that simplicity is good for businesses generally, but is it also good for individual leaders? The answer appears to be a resounding "yes." Several years ago, Steve Strelsin, an experienced CEO who also helped found the online law service Axiom, performed a research project studying CEOs in collaboration with Harvard Business School. Strelsin compiled a sample set of executives from various industries and asked them questions about the way they approached their leadership role. Then he mapped their answers against their records of achievement.

What he found was remarkable.[2] Strelsin asked CEOs an easy question: "How would you describe the most important aspect of your role in the organization?" The CEOs whose companies were *inconsistent* in their performance prioritized creating a vision, building a specific corporate culture, and developing a specific business strategy. But when Strelsin posed the same question to CEOs of industry-leading companies, most said that they had made it their personal mission, above all else, to *simplify* the lives of those who worked below them. They pursued simplification in a number of ways: they simplified their strategies so their peers and subordinates could focus on the most important challenges. They simplified their hierarchies, so that their companies could execute their strategies more effectively. They made it a priority to communicate in clear prose that inspired everyone to join in their company's respective mission. In short, the most successful executives in Strelsin's study excelled in their jobs because they regarded themselves not merely as CEOs, but as chief simplifiers.

Strelsin's results suggest two important corollaries for organizations. First, simplification can't just be a onetime, spring-cleaning kind of event. The impulse to embrace work that is minimal, understandable, repeatable, and accessible needs to be cultivated, ingrained, and deepened over time. Simplification needs to be a habit and a way of looking at the challenges we face every day. It needs to be part of every moment and every decision, woven firmly into the culture of business and defining the ethos of each and every employee. Many companies fail at simplification because they don't integrate it deeply enough into the organization. They don't simplify the work that *everyone* does, in turn making simplicity a defining part of the culture.

We talk a lot about corporate culture, but I believe we've lost sight of what that truly is. Culture is not colorfully painted walls. It's not collaboration rooms with large whiteboards. It's not the organic food stocked in the common room. It's much more than that. Most fundamentally, it's behavior—the way work gets done. It's the stress level at various kinds of meetings and the time people get to the office each morning. It's the informal sense of what behavior is allowable and what's beyond the pale. Communication plays a role—policies, handbooks, posters, and the like—but that's not the only place where culture is defined. Most of it is developed through the daily interactions that people have with their peers on a routine basis. Culture is the work we do every day.

> Culture is the work we do every day.

A second point hinted at by Strelsin's research is that any organization interested in simplification requires strong engagement at the top. When you discover that an organization has failed to simplify work processes at all levels, you often find a leadership vacuum: senior executives haven't oriented themselves and their work around simplicity. They might affirm simplification's value, but they do nothing to clear the barriers that prevent it. They let behaviors persist that create and reinforce complexity on a daily basis. Employees perceive that simplification isn't a core initiative, one that the entire organization must support. It becomes much more difficult to convince people at lower levels to reform their own work habits and part with practices and procedures that feel comfortable but that bog down their colleagues.

When leaders don't embrace simplification, it's often because they don't quite know how, rather than that they don't want to. For all that has been written about simplification, leaders have lacked a coherent playbook that lets them work simplification deep into the way people under them work. This holds true for leaders at *every* level of an organization, not just C-suite executives. If you're a frontline manager or a department head or a vice president of a business unit, you too have the opportunity to cut away complexity and help your team get to work that matters. The exercises in the preceding chapter might help you undertake a onetime simplification initiative, but they don't tell you what to do to make simplicity a habit.

Rest assured, there's a *lot* you can do right now, without waiting for a formal review process to run its course. This chapter provides a dozen strategies for building simplicity into the *ethos* of the organization— whether that's an organization of a hundred thousand employees or just a few. Arising out of my work with hundreds of companies and my interviews of executives and managers at all organizational levels, these strategies reflect my firsthand knowledge of what works and what doesn't. Not every one of my strategies will be appropriate for every organization or individual, but taken together, they give those leaders who want to simplify the know-how to press on.

When working with these strategies, I'd like you to imagine that you have been assigned the role of chief simplifier—not of your company, but rather of the domain that you control within your organization *today*. If no one reports to you, think about how you can use these strategies to eliminate complication in your own work. If a handful of people report to you, consider which of these strategies might help you eliminate complications in *their* routines. And if you're nearer the top of an organization, extract from these twelve strategies some general ideas for ensuring that each member of the workforce below you has an opportunity to do more meaningful work every single day.

Strategy #1: Set a Vision

It's easy to proclaim that you want to simplify your work, but to get sustained buy-in from the people you work with—to make simplicity a common ethos—you need to paint a picture of what simplification will entail and help achieve. Taking the time to craft your vision will eliminate potential confusion, giving your peers a clear understanding of what they can do to meet your expectations. By clarifying *why* you're so keen to embrace simplicity, a vision can motivate your subordinates to make better decisions. Finally, a clear definition wins hearts and minds by highlighting your intent, namely your desire to see your team do meaningful, valuable work.

To further build excitement around simplification, engage others in shaping the details of your vision. A vision is more likely to stick when everyone has a say. Start by surveying team members, formally or informally, to get their input. Ask them how *they* think simplification could benefit your common enterprise. And then incorporate their insights, making sure to give them credit among their peers.

Recall how Brad Katsuyama, the hero of Michael Lewis's *Flash Boys*, founded his company IEX explicitly to combat the purposeful complication that had invaded the capital markets. The process of buying and selling securities had become so complex that, by Lewis's telling, high-frequency traders were electronically front-running the general public, padding their own wallets at their unsuspecting victims' expense. Katsuyama wanted to build a business that promised a level playing field. How best to accomplish that goal? Through simplicity. IEX positioned itself literally "as a fair, simple, and transparent market center dedicated to investor protection."[3] As he explained it to me: "At IEX, there is a central reason people are here. It's a mission statement—we use simple language people understand and is *conflict-free*. Every decision we make comes back to our mission. It's so well documented that it makes decision-making easier—it makes the world black and white."[4]

We all intuitively understand that having and communicating a vision is important. But most leaders can find creating a clear vision hard to do. My team has developed a shortcut to help you paint the right picture. Using the tool below, you can craft a simplification vision in little more than a half hour. And you can do it either alone or collaboratively with your team.

TOOL: Simplicity Vision Statement

Step 1: Complete the Worksheet. (30 minutes)

In this first step, read the questions below and answer them honestly. First, write your thoughts under each question. When ready, polish each response to fit in the sentence starters in the answer column.

QUESTIONS (CAPTURE IDEAS BELOW)	ANSWERS (POLISH IDEAS BELOW)
1. Why is simplification important to us?	Simplification is important because:
2. What 3 things, when simplified, do we think will have the greatest impact on our jobs or business?	The 3 simplifications with the greatest impact will be: 1. 2. 3.
3. In what ways can we experience more workplace simplicity every day?	On a daily basis, we'll see small changes like:
4. If we simplify how we work, what will the result be (financial, behavioral, time-savings, etc.)?	We'll be able to measure results like:
5. How will we know when our work/business unit/function is simplified?	We'll be in a state of simplification when this happens:

QUESTIONS (CONT.) (CAPTURE IDEAS BELOW)	ANSWERS (CONT.) (POLISH IDEAS BELOW)
6. What new simplification skills will we use on a daily basis?	People will be more...
7. A year from now, how did we make simplification a habit?	Simplification will become a habit if we...
8. Looking back, what was our biggest barrier to simplification?	The biggest barrier we need to tackle is...
9. If we hadn't made simplification a habit, what would have happened?	If we don't make simplification a habit, the result will be...
10. What will simplification help us achieve—personally and professionally?	Simplification will do this for our business: For each other: For me:
11. In 1 sentence, what does simplicity mean to us?	Simplicity is...

Step 2: Share Answers and Discuss. (30 minutes)

If you're working in a group, find a partner and compare answers. Challenge one another when you discuss the following:

- What are the similarities between our answers?
- What are the differences between them?
- Which answers reflect simplification as a core value of our business?
- Of those answers, which one to three offer the most promising statements for our organization's Simplicity Vision? (Take a vote if necessary.)

Step 3: Draft a Simplicity Vision Statement. (30 minutes)

Use the collective answers to Questions 10 and 11 in the worksheet to help create a concise statement for what simplicity is and what it will do for the business.

Step 4: Solicit Feedback and Revise. (60 minutes)

Send your Simplicity Vision Statement to mentors, peers, and trusted partners from inside and outside your organization, asking them to identify weaknesses and recommend ways to strengthen them. Alternatively, invite your entire organization to collaborate on the final version. After it's finalized, share it enterprise-wide.

- **Ask for Feedback:** Ask your peers and a handful of trusted partners outside the company to give you feedback on your vision and poke holes in your answers. Is your vision clear? Jargon-free? Inspiring? Results oriented?

- **Get Buy-In:** Share your answers with your team. What's their reaction? What would they change? How would they like to make simplification a reality?

- **Turn it into a Survey:** Use the questions in the worksheet to create a survey you can give your team or larger organization if appropriate. Ask them to complete the survey, gather their responses, and compare them to your own. What were the key similarities or differences?

Strategy #2: Weave Simplicity into Your Long-Term Strategy

Once you've defined your vision for simplification, you need a strategy to get there. Many companies struggle with strategic planning, focusing on quarterly benchmarks rather than longer-term goals. As one of my clients once joked, strategic planning never really ends—we just take periodic breaks from it. And that's a shame: a part of corporate planning that should be an asset has become little more than a burden. Jeff Spencer, formerly the strategy head at Merck Canada, explained the problem succinctly: "People don't want to just hear about a strategy. They want to hear about action and results."

Books have been written about how to improve strategic planning. My point here is that you must make simplicity a vital part of the process. Simplicity can't just be the subject on a poster in the cafeteria. Long-term planning should consider what you plan to subtract from your work to better focus, not merely what you plan to add.

When companies think about how to grow, the overwhelming majority of the time their go-to approach is to show how they plan to *add* to their menu of offerings: New bells and whistles. New premium services. A fancier mousetrap. Sometimes that's a sound strategy, but all too often the complications that arise when adding products or features can erode whatever advantage you might glean. When making a strategic move, consider whether you'd be better off killing or selling off a portion of your portfolio in the name of simplicity.

In 2014, P&G decided that the best way to grow its business was to sell a narrower band of products. Within its hair-care portfolio, certain brands, like Head & Shoulders and Pantene, were growing, but others—those marketed to salons and to consumers interested in coloring their hair—were stagnant at best. Because the diversity of the company's product offerings was spreading the sales and marketing team thin, the healthy products weren't getting the proper support. Complication was stealing fuel from the company's fire.

P&G's then-CEO, A.G. Lafley, made a tough decision. Rather than pour new resources into the more peripheral beauty products, P&G would sell them to Coty. As Lafley explained, the whole point was to make P&G more efficient and streamlined. Lafley ultimately wanted to create "much simpler businesses, [that are] easier to operate, easier to grow, easier to create value creation from.... the big change has been a dramatic narrowing of the focus and choices [and] getting back to balanced innovation and productivity that really drives value creation."[5]

It's hard to abandon a brand or sell an asset. It can feel like you're waving the white flag of surrender. But simplifying your portfolio can empower you to focus more effectively on what remains. As Ron Ashkenas, longtime management consultant and expert on organizational change, explained, "Products are a good place to start when simplifying, but people are attached to them—there's ego, and it's hard to tell customers that you won't support a product anymore."[6]

Like master gardeners, outstanding leaders prune carefully because they know that eliminating waste will eventually yield better results. In 1997, Steve Jobs famously declared, "I'm actually as proud of the things we haven't done as the things we have done. Innovation is saying 'no' to 1,000 things."[7] He's exactly right.

Strategy #3: Streamline Management Layers

In 1944, the Office of Strategic Services (OSS)—forerunner to the CIA—wrote a field manual for agents looking to sabotage organizations in the name of American national security. The manual included one particular vexing strategy: complication. OSS directed saboteurs to "insist on doing everything through channels. Never permit shortcuts to be taken in order to expedite decisions... [and] multiply the procedures and clearances involved in issuing instructions.... See that three people have to approve everything where one would do."[8]

It's strange to think of complication as a means to sabotage, but it must have been a very effective tool. As management layers pile on, it takes too long for good ideas to make their way up the chain of command, and too much time for sign-offs to make their way back down. People in positions of authority become far removed from realities on the ground. Explains Ashkenas: "Senior managers become insulated from what's really going on when there are too many layers. Each one spins the reality in a different way, so that the senior manager doesn't actually know the truth."[9]

It's not that every organization should flatten its management structure altogether; a boss with too many reports can't give anyone sufficient attention. Yet extra layers cost money, waste time, and delay decisions.

One study found that adding a new manager creates, on average, an employee-and-a-half's worth of work. That's not because the new manager is coming up with more ideas; it's because the new layer adds a whole new layer of complication.[10]

"De-layering," as Bain & Company and others have called it, is now a staple for those looking to eliminate redundancies. But you don't need to bring in outside advisors to help you identify what you already understand. Streamline your own management. Look at each person's role in the existing reporting structure. Are there any redundancies? Are people siloed? Compare your reporting structure to industry norms. When you compare yourself to the competition, are more sign-offs required for each discrete decision? Make reasonable changes. With a careful eye not to overwhelm your employees, could you increase the range of control for certain roles and functions? Answer these questions carefully, and then see if you can beat the competition.

Strategy #4: Simplify Decision-Making

As Merck Canada prepared for a company-wide simplification initiative, the leadership team identified an ongoing challenge. In all too many cases, employees authorized to make decisions were asking their bosses to sign off on them. This was driving unnecessary delays and burdening managers. Senior leaders didn't know why employees were so reluctant to take personal responsibility, but they eventually concluded that employees feared making a bad move. By pushing the decision a level up, they were passing the buck.[11]

One of my other clients, a senior manager heading up risk analytics at a large financial ratings company, noticed something similar happening in his organization. He was so frustrated that his ten direct reports refused to make decisions independently that he instituted a new policy: each report *had* to make two decisions each week without his sign-off. Initially, he continued to get e-mails like, "Can I invite Robert to tomorrow's meeting?" He would reply, "That's exactly the type of decision you can make on your own." Eventually, his peers got the message, and my client was elated to find that he had twenty fewer decisions to make each week. Over time, he upped the ante, requiring that more decisions be made without him. Six months later, he discovered that he had to ask more questions of his subordinates just to stay abreast of the latest developments.[12]

At Merck Canada, employees with direct reports began refusing to make decisions that subordinates were authorized to make on their own. The results were powerful. Employees who once looked for cover began taking responsibility for their own decisions. They were more invested in making sure they made the right choice in a timely manner, and they felt more ownership over the outcome.

Leaders can simplify decision-making by empowering frontline staff as well. Commerce Bank's leadership wanted staff to respond better to customer requests, so it made the process of turning down a request in the moment more burdensome than fulfilling the request. If an employee was inclined to do what a customer wanted, the employee could make that decision on her own. Simple! But if she wanted to turn the customer down, she had to get her manager's approval. In essence, it was "One to say YES, two to say NO."

At too many companies, the failure to clarify who should make which decisions drags down decision-making and execution. If firms devote less time to managing the matrix, they have more time to do work that matters. As SAP's Jeff Woods has explained: "We did a simplification study with Wharton to understand technology and complexity. In the research data, we asked employees what kind of complexity was holding them back. People cited decision-making and process complexity more than technology complexity. It's not the tech itself but how it's used that's creating the complexity."[13]

Take time out to review the decision-making processes at *your* organization. Challenge yourself and your colleagues to reduce or eliminate the number of people required to sign off, approve, or review particular decisions. To get the process going, ask yourself:

1. What's the *smallest* number of people we could feasibly require to sign off on a report/document/expense?
2. How much money can I let someone spend without requiring paperwork or a report?
3. What reports/paperwork/requirements could we eliminate from our approval processes immediately?

Strategy #5: Establish Clear Metrics

Before embarking on any sort of simplification, you need some sense of how you'll measure the outcome. Few things scuttle a promising initiative more than the absence of proof that it worked. Without proof, others try to credit unrelated factors for the improvement or blame the initiative for unrelated failures.

What's the best way to track progress in simplification? In my experience, metrics can be soft and qualitative as well as hard and quantifiable. They should not only measure progress on eliminating complexity but also encourage positive changes in behavior. Most important, they should make clear whether simplification is contributing to actual business results.

When working with clients, Ron Ashkenas often recommends that businesses avoid implementing new metrics. Instead, he suggests that they "ratchet up the expectations on the current metrics. So if sales are at a certain level, then increase the goal by 15 percent—which might require doing business in very different ways."[14] The point, after all, isn't just to be simple, but to use simplicity as a tool to improve your performance. Heightening expectations can compel employees to reduce complexity in the pursuit of better results.

The tool that follows, "Simplification Metrics," helps individual leaders, teams, and business units build the metrics they need. As I mentioned, trackable metrics can be hard and quantifiable or soft and qualitative, but each one should focus on a part of your business that needs to be simplified. From reducing reports or management layers to increasing employee retention, the right metrics will support your business goals and encourage positive behavioral change. "Simplification Metrics" will serve as your guidepost—and ideally, provide you with proof of your simplification success.

Simplification Metrics

Step 1: Identify and Discuss Simplification Objectives (60 minutes)

As a group, use the questions that follow to discuss your simplification objectives and which metrics will track your efforts.

- In which areas of our business will simplifying have the biggest impact?
- Which key processes and systems should be simplified to create that impact?
- What short-term changes will achieve the quick wins we need to gain momentum for simplification?
- What long-term changes do we expect to accomplish through simplification?
- Which behaviors inside our organization need to change? Which simplification behaviors should become habitual?
- What types of results will indicate that we've reached our simplification goals?
- How will we make our selection and monitoring of metrics visible to everyone in the organization?

Step 2: Select Simplification Metrics (30 minutes)

Assign a leader to capture the group's metrics on a whiteboard or ask participants to write their top selections on sticky notes. Choose a manageable five to seven metrics to track, and feel free to create custom metrics. Keep the following in mind:

- **Connect Metrics to Your Organization's Overall Strategy.** Choose metrics that benefit both your business unit and the entire company.

- **Be Mindful of Unintended Consequences.** If you want to track "amount of cost savings resulting from eliminated meetings," make sure that metric doesn't push people to blindly eliminate as many meetings as possible. For example, an existing daily huddle for a project team may be preventing redundancies and increasing workflow. Eliminating a valuable meeting like this could end up costing the organization money, so communicate objectives along with metrics. Consider customizing any metric (e.g., track cost savings by eliminating *long* meetings) with the potential for negative side effects.

VISION/COMMUNICATION METRICS	ORG STRUCTURE METRICS	HR METRICS	STRATEGY/PLANNING METRICS	OPERATIONAL METRICS	
☐ Decrease in time spent communicating on irrelevant social media channels	☐ Increase in staff decision-making due to simplified org. structure	☐ Decrease in number of approval layers for hiring qualified candidates	☐ Decrease in number of approval committees	☐ Number of contracts shortened	☐ Employees are actively cutting red tape out of their day-to-day activities
☐ Decrease in number of jargon statements in communication from senior leaders to employees	☐ Increased communication between teams or divisions due to simplified org. structure	☐ Decrease in number of performance assessment criteria	☐ Amount of time saved from decreasing number of approval committees	☐ Amount of time saved through shortened contracts	☐ Decrease in number of required sign-offs/signatures for approval
☐ Increase in conversations about elimination and simplification among senior management	☐ Increased sense of empowerment among employees due to simplified org. structure	☐ Amount of time saved from reducing performance assessment criteria	☐ Decrease in amount of time to finalize and approve annual strategic plan	☐ Decrease in employee help-desk requests for basic troubleshooting	☐ Increase in consistency of processes within and across lines of business
☐ Increase in staff comprehension of why simplification is valuable to the business		☐ Increase in number of bonuses or rewards administered for simplifying	☐ Decrease in amount of time to finalize and approve annual fiscal budget	☐ Increase in time employees now spend interacting with clients/customers	☐ Decrease in time to process requests or approvals from employees or customers
		☐ Decrease in full-time equivalents (FTEs) from simplification effort		☐ Decrease in customer-service response time to customers/clients	☐ Number of policies, processes, or procedures simplified
		☐ Increase in number of employees trained in simplification		☐ Decrease in number of active vendors	☐ Number of processes automated
		☐ Number of duplicate functions eliminated		☐ Decrease in customer/client/vendor questions about our contracts	☐ Amount of time saved from automating processes
		☐ Amount of cost savings from eliminating duplicate functions		☐ Amount of time saved from eliminated forms	☐ Number of stupid rules killed
		☐ Increase in number of people recognized for simplifying		☐ Number of redundancies eliminated	☐ Number of stupid tasks killed
		☐ Decrease in number of new or existing HR policies		☐ Amount of time saved from eliminating redundancies	☐ Number of forms eliminated
		☐ Increase in positive feedback about culture in employee surveys		☐ Increase in number of projects completed on time	
		☐ Increase in employee-retention rate			
		☐ Decrease in regrettable turnover			
		☐ Increase in employee satisfaction			

PRODUCT/SERVICE METRICS	MEETINGS METRICS	EMAIL/CALLS/ VOICEMAIL METRICS	REPORT METRICS	PRESENTATION METRICS	VALUE OF STAFF TIME METRICS
☐ Number of steps or layers removed from our product-development process	☐ Number of meetings eliminated	☐ Decrease in total volume of internal emails	☐ Number of reports killed	☐ Amount of time saved by eliminating PPTs from internal meetings	☐ Number of activities eliminated to make room for new ones
☐ Decrease in number of steps to access or interact with customers	☐ Decrease in amount of time employees spend in meetings	☐ Amount of time saved from decreasing internal calls to 12 mins., 25 mins. or 50 mins.	☐ Amount of time saved from eliminating unnecessary reports	☐ Amount of time saved from implementation of Google docs or other collaboration tools	☐ Increase in productivity due to establishing black-out periods for uninterrupted ideation time
☐ Number of underperforming projects eliminated from development pipeline	☐ Amount of cost savings from eliminated meetings	☐ Amount of time saved from limiting cc's on internal emails	☐ Reduction in number of reports reviewed in decision-making process	☐ Amount of time saved from using simple formatting and fewer graphics in presentations	☐ Amount of time saved from channeling similar tasks to 1 source
☐ Decrease in customer concerns about our products, services, or website	☐ Amount of time saved from simplifying materials for internal meetings	☐ Amount of money saved from eliminating voicemail	☐ Reduction in duplicate information gathered for reports		☐ Amount of money saved from channeling similar tasks to 1 source
☐ Decrease in time to market for new products/ services	☐ Decrease in overall volume of internal meeting invitations	☐ Amount of time saved by shifting weekly calls to bimonthly	☐ Amount of time saved from reducing duplicate work for reports		☐ Number of tasks eliminated through simplifying sessions or bureaucracy busters
☐ Number of products, services, or SKUs phased out	☐ Increase in number of people declining meeting invitations	☐ Increase in productivity due to establishing email-free time zones			☐ Amount of time saved on tasks eliminated in simplifying sessions or bureaucracy busters
☐ Increase in positive feedback from customers or clients	☐ Increase in conversations and comfort levels around eliminating meetings	☐			☐ Employees appear less overwhelmed by their workload

Step 3: Discuss Proposed Metrics. (30 minutes)

Discuss the following as a group:

- Which five to seven metrics did each of us choose?
- Which of these metrics address our objectives for quick wins, long-term changes, or behavior shifts?
- Do we agree on our five to seven metrics? (If not, take a team vote.)

Step 4: Establish Baseline, Goals, and Timing. (20 to 60 minutes)

You'll need a current baseline to track progress for each simplification metric. If "number of reports killed" is one of your metrics and your business unit currently generates thirty reports a year, then thirty is your baseline (additional research may be needed to complete this step). As you establish goals and timing, be realistic. You want to motivate teams, not set people up for failure, so share goals and timelines across the organization, and be open to feedback.

Tips for Success

We designed the steps in this tool to give you the best chance of weaving simplicity into the way your company works. But certain nuances can influence whether any metrics regimen provides the feedback a company needs. Remember, the key to most simplification regimens is to build some momentum—to parlay a few quick wins into something more sustainable. Much as the failure of metrics can stymie your progress, success right off the bat will spur more of your colleagues and peers to buy into the effort moving forward.

The following tips might help:

- **Test Your Metrics.** Do employees actually understand the metrics, the goals, and their individual role in tracking simplification? Pilot your

OUR METRICS	CURRENT BASELINE (Where does it stand today?)	GOAL (Where do we want it to be?)	TIMING (When should we achieve this?)
Example: Decrease in amount of time spent in meetings.	*40%*	*20%*	*One year from now.*
Example: Decrease in number of approval layers for hiring qualified candidates.	*3*	*1 approval layer below director level; 2 for levels above.*	*Immediately.*

metrics with a small group before your formal rollout and make adjustments if necessary.

• **Designate Trackers.** Avoid underreporting by channeling data for each metric back to one source and communicating who's responsible for tracking what.

• **Evolve Your Metrics.** Check in with your metrics. If your goals were easily achieved with time to spare, be more ambitious with the goal itself or its timing.

• **Stay Informed.** Package a single sheet of your current metrics for senior leaders at every quarterly meeting. With data in hand that is succinct and well organized, leadership can easily make decisions that guide simplification in real time.

Strategy #6: Create a "Simplification Code of Conduct"

Simplification works in part because it specifies guiding principles instead of prescriptive rules. It steers us to define the outer limits for conduct rather than to dictate exactly how subordinates must handle every situation. Simplicity thus invites individuals to take greater responsibility for their own choices and to apply their own ingenuity to solve problems. The challenge, of course, is to make sure that individuals don't use their newfound authority to create still more complexity. As we've seen in previous chapters, individuals choose complexity for all kinds of reasons, including fear, risk aversion, and ego.

To push back on that impulse, my team has created a "Simplification Code of Conduct"—a pledge that every member of an organization should endorse. We were inspired by Google, which, in an effort to drive productivity, published a manifesto that spelled out "nine rules for e-mail."[15] Our code of conduct is more general, setting a standard that encourages each individual not to waste anyone's time or create unnecessary work. Moreover, our code of conduct empowers people to point out others' complexity. In essence, the "Simplification Code of Conduct" works because it makes it shameful to choose complication. It also establishes a set of behaviors or "permissions" everyone can point to when trying to make simplification happen every day.

TOOL: Simplification Code of Conduct

I commit to simplifying everything I do.
I will:

1. Eliminate redundancies and unnecessary work, and empower my team to do the same.
2. Not create false urgency.
3. Push back if I think something is unnecessary.
4. Use clear, jargon-free language when I communicate.
5. Keep my e-mails, documents, meetings, and conversations short.
6. Be decisive and limit the amount of information I need to make a decision.
7. Empower others to make decisions without me.
8. Make information available to others (unless illegal).
9. Say NO whenever possible.

This code is very specific, so it might not apply perfectly to your own situation. For that reason, my team has created a tool designed to help you develop your *own* code of conduct. This tool, which should take you no more than an hour to complete, enables you to communicate the specific simplification behaviors and choices that your particular organization should embrace. It also identifies which behaviors you should avoid in order to reduce unnecessary work and respect one another's time. By the end of this exercise, you'll create and distribute a "Simplification Code of Conduct" that every member of your organization will be encouraged to endorse.

Step 1: Answer the Code of Conduct Questions. (15 minutes)

Answer the following questions with statements that are short and specific, focusing on the behaviors and habits you want to transform. If conducting this exercise in a group setting, work through these questions together.

- Which simplification behaviors should people in our organization employ on a daily basis?
- Which behaviors add unnecessary work and should be avoided from this day forward?
- What prevents people in our organization from simplifying? What change can we make to remove these obstacles?
- Starting today, which specific tasks should people in our organization do less of?

Step 2: Draft a "Simplification Code of Conduct." (30 minutes)

Use the example on the previous page and your answers to the questions from Step 1 to draft your organization's "Simplification Code of Conduct." Tip: Avoid two-part statements like "If X, then Y" or "I will do X unless Y."
I commit to simplifying everything I do. This means I will:

1.
2.
3.
4.
5.
6.
7.
8.
9.
10.

Step 3: Finalize and Share with the Organization. (15 minutes)

Once you've finalized your "Simplification Code of Conduct," share it with the organization along with a short, personal message about why simplification is essential to the company's overall health and happiness. Urge recipients to sign, date, and display the code as a unifying reminder of everyone's long-term approach to daily work.

Strategy #7: Build a Simplification Team

Who should lead the charge in driving simplification? You need immediate buy-in at the very top, but making simplification a habit requires something more: the right *team* of people to lead the charge. You're not looking to hire a corps of simplicity police; you don't want an honor guard of middle managers looking over everyone's shoulder, slapping people on the wrist for nurturing complication. Rather, you need to find ways to facilitate simplification so that grassroots employees and managers take ownership for what actually happens.

In an interview with me, Michael Bungay-Stanier from Box of Crayons explained that "You need a core group to drive simplification, but the ultimate goal is for that team to rotate or fade away. Their job is to facilitate and make everyone a simplifier; otherwise, people will assume it's not their job but rather the simplification team's job. As soon as you hive it off, it's too easy for people to say, 'Great, let someone else worry about this, I'll stick with business as usual on my team.' Then it just won't work."[16]

Companies should think carefully about whom they empower to facilitate organization-wide simplification. Jim Daly at Affinion Group once argued that "incumbency or tenure work against simplicity. It is very difficult for someone who has made decisions to do things a certain way to give those things up or replace them. It takes a lot to overcome inertia from past choices even when a new way would make things simpler."[17] Small firms can often change cultures without creating new task forces or departments, but for big companies that might not be possible. One option is to create a team of project managers who:

- Survey business units or functional teams to learn what needs to be simplified
- Compile, manage, and monitor an inventory of potential simplification areas
- Ask for volunteers to spearhead simplification initiatives in parts of the business
- Provide techniques and tools to attack complexity (see chapter 6)

Some companies may want their simplification team to fade away as simplicity becomes part of the fabric of the organization. Often, though, employee churn will require a more formal approach. To keep the group fresh and employees engaged, institutionalize the team but fill out its membership on a rotating basis.

Absent a group devoted explicitly to simplification, the demands of everyday work can make it impossible for anyone to look to other companies for best practices or to customers for insights and feedback. In addition, intellectual barriers can prevent employees in one area or department from appreciating complexity's broader impacts. IDEO general counsel Rochael Soper Adranly emphasizes the importance of breaking free from narrow, siloed perspectives. Reflecting on her team's work, she observed that "Too often legal groups in organizations are kept separate or even isolated from the rest of the company. To be effective at IDEO, we need to identify all the stakeholders that touch the legal team and integrate ourselves within the rest of the organization. In our approach, legal terms and positions are driven by the business needs and not the other way around."[18]

While a simplification team may prove vital, be sure not to let it do all the work. The ethos of simplicity ultimately demands that employees take ownership of their "piece of the complexity pie." Those who will eventually live with the new, streamlined regime need to feel invested in its success. After all, the point is for *them* to get to work that matters. Simplicity's facilitators, therefore, should look to build coalitions of the willing, encouraging people to devise their own solutions. They should also be sure to publicize and promote solutions when they emerge. As the former head of strategy at Merck Canada, Jeff Spencer, advises, "Celebrate the heck out of it!"[19]

It's important to select people for the simplification team who can champion simplicity energetically. When I asked Spencer what kinds of attributes make someone a simplifier, he was very direct:

> They are not the sheep. They don't seek the comfort and security that comes with complexity. They don't hide behind complicated things. They are change agents. They are prone to go against the grain, and they are resilient. They also have a strong results focus. They like the elegance and sense of timelessness that comes with simplicity.... They are pragmatic and results oriented, because they know that simple things survive, whereas complicated things break down, and are much less scalable. They need to have a solid understanding of the problem and have lived it or worked hard to understand it. Otherwise it doesn't work.[20]

Spencer is in turn quite deliberate in engaging the simplifiers:

> You need them to set an example, but don't be overly reliant on them. Enable them to simplify something that they care about, support them, help them to deliver something tangible, thank them, and then use their accomplishments as a way to create momentum and motivate and engage others. While the reflex might be to go back to the same people again and again, doing so will burn out your supporters, without having instilled the simplification mindset in the broader organization.

My team has constructed a series of questions you can use when hiring people for your simplification team (or indeed for *any* position as simplification becomes a core part of your culture). Is it possible to recognize a simplifier during a first interview? Absolutely—when you're armed with these questions. You don't need to ask every single one; select those that resonate with you the most. These questions can help you discover how good a prospect will be at different parts of the simplification process, such as identifying and culling unnecessary complexities. The whole tool should take no longer than an hour and fifteen minutes to complete.

TOOL: Interview Questions for Hiring Simplifiers

Step 1: Choose Ten to Fifteen Relevant Hiring Questions. (30 minutes)

Review all thirty-four questions and check the box beside the questions that specifically address behaviors you want to encourage in your business. If empowering employees to challenge complexity is a goal, choose an EXECUTION question, like "When you experience resistance to your simplification efforts, how do you respond?" If you need employees who recognize and eradicate complexity in their daily work, choose an IDENTIFICATION question, like "What would make it easier for you to do your current or previous job?" Feel free to add custom questions.

AWARENESS

☐ Can you name an individual who has successfully simplified a complex business or industry?

☐ Which company or individual is the portrait of simplicity? What about complexity?

☐ In your opinion, what are the major causes of organizational complexity?

☐ How do you know if you're working in a simplicity-centric organization?

☐ What are the characteristics of a simplicity-focused organization?

☐

IDENTIFICATION

☐ Can you name a few red-flag indicators of complexity?

☐ If you were put in charge of our simplification efforts, where would you start?

☐ In your opinion, where does complexity typically live in an organization? Why?

☐ Can you name a situation in which you encountered excessive complexity and nobody else recognized it?

☐ What gets in the way of accomplishing your workplace goals?

☐ What is the most basic issue that interferes with your job performance?

☐ What would make it easier to do your current or previous job?

☐ In the last month, were you asked to do any work that proved to be a total waste of time? What do you wish you would've done or said to avoid it?

☐ If your colleague is performing a task that doesn't add value to the business, do you speak up? Why or why not?

☐ Can you remember a situation where it was evident that your team or organization had a complexity problem? How did you resolve it?

☐ What sorts of reasons do people use as an excuse for not simplifying things that are unnecessarily complicated?

☐

PRIORITIZATION

☐ If you could do 1 thing at your previous or current company to instantly simplify your work, what would it be?

☐ What 2 time-suck tasks would you eradicate from your previous or current job? Why these tasks?

☐ Can you share an example when you were frustrated by a company that made things purposefully complicated?

☐ We're redesigning our company's website to reflect a simplified approach. Which current elements would you eliminate to achieve this?

☐ In 140 characters or less, what would you tweet to persuade us that you're a simplifier who should be offered this job?

☐

EXECUTION

- [ ] Can you share an example of a successful workaround you created to simplify a frustrating process or system? Was it adopted as the new protocol?

- [ ] When you encounter an individual who makes things needlessly complex, how do you respond?

- [ ] How would you measure simplicity in an organization?

- [ ] What circumstances are optimal for achieving simplicity?

- [ ] Would you rather construct a new, simple product/service from scratch or simplify a current product/service that's plagued with complexity?

- [ ] Can you share a situation—either in your personal or professional life—where you were utterly overwhelmed by complexity and found a way to simplify things?

- [ ] In your opinion, what prevents people with unnecessarily complicated schedules from simplifying and freeing up their time?

- [ ] When you experience resistance to your simplification efforts, how do you respond?

- [ ] From the existing job description for this role, which 3 objectives should we cut and why?

- [ ]

HABIT FORMATION

☐ In your opinion, what individual behaviors contribute to simplification?

☐ What are the managerial habits or behaviors that contribute to complexity? How could these be modified?

☐ When you encounter an inefficient policy or process, do you offer to find a better solution?

☐ If hired, what are a few ways you might make simplification a habit within your group?

☐ _____

_____

_____

Step 2: Incorporate Questions into the Hiring Process. (45 minutes)

During interviews, look for examples of the candidates' approach to simplification in their answers. True simplifiers can easily and passionately explain their philosophy, and they can share stories about a process or task that they proudly streamlined or eliminated. They're honest about the resistance they faced along the way, and can offer detailed, firsthand accounts of their experience.

Conversely, beware of candidates who generalize or toss around business jargon in lieu of specifics. If you hear language about "minimizing bureaucracy" or "getting rid of red tape" without personal examples, you're likely interviewing a status quo complexifier. If the only anecdotes they can share are business news stories or secondhand descriptions of simplicity in action, that's also a red flag.

By utilizing the hiring questions in this tool, and hopefully adding a few of your own, you'll increase the chance of hiring your next simplifier, instead of another complexifier.

Strategy #8: Focus

Once you've seen simplicity's power and potential, it's hard not to want to spread the gospel and undertake yet another simplification initiative. Slow down and take your time. People have short attention spans. Trying to spread simplification *everywhere* can backfire, preventing you from spreading it *anywhere.* Simplification can become background noise. People will nod their heads when someone highlights its virtues, but they'll return to business as usual as soon as the conversation ends.

To sustain momentum around simplification, you must prioritize and build a chain of substantive wins. Decide first which systems and processes most require simplification. From there, go on to choose a key group of projects that deserve the simplification team's attention from one quarter to the next.

Focus was a big part of Merck Canada's success. As Jeff Spencer explained, "There is only so much change that an organization can process at one time. Take the time to install and realize one change before proceeding with the next. Otherwise, the change doesn't stick."[21] During the first three months of Merck's simplification initiative, the simplification team initially focused on a single change: simplifying meetings. This meant developing best practices for who should be invited to each meeting, what participants should read before attending, how to set the agenda, how to resolve a conflict quickly, how to define the desired outcome, and how long each meeting should last. "Having everyone focused on one change at a time helped to create the focus, energy, and the 'personal permission' necessary to create real change," Spencer said.

Chetan Chandavarkar, a senior director at Pitney Bowes, took a similar approach when working to instill simplicity among his team members. "I keep telling my team that the best way to simplify is to focus on three things. Force yourself to articulate—on every e-mail, every meeting agenda, every project charter, every PPT deck: 'I want to outline/solve/explain THREE things.' Starting with this rule of three from the onset has helped me focus my thinking and articulation."[22]

In prioritizing, look for opportunities to notch quick wins that can galvanize the organization. It may well be that your company's travel policy is the most vexing complication you face but fixing that policy will be terribly difficult. In that case, start with another, easier project first. Try these tips:

- Eliminate annoying tasks that take time, yet add no value (see the chapter 6 tool "Killing Complexity").
- Get rid of redundancies.
- Kill reports that don't add value or no one looks at.
- Question the need for any recurring meetings.
- Shorten presentations.
- Reduce the number of sign-offs and approvals.
- Do a meeting audit for every meeting you have during the year and cut the list by 50 percent.
- Reduce the number of forms or the information required on forms or documents.
- Have a cleanup day. Reducing clutter can create focus. Have everyone stop work for half a day and throw out everything they don't need or have accumulated. This includes e-mails, contacts, work documents, and more.

It's amazing the difference a few small changes can make. If you can shed a few annoying steps, you will create some new bandwidth that you can use to focus on more substantial simplification opportunities. The momentum will build in turn.

Liz Tinkham, a senior managing director at Accenture, bravely made herself the target of the first round. She brought her leadership team in from all around the world—people who worked on one of the company's most important accounts—to discuss ways to drive innovation. And she asked them to openly discuss the rules that stood in the way of pioneering ideas—even if she had put some of those in place herself. It wasn't easy for Tinkham to make herself vulnerable, but it was certainly effective, and it's what great leaders do. Once she made it clear that she *wanted* her team to reveal what was holding them back, they brought all sorts of bottlenecks to light.

In many cases, her team's frustrations weren't driven by rules at all. They were driven by misperceptions that Tinkham could easily dispel. In a few instances where seemingly unnecessary rules *were* holding the team back, Tinkham explained that the guidelines had been created at the corporate level, but that she would willingly bring the matter up the food chain in the hope that they could be eliminated or modified. The rapid progress from just one exercise got her team fired up to tackle still other simplification challenges. And in overcoming the urge to react defensively, she set an excellent example. As a result, when her leadership team returned to their own teams, they were more open to stripping out unnecessary complication. Many of them used the "Kill a Stupid Rule" tool with their staff and also with clients.[23]

Strategy #9: Increase Employee Engagement

Agnelo Fernandes, senior vice president at Destination Hotels, once pulled me aside to highlight the fact that "*people* are the heart of any business, and as a result, any complexity. Influence their behavior and results happen."[24] To keep employees riveted on simplification, tie their accomplishments in this area to their compensation. How good are employees at identifying and eliminating complexity? Do they suggest ways to simplify work? Do they question if rules or processes are really necessary? How well do they uphold the "Simplification Code of Conduct?" Imagine a company with rewards for achievements like:

- Most meetings eliminated
- Most time saved through the creation of standardized, streamlined reports, contracts, or processes
- Number of rules killed that resulted in higher customer satisfaction
- Most effectively streamlined business unit/effective business unit
- Least amount of time spent in meetings/e-mails while still hitting goals

But rewards and recognition are just one side of the engagement equation. If you're in a leadership position, another way to sustain employee engagement around simplification (and to hold yourself accountable) is simply to ask employees how things are going. Gather feedback to get a read on how much progress people think the team—and you—are making in simplifying the team's work experience. You can ask true–false questions or have employees rate your efforts on a scale of 1 to 4, ensuring that there's no neutral option in the middle. Sample questions to consider:

- Does management support my effort to simplify?
- Do my leaders articulate a clearly defined vision of what simplification is and what it will do for the organization?
- Am I encouraged to identify and eliminate redundancies or unnecessary policies and reports wherever possible? Do I encourage my team to do the same?
- Are decision-making processes within the organization clear and quick? Can I say with confidence that they do *not* require excessive layers of approval?

Your goal is for everyone on staff to buy into the ethos of simplification. Everything should be aligned: the messages they get from above, the incentives they have in their own work, and the examples they set for their own teams. The challenge is to make simplification a sustained effort, not a one-off. Weaving it into day-to-day and year-to-year routines will help keep simplification an important priority for your people.

Strategy #10: Communicate with Clarity

Kelly Leonard, former executive of the improvisational comedy company Second City, once spoke with me about the importance of simplicity to comedy. As an expert who has worked with the likes of Stephen Colbert, Tina Fey, and Steve Carell, he explained, "The best comedy is reductive. When something is not working, you've probably done too much. Get to the quickest, easiest way to deliver something. And then move on."[25] In any organization or for any purpose, keep your messages clear and concise, modeling that behavior for colleagues while also taking steps to ensure that communication is simpler company-wide.

Richard Branson, the wildly successful founder of the Virgin Group, insists that any proposal presented to him be succinct enough for an ordinary consumer to comprehend: "These days, when somebody pitches me a business idea about doing something better in an established industry, I ask if a summary can fit on the back of an envelope. If it is too complex to be explained in just a few words, then it is unlikely that consumers will understand it, and even more unlikely that they will buy it."[26]

When Alan Siegel founded his firm Siegel+Gale in 1968, one of his first assignments was to redesign all of Citibank's retail forms (the paperwork the company used to explain and process installment loan notes, the rules for savings accounts, and so on). These documents had become so complex that even the bank's employees couldn't understand them, let alone explain them to customers. Over the course of a year, he and his firm entirely redesigned everything, starting with the mortgage documents; in plain and simple language, the new documents described how to make payments and what the penalties would be if customers failed to pay.[27]

For example, the "default clause" Siegel inherited (the section of each mortgage agreement written to detail when a customer could be considered to be "in default") was a run-on sentence of roughly 250 words, with many clauses, a whole slew of semicolons, and phrases like, "In the event of default in the payment of this or any other Obligation or the performance of observance of any term of covenant contained herein or in any note or other contract evidencing or relating to any Obligation or any Collateral...." Working with Dr. Rudolf Flesch, a Columbia-trained library scientist who had written *The Art of Readable Writing*, Siegel boiled the whole thing down to a few lines: "I'll be in default: (1) If I don't pay an installment on time; or (2) If any other creditor tries by legal process to take any money of mine in your possession."[28]

Think of the impact those streamlined documents must have had. Suddenly, banking with Citi wasn't a mystery but an intuitive process. The forms weren't black boxes but rather guides to what was happening and what would happen if you adopted a course of action. As Siegel later explained: "We learned the valuable lesson that the content must be questioned first, before rewriting. In this case, we revealed that the most important issue that triggered default was a failure to pay on time, and the rewrite emphasized that effectively." Bankers no longer had to explain terms but could instead focus on the customer's needs. *That's* the sort of experience that will have employees celebrating simplicity. *That's* the sort of story that will make other departments eager to jump on board.

Strategy #11: Train the Next Wave of Simplifiers

Another step in spreading the ethos of simplicity is to train *others* to spread the gospel. Every company's human resources department should teach employees a range of tools and behaviors designed to save time and reduce the number of e-mails and meetings. Start by presenting employees with the tools detailed in chapter 6 (ways to get started on the road to simplification) and by training individuals in how to implement simplicity initiatives. Go on to teach techniques that allow both individuals and departments to simplify faster. These techniques include:

• **Practice EOS**—Eliminate, Outsource, Streamline—by making it part of your ethos. With every complexity you attack, use these three actions as a guide. Can the problem be **eliminated**? Can it be **outsourced**—done by someone else so I can better use my time, without costing more? If it can't be eliminated or outsourced, can it be **streamlined**? Some people prefer to say "improved," but I prefer streamlined because it implies a mindset of subtraction. Improvement often results in reshuffling, adding more steps to fix a bad one. Sometimes addition drives an improvement, but more often it doesn't.

- **Use More Extreme Criteria.** Think of what happens to our closets when we use the broad criteria: "Will I wear this someday?" The closet becomes cluttered with clothes we never wear and probably never will. If you ask, "Will I *absolutely* wear this in the next six months?," you're more likely to get rid of an item to make space for something better. Simplification works especially well when you use extreme criteria to challenge how things are done. Some examples:

  - To solve this problem, give me a solution that would shock people.
  - To solve this problem, give me an idea that would get you fired.
  - To solve this problem, give me an idea that would eliminate *all* or a seemingly impossible amount of something. Example: A group within a telecom company wanted to cut meetings, so they challenged each business unit to eliminate 50 percent of their meetings, knowing full well that this would be near impossible. In the end, managers reporting cutting 15 percent of their meetings, greater than the 5 percent they originally expected.

- **Stop Being So Nice.** One pattern that causes or exacerbates complexity is the tendency not to speak up when something isn't working. We all hesitate sometimes to challenge senior people when they run long, unnecessary meetings, give confusing assignments, send needless e-mails, demand pointless overanalysis, and perpetuate other complicating habits. But you shouldn't let "being nice" prevent you from providing honest feedback.[29]

Strategy #12: Walk the Walk

If you're a leader, you're in the public eye, and people will follow your example. So in addition to the preceding strategies, build simplicity into the way you live and work. As your team's chief simplifier, you need to practice what you preach. Let people see your own success and understand it as evidence of simplicity's upside. Make them feel the same personal responsibility that you feel to keep work simple. Let them feel excited to clear out meaningless or useless *stuff*, because they see how excited you are. Here are some tactics that will help you simplify your own work:

• **Do a Time Inventory:** How do you really allot your time? Log your time usage for a week or month. Write down all the things you did, and how many times or how much time you spent on each. What would you change or eliminate? What else could you do with that time?

• **Delete Toxic People:** Delete them from your social networks, contact lists, and phone—right now. Stop hanging out with people who suck your energy, are rude, add no value, or make you feel lousy each time you interact. Say good-bye to bad clients, business partners, and team members. Some guidelines:

  • If the person is distracting or continually sucks up your time—delete.
  • If it's a one-way relationship in the other person's favor—delete.
  • If people don't appreciate you for who you are or what you have to offer—delete.
  • If you can't remember who they are or where you met them—delete.
  • If they communicate with you too much or they clog your inbox—delete.

• **Practice "Two Today":** What two things do you want to get done today? Focus your mind by starting each day intentionally. This will help you make choices, avoid distraction, and control your impulses.

• **Practice "What if I Didn't?":** Stop fulfilling unnecessary obligations. Look at your calendar or to-do list. Want to eliminate something? Ask yourself: "What if I didn't do that? What is the worst that would happen?"

• **Automate and Systemize:** If there's something you can automate (for instance, your online grocery list, which can be saved and made into a recurring delivery from your online grocery service), do it. But don't confuse being organized with being simplified. Always try to eliminate first.

- **Throw Things Out. Now:** If you have kids or pets, or you just like to buy things, you know that your home can feel like a house from the TV show *Hoarders* in the blink of an eye. Be diligent about decluttering. Get rid of anything that doesn't have a memory attached or that you can find online. Creating physical space helps create mental space.

- **Unsubscribe:** Over the course of a week, unsubscribe from every e-mail newsletter you don't read that comes into your inbox.

- **Pare Back Apps and Social Media:** Just because you can, doesn't mean you should. I can be on Facebook, Twitter, Skype, LinkedIn, Gmail, Instagram, WhatsApp—but why? Social media is a huge waste of time. Get rid of the sites, social media platforms, apps, and other things you just don't use.

- **Delete Old E-mail Accounts and E-mail:** Get rid of e-mail accounts you don't use. Delete old e-mails taking up space. If it's important, store it in the cloud.

- **Create a Simplicity Statement:** What do you want your simpler, better life to look like? Write it out. Goals create intention, and intention creates action.

- **Experiment with Eliminating Something:** Remember the story of the publishing employee who decided to complete his "Monthly Operating Reports," but then chose not to submit them? He was testing to see whether anyone would notice their absence. It took three months for anyone to ask! That told him that the reports, which were time consuming to complete, were of very little use. Try to eliminate something in your personal life, just to gauge the impact. Get rid of a food, a possession, a process, a status meeting, a signature, a report, a commitment...and see what happens. Were there repercussions? Did you really miss it? Can you eliminate this item or task altogether now?

As you apply some or all of these tactics, you might not find as much time as you would like to simplify. Don't worry. Simplification is a marathon, not a sprint. Do what you can, and pay consistent, proactive, and regular attention to it over the long term. You'll be amazed at the difference in your own life, and the people around you will notice, too. Soon they'll catch the simplification bug themselves.

Simplification Success Story: General Electric

General Electric has long been at the vanguard of global efforts to improve the way business works. And that tradition continues with GE's recent focus on simplification. There's no denying that the products GE produces—airplane engines, steam turbines, industrial computers—are very complex.[30] But GE's CEO, Jeff Immelt, believes that the processes that govern how those products are produced need to be made as simple as possible. He has done what I've suggested in this chapter. He's made it a strategic priority to weave simplicity into everything GE does. His goal: reduce overhead from 18.5 percent of revenues to 12 percent over a five-year period.[31]

Initially, that meant asking GE's leaders to de-layer, stripping out unnecessary levels of management and oversight. It also meant reducing the number of approvals and sign-offs required to complete various tasks. From there the company developed and implemented a program called FastWorks that brings its customers into the production process, allowing those who have hired GE to provide feedback throughout a product's lifecycle. And GE didn't stop there. Next, the company set off to change the company's culture, encouraging employees to reduce complexity wherever possible. To help people focus, the company established a set of clear and simple "GE Beliefs," incorporating them into leadership development, recruitment, management, and evaluation programming. These beliefs included items like "customers determine our success," "stay lean to go fast," "learn and adapt to win," and "empower and inspire each other."

Finally, GE incorporated its commitment to simplicity into the process it uses to manage its performance. The company has replaced the usual litany of goals with a few key priorities, a shift that directs the company's employees to adapt their own work as their customers' needs evolve. Rather than telling employees to "do more with less," GE advocates doing "fewer things better." This renamed process, Performance Development, has put simplicity right at the center of the way each individual employee approaches the tasks at hand.[32]

GE's methods for driving simplicity deep into the business might not work for every organization. But GE's story confirms that, in an age when technological breakthroughs, global interconnectedness, and stiffened compliance requirements have added complexity to nearly every aspect of our work, simplicity has become a key strategic imperative. No company can afford to maintain a working environment where disengaged employees do subpar work, fail to innovate, and provide lousy customer service. And in a working environment defined by complication, that's what will happen.[33]

You now have the tools required to make simplification the norm for yourself and your peers. No matter how many people report to you, get simplification started, press the advantage, and make simplification a habit. Battling complexity is never easy, but *any* barrier that keeps your employees from doing work that matters demands your sustained attention. Someone has to take the lead on simplification, so why not you? You can beat complication. Go ahead and become the chief simplifier right now.

CHAPTER EIGHT

Getting Simplification Right

"Simplicity is the final achievement. After one has played a vast quantity of notes and more notes, it is simplicity that emerges as the crowning reward of art."

—Frederic Chopin[1]

Let's return to an observation we made at the beginning of this book: although many firms have talked about simplification, and some have embarked on simplification initiatives, very few have succeeded in reaping the full benefits that simplification can offer. Any team or organization can employ the tools presented in chapter 6 and the structural tips presented in chapter 7 to embark on a simplification initiative. But simplification for an organization of any size is also an ongoing *process* that unfolds organically in real time. As such, it will spark common fears that people have, trigger the usual political dynamics, and in general reveal both the latent strengths and weaknesses present in any organization. When obstacles crop up, managers and leaders have to *step up*, calling upon their deep stores of grit, determination, vision, and perseverance to get the job done.

Your ability to gain the benefits of simplification for your organization hinges on your ability to succeed where others have failed. To close out this book, let's consider how one organization has managed to reinvent itself and its culture over a period of years, turning simplification into a significant competitive advantage. To make it *really* interesting, let's pass over the usual companies that people tend to look at when describing "state of the art," innovative thinking—Apple, Southwest, Virgin, and so on. Let's look at a company from an industry that isn't "sexy" by conventional standards. Let's look at a company in a regulated industry, with a considerable amount of mandated complexity to contend with. Let's look at a midsize company, one without endless resources to put toward simplification, but one whose business is also large enough to spawn considerable complexity. Let's look at an established company, not a nimble start-up with a license to innovate and creative energy to burn. In sum, let's look at a company that on the surface at least would seem highly *unlikely* to succeed at simplification. If this organization can do it, then yours can too.

Coming Up Short on Simplicity

Vancouver City Savings Credit Union (Vancity) is Canada's largest community credit union, with more than a half million members, $19.8 billion (Canadian) in assets, fifty-nine branches, and 2,500 employees. Although that might sound big, Vancity in 2015 was but a small fraction of a giant like TD Bank, with $264 billion in assets and more than 26,000 employees.[2] On the other hand, Vancity is no start-up. In the early twentieth century, traditional banks were often reluctant to lend money to average citizens. To fill that void, citizens began to form credit unions, each designed to help their members invest in the future. In 1946, fourteen residents of Vancouver established what was then called an open-bond union, dubbing it the Vancouver City Savings Credit Union. They opened up the first branch in a former machine shop at the corner of Broadway and Quebec, in downtown Vancouver.[3] Right from the beginning, the company prided itself on helping to nurture healthy communities by offering good, balanced products to individuals and families looking to join its ranks.[4]

Like many other financial institutions, Vancity saw complexity creep up on it slowly but surely over a period of decades; as the credit union went through mergers and acquisitions, product development, management and strategy shifts, and other changes, the organization's core processes and systems were tweaked. More layers, features, and functions were added, and few were taken away. In recent years, on the advice of external experts, the organization had embarked on process improvements with the goal of becoming more efficient. The results did not materialize, in large part due to a lack of organizational alignment and employee engagement. Process improvements occurred in one part of the organization, while decisions to change systems occurred in others. Frontline employees were left to adapt to greater complexity.

By 2013, it seemed clear that this IT redesign wasn't working as the organization had hoped. As executives saw it, the credit union was spending a lot of money, and it was getting a relatively superficial update to what the organization already had.

The organization could have thrown up its hands, taking comfort in the notion that "simplification is hard," that banking systems are notoriously complex, and that many have struggled with similar issues. But leaders knew they couldn't just give up. The organization needed to streamline customer experiences and minimize internal processes; otherwise it would fall behind the competition. Leaders stepped back and asked some deeper questions: What did Vancity *really* hope to gain from the effort to update its core processes, and what could leaders do to turn this challenge to the company's advantage? How might Vancity's ongoing commitment to a truly unique member experience inform the way it approached improvements for its people, processes, and systems?

To answer these questions the company's executives charted a course to define what a new core system could do in a more simple and effective way. In doing so, they decided to first define what was needed to make the right connection between people, process, and technological change.

Corporate Hoarders

Jay-Ann Gilfoy, Vancity's senior vice president for banking applications renewal, joined the organization after it had recommitted itself to using technology where necessary and putting equal focus on the people and process side of change for the sake of improving its member experience. When I spoke with her, she was direct in discussing how Vancity's previous effort to overhaul its core processes hadn't worked. The problems derived from "the rise of the expert, or the rise of the specialist...and each time you apply a new set of experts, whether it's technical experts or process experts or people experts or whatever, the problem is misalignment and miscommunication and misunderstanding. We brought in the experts to figure it out *for* us and not *with* us." Vancity was hardly alone in struggling with its use of experts. In many cases I've seen, people come in with knowledge about a specific area (such as technology), yet they know little about the vital perspectives of employees and customers. As a result, redesign efforts cause as many problems as they solve. Efforts to simplify the organization and improve wither on the vine.

In asking themselves what they wanted to accomplish, members of the executive team came to an unexpected conclusion: they did not want the company's technology to take over tasks that people were better suited to complete. As they saw it, corporate overhauls often floundered when leaders tried to automate too much in the interest of cutting costs. Gilfoy and her colleagues weren't primarily motivated to cut costs. Rather, they wanted to upgrade the way the credit union served its members. That meant using technology not to replace staff but to empower them to do more of what they had been doing so well in service to members. Gilfoy explained: "We wanted our employees to spend a lot more time focusing on conversations with our members as trusted advisors, helping them to become financially healthy, helping our communities thrive, because we've got more time to focus on small businesses, community organizations, and the health of our membership."

To empower employees, Gilfoy and her colleagues on the executive leadership team took a new approach. Rather than look for efficiencies with only technology or processes, they would rethink the credit union's general "policies and procedures" (P&P), bringing together people from across the organization to challenge the "why" of the way work got done. As they saw it, the two previous attempts at reform had failed because they had bypassed the most fundamental problem of all: complexity. Like other companies operating in regulated industries, Vancity had tended to address issues that cropped up by adding policies, procedures, and forms.

It hadn't thought much about how these new policies, procedures, and forms would affect the organization, or more importantly, the member experience. They'd certainly never bothered to "clear away the under-brush" of obsolete or unnecessary processes. The result was an operational system creaking under its own weight.

Once the executive leadership team had identified excessive policies and procedures as part of the complexity problem, the haze began to clear, and things came into focus. The C-suite bought in entirely, and was committed not just to undertaking a short-term simplification initiative but to making simplicity one of the company's key strategic priorities. With the support of the CEO, Gilfoy and her team also received initial buy-in from the board of directors. At that point, Gilfoy redefined her mission as addressing Vancity's overreliance on technological complexity to solve process and people problems. The cure indicated for this diagnosis—simplification—was not esoteric or highly technical. Everyone could intuitively understand what it meant to pare back needless processes and steps, and everyone could help do it. Vancity's strategy was to start at the grassroots level and drive simplicity throughout the entire organization, reforming specific operational areas while also creating a *culture* of simplicity. "It's like an episode of [the TV show] *Hoarders*," Gilfoy explained matter-of-factly. "You gotta start by getting rid of some stuff. So that's what we did." Gilfoy decided to focus on the areas that had gone untouched for years—areas that caused frustration for employees, but corporate leadership had regarded as less important.

Structure for Simplicity

In ramping up, Gilfoy and her team had to develop a specific game plan for instilling simplicity throughout the organization. Gilfoy was determined not to set up a permanent "department of simplicity" that would "own" simplicity and impose it from on high. She wanted to develop a process that would encourage *everyone* in the organization to use his own capacity to simplify his work on an everyday level. To that end, she and her team created a new opportunity for implementing simplification called "rapid cycling." Gathering together in two-day workshops, small, cross-functional groups of employees and managers would identify and then endeavor to fix discrete and unnecessary complications. These employees and managers actually performed the work that the group was trying to simplify. They were intimately familiar with the problems at hand and vested in fixing them. At the end of each cycle, after getting sign-off from a group of senior operational leaders, the group would implement the simple solutions they'd crafted together. Every two weeks, a new cycle began.

The workshops themselves were highly structured, each one led by a facilitator whose job it was not to drive or dominate the discussion, but rather to help the employees and managers do the real work of simplification. Gilfoy explained: "Given that our people are in the best position to simplify and change the process because they are closest to it, providing the context and right information will enable them to solve problems and find the best solution as the conditions for them to be successful have been set."

On day one of each rapid cycle workshop, participants spent time generating some very broad thoughts for simplification. They narrowed down this list and "acid tested" them with phone calls to other employees whose work would be affected by the change to see if these changes could work. Members of the team would ask for feedback and concerns. As Gilfoy told me, these phone calls helped group members identify potential problems that they could then address before implementing the solution. Also, outreach helped each workshop team gain buy-in from employees who were the most skeptical of the process. Acid testing made clear to everyone that simplification was real and not just another well-intentioned but ultimately ineffective directive.

On day two of each workshop, participants focused on simplifying in a number of discrete areas that had been selected, with participants gathering details on those themes. Examples of complexity raised by employees ranged from "If we didn't need this signature on this document, it would save ten minutes" to "If we all had access to the same scheduler, we could be more efficient in terms of scheduling a member's handoff from one employee to the other" to "Wouldn't it be great if we could send all of our forms electronically to our members and there was a secure way of doing that?" Senior leaders came in at the end of the day to debrief the workshop groups and listen to the solutions the team had come up with.

Rapid Cycle Innovation Methodology

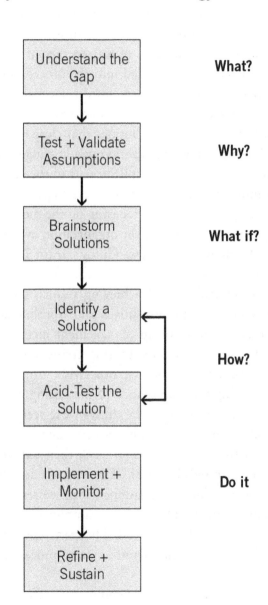

What is our current approach to doing this work? What is the gap or the problem we are trying to solve? What does this mean in terms of our ability to deliver a differentiated member experience?

Understand the Gap — **What?**

Why do we do it this way?

Test + Validate Assumptions — **Why?**

What are possible options for closing the gap?

Brainstorm Solutions — **What if?**

Which is the best solution? Will it close the gap?

Identify a Solution

How?

How can we make it work? How can we make it sustainable? What would we need to do to break it? What does this tell us?

Acid-Test the Solution

Has the solution closed the gap? Are the expected benefits being realized? Why or why not?

Implement + Monitor — **Do it**

Refine + Sustain

Then they moved to implement them immediately, and in many cases solutions rolled out to the organization within one to two weeks.

As Gilfoy's team explained to Vancity's employees at the beginning of the program: "The principal idea of Process Simplicity is to implement a simple, repeatable agile methodology with intact and cross-functional teams that can be easily replicated, to become a key practice for the way we do work."[5] Elements of Kaizen theory and Agile methodologies were considered and embedded into the process, but they were "Vancityized" so that people focused on learning in real time rather than on the theory. The rapid cycle methodology was "about problem solving at the root cause and developing solutions that close the gaps and enable realization of benefits." The organization would gauge the method's success against three goals: making simplicity part of the organization's culture, keeping banking transactions down to five steps or fewer for employees (so they could spend more time focusing on the members themselves), and bringing a positive energy to the organization overall.

To monitor progress, Gilfoy's team installed a rigorous system to generate quantitative data. Vancity already understood the importance of accountability and achieving results, with metrics deployed among the company's top executives and frontline staff alike. Progress reports figured prominently in management meetings, town halls, and on the credit union's website. In this context, Gilfoy's team needed metrics to document its success; otherwise, simplification would lose steam. Describing the importance of measuring progress, Gilfoy asked: "How do we make sure that the things we're seeing from a qualitative or anecdotal perspective actually translate into increased capacity, and how do we, at the senior leadership level, then redirect that capacity into doing more meaningful things?" The team eventually settled on a series of metrics that included the number of processes and procedures simplified or removed, the number of forms simplified or removed, and the number of steps simplified or removed. The team would hold off on metrics relating to the business impact until system process reforms were more fully in place.

To administer the ongoing rapid cycling process, Gilfoy created a small office led by Seema Dhanoa, the "director for simplicity." This manager led a three-person team that included a senior consultant, Christina

Fai, whose job it was to be a key facilitator and coach others at Vancity to lead the methodology, and a consultant, Ali Anderson, to coordinate workshops, capture ideas, manage the details, and work on the implementation of the rapid cycles. Rather than staff the team with permanent employees who again would come to "own" simplicity, she rotated employees in and out of the team on temporary assignments to facilitate workshops. Team members were volunteers selected on the basis of their cross-organizational experience, ability to facilitate discussions, ability to learn new processes, and overall curiosity. As they left and went on to other assignments, they would take their simplification experiences with them, helping to build a simplification mindset, competency, and culture within the organization.

As for the simplification team, Gilfoy's goal was very clear: she wanted it to fade away over time. If the initiative succeeded, simplicity would be spliced so seamlessly into the company's DNA that the facilitation the team provided *would no longer be necessary.* The team was just a triggering mechanism. The heart and soul of simplification was the process that the team helped teach, as well as the accompanying mindset.

Getting Simpler, One Cycle at a Time

Gilfoy and her team believed in the power of simplicity, and they had high hopes for the rapid cycling model. But they knew people had to experience it, so they just dove in. As they saw it, why wait? What was stopping them? The simplicity team prioritized the list of possible topics to work through in the various workshops, considering two key factors: whether the process being examined had a direct impact on Vancity's members and whether the process addressed one of the company's greatest needs.

With priorities in place, the rapid cycling began. The first several cycles seemed to go successfully. After just a few months, anecdotal evidence piled up suggesting that the changes were becoming pervasive across the organization. For example, some managers noticed a decreased acceptance of silos across the organization and an increased sense of staff engagement and acceptance of change. Processes across the business were becoming clearer and more consistent, and employees were beginning to apply simplification methods on their own initiative to work areas not included in rapid cycle workshops. Becoming aware of all the progress, departments that hadn't yet conducted rapid cycle workshops were very interested in how to conduct workshops of their own. Fai, the lead facilitator, said, "We knew things were working when the main question people asked us shifted from 'Why are we doing this?' to 'How quickly can you do this with my team?'"

Through these rapid cycles, Vancity also began to cultivate a group of people who knew how to simplify work and who could replicate it elsewhere in the business. Meanwhile, the organization began to take a look at how other financial institutions were doing business, just in case those experiences could enhance their own simplification effort. Like a muscle slowly being built up over time, Vancity became increasingly adept at making progress through the rapid cycles. As more people directly experienced the rapid cycling methodology, broader swaths of the company's employees began to buy in. As Gilfoy explained: "Unless people experience something, their willingness to lean into it and be an advocate for it is lessened."

Gilfoy noticed that frontline employees were often offering the best ideas. Not surprisingly, having hands-on experience with any given complication provides a unique perspective on how best to eliminate it. The contribution of good ideas from the front line inspired everyone. As junior staff members began making meaningful contributions to *how* the company operated, they became excited, and their excitement got leaders excited, too. Leaders also were won over by a few early quick wins that the simplification initiative notched. They saw the impact—it was there in black and white. Although some had doubted it at first, it became clear that a systematic model focusing on small steps within an organization could be aggregated into something even more useful and sustainable. Quick changes based on the insights of people who had experienced complexity firsthand could make a big difference.

Members of the simplicity team were unsure at first about the impact they were having. Some had expected that the rapid cycles would "hit gold" right from the start, magically transforming the organization all at once. The team was a bit disappointed when that didn't happen, but they didn't get too discouraged. As implementation picked up steam, they saw the difference simplification was making. The anecdotal results were steady, and they were impressive. Through a couple of surveys, the simplicity team learned that the culminating effect is that they have more time to spend helping members with financial services needs.

That is not to say there wasn't room to improve the workshops. Soon after they began in earnest, Gilfoy and her colleagues detected an important barrier to their long-term success: fear. When introducing the initiative across the company, they wanted employees to understand that the simplicity team had no intention of running a program that would eliminate roles; in fact, the idea was quite the opposite.

Through the process, Gilfoy discovered the most fundamental way to overcome the workforce's inherent fear of simplicity was to explain the link between simplifying processes and expanding the company's capacity. Simplification was a way to ensure employees could be released from administrative tasks and turn their attention to the company's strategic priorities and, in the case of Vancity, the member experience. Less time focused on policies and process would make any company more efficient, but only as a side benefit. The real hope was that rapid cycling would empower individual employees to return to the work that matters. As Gilfoy explained, without addressing the fear that people were going to be pink-slipped at the end of the process, "We couldn't get the same level of participation or the same level of thinking. And we certainly wouldn't get the same level of output."

In addition to expressing their concerns, workshop participants sometimes reacted defensively because the processes being streamlined had been their brainchildren. When someone suggested a simpler alternative, they might respond with, "What do you mean you want to 'change how we do it'? Who are *you* to come in and try and fix..." It was precisely to meet this challenge head-on that the simplicity team had insisted that senior leaders be present at the end of each session. This represented a heavy lift for some of the more senior people; their schedules were already overloaded. But unless employees believed that top leaders backed the program, Gilfoy's team would be viewed like outside consultants with little authority to effect change. Thus it was that when one senior leader came to Gilfoy and asked to simplify processes without convening a group, Gilfoy refused. "No, you have to go back and do it with the group," she said. "We need everyone to be invested in what we're trying to accomplish *together*."

With leadership's backing, the program's early skeptics often became the most effective participants. Those who had set up the incumbent rules usually didn't volunteer at first to join a workshop. But the acid-testing process, in which those participating in the workshops called their peers to get feedback on various ideas, woke up many of the skeptics. In later rounds, they *did* volunteer, if only because they wanted to have a voice in shaping the next iteration of reform. Seema Dhanoa, the original director of simplicity, knew that it might be hard at first getting people to embrace change. To win over skeptics, she continually demonstrated to colleagues and leadership that pushing for simpler solutions to problems would create meaningful results for both employees and members. In one of the best examples of how much leadership was buying in to simplicity as an operating principle, Dhanoa, a talented leader, was promoted to vice president partly because of this work.

Within a year, Vancity had executed twenty-five rapid cycles, simplifying and removing steps, forms, policies, and procedures that had long encumbered processes as diverse as preauthorized payments and scheduling appointments.

For example, when an employee in the Vancity call center, or one working the mobile sales channel, wanted to help someone open a new account, he couldn't just book an appointment for the potential member with an account manager at a branch. Instead, the employee would have to call or e-mail the branch nearest the prospective member and inquire when an account manager would next be available. This process added steps, and often had members waiting on hold as branch staff and the call center employee worked to identify potential times.

A rapid cycle quickly identified this as an issue and proposed a solution: What if call center and mobile staff could access Outlook calendars for all account managers and book the appointments directly? Working with IT, Vancity introduced this functionality, and now employees can work quickly and directly with potential members to identify the best time and place for an account opening to happen.

Imagine the impact of *twenty-five cycles,* each of which brought a number of changes just like this. Eliminating or streamlining scores of excessively complex processes that had piled up over time gave frontline workers an opportunity to do much more meaningful work. Taken together, the results of these workshops were powerful:

- Number of processes and procedures simplified: 133
- Number of processes and procedures removed: 134
- Number of forms simplified: 41
- Number of forms removed: 53
- Number of steps simplified: 80
- Number of steps removed: 35

The *emotional* effects were even more profound. Fewer boxes to check led employees to *feel* empowered, and that benefited everyone because, as Gilfoy explained, it allowed Vancity to "direct the company's collective mindshare into the things that everyone wanted the employees to be doing," like taking care of their members. As one analysis found: "By reducing additional approvals and signatures, processing time is reduced by nearly 50 percent for some transactions. Streamlining the process and removing restrictions will allow staff to meet members where they are and have more meaningful conversations with them."[6]

Keys to Success

As Gilfoy would be the first to confirm, there was no magic formula to Vancity's success. Simplification requires leadership, resilience, tenacity, flexibility, and hard work. But there are certain lessons we can draw from Vancity's experience, lessons that can put any organization's simplification efforts on a surer path to success. These include:

1. **Establish Simplicity As a Key Strategic Priority for the Organization:** Simplicity can't be an add-on; it can't be an afterthought. Simplicity must be the lens through which you view every problem—starting now.

2. **Clearly Define and Communicate What the Process Will Look Like, Enabling Employees to Adjust:** Simplicity can be frightening to the average employee—particularly if it's viewed as a cost-cutting exercise. That means that those leading the exercise need to make a significant

effort on the front end to allay any concerns. The more employees understand about what is going to happen over the course of a simplification initiative, the more they will invest in making the outcomes work. Any employee worth having wants meaningful work. Giving each person sufficient insight into the why, what, and how will make her participate more eagerly over the long term.

3. **Maintain a Very Small, Central Team Charged with Facilitating Simplification:** No simplification effort will survive on its own; it needs people to drive it through to fruition. Yet the work of simplifying can't be done by a group of internal (or external) consultants; the people in the trenches need to feel as though this is *their* fight. In larger organizations, a small group should facilitate the process without claiming sole ownership.

4. **Focus on a Few Things, Not Everything:** It's often hard to determine which areas most need simplification, and so companies tend to tackle them all at once. That's a mistake. The most effective approach is to address each problem in succession. As each simplification makes a marginal difference, employees begin to feel it, and momentum builds.

5. **When Tackling Complexity Problems, Maintain a Mix of Specialists and Generalists:** In most cases, complication comes to the fore during conversations between people who understand the big picture and those who work in the weeds. Generalists and specialists often fail to understand the other's perspective—and in their mutual lack of familiarity, they *assume* complications are necessary. Bring them together, and everyone can spot complications that are ripe for elimination.

6. **Coach Leaders to Become Facilitators:** Simplification isn't always an innate skill. As previous chapters have explored, people *choose* complexity for many reasons. But simplification initiatives can prove contagious once they get going. Quick wins can engage an entire workforce. In that case, developing the next generation of facilitators is key to keeping the momentum alive.

7. **Get Started:** The best way to get started is...to just get started. Clear away the underbrush. Dive in. Do it.

Gilfoy's task was far from easy. She had to push change, but she also bore responsibility if her organization's core processes failed. David Perri, who became the director of process simplicity after Seema Dhanoa's promotion, explained that the group's mandate was akin to driving a car at sixty-five miles per hour while changing the tires. But with some of its core processes streamlined and a new culture of simplification taking shape, Vancity is now positioned to drive even faster than it was before. The organization's methodology teaches people to solve problems across divisional boundaries quickly, effectively, and without the added complexity that can come with relying on outside experts. As Perri said, "When I joined the team several months into their process, I could see the progress they were making. I knew that my role was to take the process in place and get even more capacity out of it. The potential for positive change and impact was huge."[7]

Maintaining Focus over the Long Term

Vancity is still changing the tires. Simplification is a constantly deepening process—what we might call an "innovation competency"—that can be constantly applied in new ways and in new areas of the business. Although, as of this writing, Vancity was still completing its first round of rapid cycling, Gilfoy and her team were already thinking of the next step. They had applied simplification to Vancity's core processes, and when that was complete, they planned to use the same methodology to simplify additional back-end parts of the business, such as the way the organization tracked and collected accounts payable. They also envisioned putting simplification to work in developing new products and services and in engineering the new, underlying processes and technology to support them.

As helpful as those changes will probably be, Gilfoy had even greater ambitions. She hoped that Vancity's employees would feel so empowered by the organization's embrace of simplicity that they would proactively weave simplification principles into their everyday work—without the organization's prodding. Early indications suggested that this had already begun to happen; groups in areas such as finance and risk management had asked to be part of the process and were starting to streamline on their own. When Gilfoy and her colleagues on the simplicity team asked staff what they thought of the process a few months in, they received an overwhelmingly enthusiastic response. That led many of Vancity's executives to believe that a huge opportunity existed to get employees asking themselves in every situation, "How can we simplify this work?"

Standard approaches to process improvement won't work for every organization and every situation. Traditional change processes like Lean Six Sigma have an important place in nearly any business if done correctly. But such processes can falter in the execution phase (for example, when process improvement tries to tackle more than originally intended, or when those leading the improvement initiative fail to consider the perspectives of frontline employees). Sometimes it's best to bypass process improvement and focus on simplifying daily work process. As Gilfoy related, simplification in Vancity's case "wasn't about improving things. It was about making it simpler. The goal was to remove things... simplicity through subtraction." But of course, simplification served precisely to improve the credit union's operations, because complexity had been bogging them down all along. It also served to energize the workforce. "This is as much about employee engagement and change leadership," Gilfoy mused, "as it is about the outcome of simplicity. We have seen some of our first cohort of employees gain the confidence they needed to apply for higher roles in the organization. That is as powerful as the actual process."

As Gilfoy will attest, simplifying is such a powerful, cheap, and accessible approach that it can dramatically improve results at any company, just as complexity can accelerate a company's death knell. Don't wait—start simplifying. Don't let anyone waste your time anymore. Get back to the meaningful work that will provide you with real satisfaction. Whether as organizations or as individuals, the investments we each make in simplifying our lives are well worth the cost. Gilfoy summarized what she's learned this way: "Employees feel empowered and the organization benefits because we can direct mindshare into things we want employees to be doing." Improve the work, and you improve the culture. Both of these together allow you to improve the organization—for everyone.

Acknowledgments

The irony of writing a book on simplicity is that it has been one of the most complex things I've ever done. With so much to research and so many angles to explore, it became glaringly apparent that answering even the most basic questions on the topic wasn't going to be easy. From the beginning, I noticed there was a wealth of information on the concept of complexity, but surprisingly little on simplicity. In fact, there was tremendous confusion around *what exactly is simplicity, anyway*?!

It all felt so...complicated.

Full disclosure: I wasn't sure that I even wanted to write another book. My publishers, clients, and friends all asked me when I was going to do it, and I always told them—*wait for it*—that I was too busy. In fact, I told my husband and close friends to please slap me if I ever mentioned doing it again—it's a tremendous amount of work, and it takes a ton of time—something I just didn't have. But once I committed, I was a person on a mission with a publishing date to make...and about eighteen months later, here we are.

I write books not because of some résumé-building goal I've had since high school or as a way to gain notoriety. I do it to solve a problem. I hate having problems, and I like to get rid of them as soon as humanly possible. And because I own my own business, "work" problems and "personal" problems are often intricately linked (as I'm sure they are for many of you these days). When I'm confronted with a problem, I fully admit and my husband will confirm that I become consumed by it. My blinders go on, and I go right into "shut-up-and-get-out-of-my-way-I-can't-hear-you-I'm-busy-now-can't-this-wait" investigative research mode to figure it out. And recently, I felt that work (and life) just kept getting more complicated for me, for my clients, and for everyone around me—and I wanted to know what the hell was causing this. *I mean, aren't we all competent adults who make smart, rationale choices and know what are priorities are?* Um, no. *And by the way, when did everything get so complicated?*

I found myself sitting on the sidelines of my kids' endless sporting events, "participating" (multi-tasking?) on hour-long conference calls that took forty-five minutes longer than necessary (always), running from school event to volunteer obligation, meeting urgent deadlines for a client, and rather than feel like a superhero because I was "getting it all done," I wondered, *is all this really necessary?* How can one be so busy yet feel no sense of accomplishment beyond checking something off a list?

Turns out, there are smart ways to take more control over the complexity in our lives. Some are easy, and some take more guts and focus. I learned so much in the process of creating this book, and simplified my life along the way. I learned that the art of subtraction can be far more powerful, and freeing, than the pervasive culture of "more is more" that we live in. That by getting rid of mundane tasks, meaningless work, and unnecessary social obligations you really could focus on what matters. You learn where your time is being well spent, and where it's not.

While writing this book, my time was well spent getting insights from a lot of smart people, without whom I would still be training for a gold medal in "maintaining complexity," and a silver in "inability to get out of my own way." First, I must thank a specific group of clients, partners, and friends who helped me on the journey to eradicate complexity. These people shared their tricks, tips, and experiences without hesitation. These people include: Adam Grant, Alexandra Yaghoobi, Amy Ikonich, Andrew Malkin, AJ Pape, Andy Gurnett, Ayuko Mueller, Urs Mueller, Bill O'Leary, Blair Faulstich, Bob Reinheimer, Camille Mirshokrai, Carter Busse, Cheryl Sorenson, Daphne Carmeli, Elaine Bowers Coventry, Eric Lowenstein, Erin Seuffert, Heiner Koppermann, Howard Prager, Irene Etzkorn, James Kelleher, John Young, Jyot Chada, Linda Samios, Louis

Carter, Madlyn Del Monte, Marisa Ricciardi, Maurice Boland, Mayuri Ghosh, Judy Brown, Pam Norley, Debra Clary, Sally Lechin, Paul Sloane, Barbara Price, Joe Re, Renita Kalhorn, Robert Clauser, Patty Nusser, Michael Bungay Stanier, Ruthie Garelik, Garry Golden, Renee Anderson, Steven Bain, Todd Press, Rowena Rothman, and Nancy Singer.

Next, I want to thank my colleagues who gave me countless hours of their time to shape my ideas and light my fire. To start, a big thank-you to my New York–based team, including Katherine Grant and Trevor Roten, who read countless chapter drafts, brainstormed dozens of simplification tools, and proofread documents until they were blind. Thank you so much. Next, the dynamic type-A creative duo of Tré Miller Rodriguez and Katie Webb. Tre, you are magic with words on paper. You are a pro at pushing my thinking, and with turning the simplification tools into something truly powerful, useful, and always—fun. Katie, you design god! Your dedication and countless weekends spent making everything look good and work well has been tremendous. And I must also thank my dear friends Robert Clauser and Patty Nusser, who gave me their humor, support, and wine throughout the entire process.

Interestingly, I've always fancied myself to be a strong writer. My creative thoughts, clever sound-bites, and sarcastic humor often enable readers to overlook my use of slang words and occasional grammatical errors. When writing a book, however, slang and grammatical issues are not viewed as such a great thing, which brings me to my need to thank my wonderful writers. There are two people in particular whose brainpower, eloquent use of the English language, and genuine interest in simplification made this book, well, great. First, Seth Schulman—thank you. You continually encouraged me to come up with fresh insights in order to avoid what could have been "just another boring business book." You continually probed for personal stories when I thought I just didn't have any more to give, and challenged me with thought-provoking questions and clever ideas on how to present my points of view. Second, I must also thank Marc Dunkleman. Your ability to take my hundreds of pages of semi-unintelligible crap (aka my in-depth research and notes) and make it sing is nothing short of artistic. I appreciate your pithy phrases, smart summaries, and pushback on anything that was too mundane. I would like to thank also my publishers, Erika Heilman and Jill Friedlander.

My sincere gratitude for once again being extremely supportive, open to change, and flexible with ideas (and deadlines).

And finally, I must thank my husband, Brian. No one's feedback quite encourages me, enlightens me (and frustrates me!) like his. Why, you ask? Because in one quick paragraph he can express a thought that takes me pages of run-on rambling to articulate. Importantly, his feedback is always straightforward, honest, and smart. With every draft and precious little free time of his own, he continually gave his insights and experiences on this topic. Because of our very different work backgrounds (I'm the creative person and he's the fintech entrepreneur) his perspective was often different than mine and therefore critical to include. I'm sure the readers will be grateful; I know I am. I am so lucky to have him in my life. Thank you so much, Brian.

If this book helps you simplify your work, or your life, and lets you spend more time on things that matter, I'll feel like it's all been time well spent.

Appendix
50 Questions for Simplifying

The following is a comprehensive list of questions for you to use when completing this exercise. Please refer to page 103 in the book for more on this tool.

Is it **Valuable**?
(Use these questions to determine what's necessary or worth your time.)

1. Which activities or tasks in my daily work add the most value for stakeholders (clients, partners, etc.)?

2. If a natural disaster struck our headquarters tonight, what's the most crucial item of business that staff would pitch in to accomplish?

3. Which activities or tasks make me feel good about my job and give me the sense that I've truly contributed to the organization's mission?

4. When I head to work, what do I most look forward to doing and why?

5. Which product or service drives the most enthusiasm, emotion, and purchases from prospective and current clients?

6. What is the most important activity for keeping employees or customers happy and engaged?

7. In terms of the 80–20 rule—where staff spends 80 percent of time on 20 percent of the work—how can I shift this ratio so I'm spending the majority of time on more valuable work?

8. I just won a trip that departs in twenty-four hours: What are the most important things I need to get done before I leave?
   1.
   2.
   3.
   4.
   5.

9. While I'm on that trip, what would I delegate to colleagues for follow-up and why? Would I classify those tasks as valuable or required/routine/time-sensitive?

VALUABLE
1.
2.
3.

REQUIRED/ROUTINE/TIME-SENSITIVE
1.
2.
3.
4.
5.

10. If I divided my meetings into two columns—those that are worth my time and those for which an e-mail update would suffice—what changes could I make right now?

MEETINGS WORTH MY TIME
1.
2.
3.

MEETINGS THAT COULD BE E-MAILS
1.
2.
3.
4.
5.
Which of the above meetings could—and should—become an e-mail today?

11. If I divided my work into tasks that delight me and tasks I find loathsome, what could be eliminated, changed, or accomplished in less loathsome ways?

DELIGHTFUL TASKS
1.
2.
3.

LOATHSOME TASKS
1.
2.
3.
4.
5.
What changes could be made to one LOATHSOME task that would compel me move it into the DELIGHTFUL column?

12. Which tasks take time or energy away from my critical goals?

13. If I could clone myself today, what's the first thing I'd assign to him/her? What's preventing me from delegating it to someone else today?

14. What one thing would I do to save this company $10,000 tomorrow?

15. What percentage of my day allows for unstructured time on work that matters? What could I change to increase my daily, unstructured time?

16. After itemizing my weekly tasks—including calls, meetings, and
e-mails—which ones actually benefit my customers or clients?

BENEFITS CLIENTS/CUSTOMERS
1.
2.
3.

NO BENEFIT FOR CLIENTS/CUSTOMERS
1.
2.
3.
4.
5.
Which of the above tasks could be eliminated to restore more time for
tasks that do benefit my clients/customers?

17. In what ways do my team members contribute to complexity? What
advice do I have for changing those behaviors?

18. If we no longer offered this _____ (product/service/pro-
cess), would we be willing to pay for it? How much?

My customized question: _____
_____

My customized question: _____
_____

My customized question: _____
_____

Is it Minimal?
(Use these questions to assess if something is streamlined or reduced to its
simplest possible form.)

19. What should I stop doing?

20. What can I start saying no to?

21. If I could kill any rule at work that holds me back from being more effective or productive, what would it be?

22. If a new CEO started at our company tomorrow, what processes would s/he immediately observe as the biggest time-wasters?

23. For every new thing we add to our product pipeline, what could be eliminated? (Which process? Meeting? Standing call?)

24. What would happen if this rule/process/etc. didn't exist?

25. If I had to eliminate 25 percent of what I do every day, what would I eliminate and why?

26. In which situations does the company require multiple approvals for an action or expenditure when a single approval or auto-approval (within certain limits) would suffice?

27. If proposals for product/service/process enhancements are required to go through layers of review, how could we dramatically reduce these layers and speed up the process?

28. If I could limit the work I provide to other functions or teams, what activity would I like to stop doing immediately?

29. Could another individual (internal or external) do some of the work I do? If so, list these below:
    1.
    2.
    3.
    What's preventing me from delegating at least one of these tasks today?

30. How could we shorten this document/proposal/contract/presentation to 1 page?

31. What are the most complex aspects of my job?
    1.
    2.
    3.

32. What redundancies could be eliminated from my job right now?
    1.
    2.
    3.
    What's preventing me from removing at least 1 of these redundancies today?

33. What is the minimal amount of data we need to satisfy our objective? If we're providing more, can we agree to stop doing this today?

34. If I had to get the same amount of work done in half the time, what would I do differently?

35. What is 1 small change I could make that would have a big impact? Is anything preventing me from proposing or implementing that change?

    My customized question: _____

    _____

    My customized question: _____

    _____

    My customized question: _____

    _____

Is it Understandable?
(Use these questions to determine if communication on a topic is as clear as possible.)

36. Could I clearly explain this to anyone outside my business group?

37. What jargon could be eliminated from this document or message?

38. How can this message be distilled down to 1 sentence?

39. How could this communication be simplified so people actually read it and take the desired action?

40. Have we clearly established the person or team responsible for this deliverable and the corresponding deadlines?

My customized question: _____

_____

My customized question: _____

_____

My customized question: _____

_____

Is it Repeatable?
(Use these questions to decide if a task or process is as automated, templated, or scalable as possible.)

41. If we automated some or all of this task/process, who would benefit?

42. Can this process be easily replicated for other teams/markets?

43. What would make it easily repeatable for other people to use?

44. If significant training is required to learn this process, what could we modify so less training is required?

45. Can we create a template for this task or process so others can use it?

46. How much time or money could we save in a year by automating this?

My customized question: _____

_____

My customized question: _____

_____

My customized question: _____

_____

Is it **Accessible?**
(Use these questions to determine if an information source is as readily available to its audience as possible.)

47. Are employees able to access information they need in real time? If not, how can we improve access for them?

48. How could customers more easily do business with us?

49. Would other departments or divisions benefit from access to our systems or data? Would we benefit by empowering them to do more of the work themselves?

50. Is there value or increased efficiency in making this product/data/service available to more employees or customers? If so, how could we do this?

    My customized question: _____

    _____

    My customized question: _____

    _____

    My customized question: _____

    _____

Notes

Chapter 1

1. Quote attributed to Confucius. See, "Life Is Really Simple, but We Insist on Making It Complicated—Confucius," habitsforwellbeing.com, accessed May 31, 2016, http://www.habitsforwellbeing.com/life-is-really-simple-but-we-insist-on -making-it-complicated-confucius/.
2. Tony Schwartz and Christine Porath, "Why You Hate to Work," *New York Times*, accessed May 31, 2016, http://www.nytimes.com/2014/06/01/opinion/sunday/ why-you-hate-work.html.
3. Todd Wasserman, "Email Takes Up 28% of Workers' Time," *Mashable*, accessed May 31, 2016, http://mashable.com/2012/08/01/email-workers-time/ #07W4SSjmGGqI.
4. Natalie Walters, "Here's What Happened When the Founders of a $100 Million Company Stopped Using Email Entirely," *Business Insider*, accessed May 31, 2016, http://www.businessinsider.com/founders-of-life-is-good-stopped-using-email -2015-12.
5. Sue Shellenbarger, "Stop Wasting Everyone's Time," *Wall Street Journal*, accessed May 31, 2016, http://www.wsj.com/articles/how-to-stop-wasting-colleagues-time -1417562658.
6. Michael C. Mankins, "Is Technology Really Helping Us Get More Done?," *Harvard Business Review*, accessed May 31, 2016, https://hbr.org/2016/02/is-technology -really-helping-us-get-more-done?utm_source=twitter&utm_medium=social &utm_campaign=harvardbiz.

7. Tim Harford, "Multi-Tasking: How to Survive in the 21st Century," *FT Magazine*, accessed May 31, 2016, http://www.ft.com/cms/s/2/bbf1f84a-51c2-11e5 -8642-453585f2cfcd.html.

8. Adam Flomenbaum, "Accenture Report: 87% of Consumers Use Second Screen Device While Watching TV," LostRemote, accessed May 31, 2016, http://www .adweek.com/lostremote/accenture-report-87-of-consumers-use-second-screen -device-while-watching-tv/51698.

9. Elizabeth Grace Saunders, "Do You Really Need to Hold That Meeting?," *Harvard Business Review*, accessed May 31, 2016, https://hbr.org/2015/03/do-you -really-need-to-hold-that-meeting.

10. Shellenbarger, "Stop Wasting Everyone's Time"; Rajesh Jha, "Microsoft to Acquire VoloMetrix to Empower Individuals and Drive Organizational Productivity," Official Microsoft Blog, accessed May 31, 2016, http://blogs.microsoft .com/blog/2015/09/03/microsoft-to-acquire-volometrix-to-empower-individuals -and-drive-organizational-productivity/.

11. Shellenbarger, "Stop Wasting Everyone's Time."

12. Mankins, "Is Technology Really Helping Us?"

13. "And So We Meet, Again: Why the Workday Is So Filled with Meetings," *Morning Edition, National Public Radio*, January 29, 2015, accessed May 31, 2016, http://www.npr.org/2015/01/29/382162271/and-so-we-meet-again-why-the -workday-is-so-filled-with-meetings.

14. Rob Cross, Reb Rebele, and Adam Grant, "Collaborative Overload," *Harvard Business Review*, accessed May 31, 2016, https://hbr.org/2016/01/collaborative-overload.

15. "Decluttering the Company," *Economist*, accessed May 18, 2016, http://www .economist.com/news/business/21610237-businesses-must-fight-relentless-battle -against-bureaucracy-decluttering-company.

16. Michael C. Mankins, "This Weekly Meeting Took Up 300,000 Hours a Year," *Harvard Business Review*, accessed May 31, 2016, https://hbr.org/2014/04/ how-a-weekly-meeting-took-up-300000-hours-a-year/.

17. Eric D. Beinhocker and Sarah Kaplan, "Tired of Strategic Planning?," *McKinsey Quarterly*, June 2002, accessed May 18, 2016, http://www.mckinsey .com/business-functions/strategy-and-corporate-finance/our-insights/ tired-of-strategic-planning.

18. *Wikipedia*, s.v. "William H. Starbuck," accessed May 20, 2016, https://en .wikipedia.org/wiki/William_H._Starbuck.

19. "Behold the Entrenched—and Reviled—Annual Review," *Morning Edition, National Public Radio*. October 28, 2014, accessed May 31, 2016, http://www.npr .org/2014/10/28/358636126/behold-the-entrenched-and-reviled-annual-review.

20. Ray Williams, "Why Performance Appraisals Don't Improve Performance,"

Psychology Today, accessed May 31, 2016, https://www.psychologytoday.com/blog/
wired-success/201402/why-performance-appraisals-dont-improve-performance.

21. Anni Layne Rodgers, "Why Performance Reviews Don't Work—and What
    to Do Instead," Inc., accessed May 31, 2016, http://www.inc.com/the-build
    -network/why-performance-reviews-dont-work-and-what-to-do-instead.html.

22. "Behold the Annual Review."

23. Dimple Agarwal, Burt Rea, and Ardie van Berkel, "Simplification of Work: The
    Coming Revolution," Deloitte University Press, accessed May 31, 2016, http://
    dupress.com/articles/work-simplification-human-capital-trends-2015/.

24. Clyde Wayne Crews Jr., "Hairball: The Cost of Federal Regulation to the U.S.
    Economy," *Forbes*, accessed May 31, 2016, http://www.forbes.com/sites/
    waynecrews/2014/09/10/hairball-the-cost-of-federal-regulation-to-the-u
    -s-economy/.

25. Joseph Lawler, "Manufacturers: Regulations Cost Economy $2 Trillion Annually,"
    Washington Examiner, accessed May 31, 2016, http://www.washingtonexaminer
    .com/manufacturers-regulations-cost-economy-2-trillion-annually/article/
    2553174.

26. Brittany Hackett, "Study: Regulatory Compliance Costs Higher Ed $27B Per
    Year," National Association of Student Financial Aid Administrators, accessed
    May 31, 2016, http://www.nasfaa.org/news-item/6352/Study_Regulatory
    _Compliance_Costs_Higher_Ed_27B_Per_Year.

27. Dimple Agarwal et al., "Simplification of Work."

28. Bill Jensen, *Simplicity: The New Competitive Advantage in a World of More, Better,
    Faster* (Cambridge, MA: Perseus Books, 2000), 19–33.

29. Yves Morieux, "Smart Rules: Six Ways to Get People to Solve Problems With-
    out You," *Harvard Business Review*, accessed May 31, 2016, https://hbr
    .org/2011/09/smart-rules-six-ways-to-get-people-to-solve-problems-without-you.

30. Morieux, "Smart Rules."

31. Timo Elliott, "What's the Biggest Barrier to Business Innovation? The Answer Is
    Simple," SlideShare Business, accessed May 31, 2016, http://www.slideshare.net/
    timoelliott/whats-the-biggest-barrier-to-business-innovation-the-answer-is-simple.

32. Steve Crabtree, "Worldwide, 13% of Employees Are Engaged at Work," Gallup,
    accessed May 31, 2016, http://www.gallup.com/poll/165269/worldwide-employees
    -engaged-work.aspx.

33. Victor Lipman, "Surprising, Disturbing Facts from the Mother of All Employee
    Engagement Surveys," *Forbes*, accessed May 31, 2016, http://www.forbes.com/
    sites/victorlipman/2013/09/23/surprising-disturbing-facts-from-the-mother
    -of-all-employee-engagement-surveys/.

34. Dimple Agarwal et al., "Simplification of Work."

35. "Simplifying the Future of Work Study," Knowledge@Wharton, sponsored by SAP, 2014.

36. Louis Doré, "The Italian Company Banning Emails to Reduce Stress," *Independent*, accessed May 31, 2016, http://i100.independent.co.uk/article/the-italian-company-banning-e-mails-to-reduce-stress--Zkms4rg7tg.

37. "Decluttering the Company."

38. Dimple Agarwal et al., "Simplification of Work."

39. Morieux, "Smart Rules."

40. "Decluttering the Company."

41. "Decluttering the Company."

42. "Our Story," Staples.com, accessed May 31, 2016, http://www.staples.com/sbd/cre/marketing/about_us/our-story.html.

43. Patrick Spenner, "Why Simplicity Should Be at the Heart of Your Small Business Marketing Strategy," *Washington Post*, accessed May 31, 2016, https://www.washingtonpost.com/blogs/on-small-business/post/why-simplicity-should-be-at-the-heart-of-your-small-business-marketing-strategy/2012/09/05/79058bfc-f769-11e1-8b93-c4f4ab1c8d13_blog.html.

44. "Staples Tests 'Easy' Virtual Button Desktop Application—Results Atypical," MarketingSherpa, accessed May 31, 2016, https://www.marketingsherpa.com/article/case-study/staples-tests-easy-virtual-button#.

45. Sarah Mahoney, "That Was Easy: Staples Ditches 10-Year-Old Tagline," Marketing Daily, accessed May 31, 2016, http://www.mediapost.com/publications/article/216503/that-was-easy-staples-ditches-10-year-old-tagline.html.

Chapter 2

1. Anita Bruzzese, "On the Job: How to Tame the Meetings Beast," *USA Today*, accessed May 31, 2016, http://www.usatoday.com/story/money/columnist/bruzzese/2013/04/14/on-the-job-too-many-meetings/2076173/.

2. Vincent Canby, "Review/Film; Steve Martin's Paean to Los Angeles," *New York Times*, accessed May 31, 2016, http://www.nytimes.com/movie/review?res=9D0CEFDB1E3AF93BA35751C0A967958260.

3. "L.A. Story, Quotes," imbd.com, accessed May 31, 2016, http://www.imdb.com/title/tt0102250/quotes.

4. Brad Katsuyama (IEX), interview with author, August 6, 2015.

5. "Everything Should Be Made As Simple As Possible, but Not Simpler," Quote Investigator, accessed May 31, 2016, http://quoteinvestigator.com/2011/05/13/einstein-simple/.

6. Wikipedia, *The Free Encyclopedia*, s.v. "IEX," accessed July 28, 2016, https://en.wikipedia.org/wiki/IEX.

7. James B. Stewart, "Gone in 0.001 Seconds," review of *Flash Boys: A Wall Street Revolt* by Michael Lewis, *New York Times*, accessed May 31, 2016, http://www.nytimes.com/2014/04/20/books/review/flash-boys-by-michael-lewis.html?_r=0.

8. Michael Lewis, "The Wolf Hunters of Wall Street," *New York Times*, accessed May 31, 2016, http://www.nytimes.com/2014/04/06/magazine/flash-boys-michael-lewis.html?_r=0.

9. Stewart, "Gone in 0.001 Seconds."

10. Mike Masnick, "To Read All of the Privacy Policies You Encounter, You'd Need to Take a Month Off from Work Each Year," Techdirt, accessed May 31, 2016, https://www.techdirt.com/articles/20120420/10560418585/to-read-all-privacy-policies-you-encounter-youd-need-to-take-month-off-work-each-year.shtml.

11. For further information, please see Apttus.com, barternewsweekly.com, https://conversation.which.co.uk, http://www.doingbusiness.org/data, www.dummies.com, http://www.britannica.com, gpo.gov, http://library.duke.edu, http://www.livescience.com, https://www.mint.com/.

12. Ronald Vogl, interview with author, August 5, 2015.

13. Jim Daly, e-mail message to author, January 25, 2016.

14. Drake Baer, "Quick: End Decision Fatigue Before It Drains Your Productivity Reservoir," *Fast Company*, accessed May 31, 2016, http://www.fastcompany.com/3009641/leadership-now/quick-end-decision-fatigue-before-it-drains-your-productivity-reservoir.

15. Victoria Clayton, "The Needless Complexity of Academic Writing," *Atlantic*, accessed May 31, 2016, http://www.theatlantic.com/education/archive/2015/10/complex-academic-writing/412255/.

16. Greg McKeown, *Essentialism: The Disciplined Pursuit of Less* (New York: Crown Business, 2014).

17. Noel Tichy and Ram Charan, "Speed, Simplicity, Self-Confidence: An Interview with Jack Welch," *Harvard Business Review*, accessed May 31, 2016, https://hbr.org/1989/09/speed-simplicity-self-confidence-an-interview-with-jack-welch.

18. Dave Moniz, "B-52 Still 'BUFF' at 50," *USA Today*, accessed May 31, 2016, http://usatoday30.usatoday.com/news/nation/2002/04/24/b-52.htm.

19. Dave Phillipps, "After 60 Years, B-52s Still Dominate U.S. Fleet," *New York Times*, accessed May 31, 2016, http://www.nytimes.com/2015/12/06/us/b-52s-us-air-force-bombers.html?_r=1.

20. Tim Weiner, "The $2 Billion Stealth Bomber Can't Go Out in the Rain, *New York Times*, accessed May 31, 2016, http://www.nytimes.com/1997/08/23/world/the-2-billion-stealth-bomber-can-t-go-out-in-the-rain.html.

Chapter 3

1. "Johann Wolfgang Von Goethe Quotes," Thinkexist.com, accessed May 22, 2016, http://thinkexist.com/quotation/things_which_matter_most_must_never_be _at_the/180010.html.

2. AnnaLee Saxenian, *Regional Advantage: Culture and Competition in Silicon Valley and Route 128* (Cambridge, MA: Harvard University Press, 1994), 59–82 *passim*.

Chapter 4

1. Leo Tolstoy, *War and Peace* (book 14, chapter 18), quoted from Goodreads, accessed May 31, 2016, http://www.goodreads.com/quotes/74099-there-is-no -greatness-where-there-is-not-simplicity-goodness.

2. Adam Smiley Poswolsky, "What Millennial Employees Really Want," *Fast Company*, accessed May 31, 2016, http://www.fastcompany.com/3046989/what -millennial-employees-really-want.

3. Poswolsky, "What Millennial Employees Want."

4. Bobbi Rebell, "Why Millennials Want to Quit Their Jobs," *Money*, accessed May 31, 2016, http://time.com/money/4199776/why-millennials-want-to-quit -their-jobs/.

5. Olga Khazan and Paul Rosenfeld, "Why We Work," video highlighting the work of Dan Ariely, Daniel Pink, and Teresa Amabile, *Atlantic*, accessed May 31, 2016, http://www.theatlantic.com/video/index/414627/why-we-work/.

6. Andrew McAfee and Erik Brynjolfsson, "Investing in the IT That Makes a Competitive Difference," *Harvard Business Review*, accessed May 31, 2016, https://hbr .org/2008/07/investing-in-the-it-that-makes-a-competitive-difference.

7. Noel Tichy and Ram Charan, "Speed, Simplicity, Self-Confidence: An Interview with Jack Welch," *Harvard Business Review*, accessed May 31, 2016, https://hbr .org/1989/09/speed-simplicity-self-confidence-an-interview-with-jack-welch.

8. Jacquelyn Smith, "72% of People Get Their Best Ideas in the Shower—Here's Why," *Business Insider*, accessed May 31, 2016, http://www.businessinsider.com/ why-people-get-their-best-ideas-in-the-shower-2016-1?utm_source=linkedin -bipage&utm_medium=referral.

9. Ronald S. Burt, "Structural Holes and Good Ideas," *American Journal of Sociology* 110 (2004): 349–350.

10. Chris Baréz-Brown, "Simplicity Is the Key to Creativity," *Guardian*, accessed May 31, 2016, http://www.theguardian.com/media-network/2015/ nov/17/creative-simple-business-management-leadership-tips.

11. Dr. Lynn K. Jones, "Simplify by Saying 'No,'" http://www.lynnkjones.com/, accessed May 31, 2016, http://www.lynnkjones.com/appreciative-coaching-blog/ simplify-by-saying-no/#sthash.ahoEe4eB.dpu.

12. Spencer Althouse, "18 of the Best Ron Swanson Quotes," Buzzfeed, accessed May 31, 2016, http://www.buzzfeed.com/spenceralthouse/18-of-the-best-ron -swanson-quotes-a078#.dm7wmaYbo3.

13. Michael Blanding, "Workplace Stress Responsible for up to $190B in Annual U.S. Healthcare Costs," *Forbes*, accessed May 31, 2016, http://www.forbes.com/ sites/hbsworkingknowledge/2015/01/26/workplace-stress-responsible -for-up-to-190-billion-in-annual-u-s-heathcare-costs/#74e1b7124333.

14. Blanding, "Workplace Stress Responsible."

15. "Stress in the Workplace: Meeting the Challenge," Healthadvocate.com, accessed May 31, 2016, http://healthadvocate.com/downloads/webinars/stress -workplace.pdf.

16. Kathryn Hayward, "The Toxic Effects of Workplace Stress," Breakfast Television, accessed May 31, 2016, http://www.bttoronto.ca/2015/11/19/the-toxic-effects -of-workplace-stress/.

17. Michael L. George and Stephen A. Wilson, *Conquering Complexity in Your Business: How Wal-Mart, Toyota, and Other Top Companies Are Breaking Through the Ceiling on Profits and Growth* (New York: McGraw-Hill, 2004), 6–9.

18. Seth Stevenson, "The Southwest Secret," Slate.com, accessed May 31, 2016, http://www .slate.com/articles/business/operations/2012/06/southwest_airlines_profitability _how_the_company_uses_operations_theory_to_fuel_its_success_.html.

19. George and Wilson, *Conquering Complexity in Your Business*, 6.

20. Gregory Karp, "Southwest's On-Time Rates: Better but Not Best," *Chicago Tribune*, accessed May 31, 2016, http://www.chicagotribune.com/business/ ct-southwest-ontime-0110-biz-20150108-story.html.

21. Steve Parker, "Pontiac, Hummer, Saab, Saturn Officially Dead; GM Dealers, Workers Slashed," *Huffington Post*, accessed May 31, 2016, http://www .huffingtonpost.com/steve-parker/pontiac-hummer-saab-satur_b_191799.html.

22. Steve Strelsin, "Simplify: The Most Important Leadership Skill," Axiom Consulting Partners, accessed May 31, 2016, http://www.axiomcp.com/simplify-the-most -important-leadership-skill-2/.

23. "The Biggest Business Comebacks of the Past 20 Years," *Fast Company*, accessed May 31, 2016, http://www.fastcompany.com/3042431/meme/the-biggest-business -comebacks-of-the-past-20-years.

24. Katie Rogers, "LinkedIn, Notorious for Sending Too Many Emails, Cuts Back," *New York Times*, accessed May 31, 2016, http://www.nytimes.com/2015/07/29/ business/linkedin-notorious-for-sending-too-many-emails-cuts-back.html.

25. Jeff Russell, "LinkedIn Stock: This Is Why the Bears Are Wrong on LinkedIn Corp," Profit Confidential, accessed May 31, 2016, http://www.profitconfidential .com/stock/linkedin-stock-this-is-why-the-bears-are-wrong-on-linkedin-corp/.

26. Margaret Molloy, "Simplifying Google: A Conversation with CMO Lorraine Twohill," Huffington Post, accessed May 31 2016, http://www.huffingtonpost .com/margaret-molloy/simplifying-google-a-conv_b_8569662.html.

27. "Capital One Rewards Barometer Reveals Consumers Might Miss Out This Holi-day Season," Capital One, accessed May 20, 2016, http://press.capitalone.com/ phoenix.zhtml?c=251626&p=irol-newsArticle&ID=1858715.

28. Jack Preston, "Richard Branson: Three Rules of Simplicity That Every Busi-ness Should Follow," Virgin, accessed May 31, 2016 https://www.virgin.com/ entrepreneur/richard-branson-three-rules-of-simplicity-that-every-business -should-follow.

29. "Global Brand Simplicity Index: 2011," Siegel + Gale, accessed May 19, 2016, http://www.siegelgale.com/wp-content/uploads/2012/02/Global_Brand _Simplicity_Index_2011_010612_v2.pdf.

30. Margaret Molloy, "Why Simple Brands Win," Harvard Business Review, accessed May 31, 2016, https://hbr.org/2015/11/why-simple-brands-win.

31. Molloy, "Why Simple Brands Win."

32. Vince Bond Jr., "New Car Technologies Often Unused By Drivers, J.D. Power Finds,"AutomotiveNews,accessedMay19,2016,http://www.autonews.com/article/ 20150825/OEM06/150829939/new-car-technologies-often-unused-by-drivers -j.d.-power-finds.

33. Jim Daly, e-mail message to author, January 25, 2016.

Chapter 5

1. Margaret Molloy, "Simplifying Google: A Conversation with CMO Lorraine Twohill," Huffington Post, accessed May 31 2016, http://www.huffingtonpost .com/margaret-molloy/simplifying-google-a-conv_b_8569662.html.

2. Interview with Roger Servison, president of Fidelity's New Business Development Group.

3. Noel Tichy and Ram Charan, "Speed, Simplicity, Self-Confidence: An Interview with Jack Welch," Harvard Business Review, accessed May 31, 2016, https://hbr .org/1989/09/speed-simplicity-self-confidence-an-interview-with-jack-welch.

4. Sue Shellenbarger, "Stop Wasting Everyone's Time," Wall Street Journal, accessed May 31, 2016, http://www.wsj.com/articles/how-to-stop-wasting-colleagues-time -1417562658.

5. Graeme Whitfield, "The Decline of Tesco: How Did the World Beater End Up in Crisis?," *The Journal*, accessed May 31, 2016, http://www.thejournal .co.uk/north-east-analysis/analysis-news/decline-tesco-how-world-beater -8407620.

6. Jenny Anderson, "Tesco Accounting Scandal Draws Scrutiny of Serious Fraud Office in Britain," *New York Times*, accessed May 31, 2016, http://www.nytimes .com/2014/10/30/business/international/another-british-watchdog-opens -inquiry-into-tesco-accounting-scandal.html?_r=0.

7. Zoe Wood and Sarah Butler, "Tesco Cuts Range by 30% to Simplify Shopping," *Guardian*, accessed May 31, 2016, http://www.theguardian.com/business/2015/ jan/30/tesco-cuts-range-products.

8. Anderson, "Tesco Accounting Scandal."

9. Natalie Walters, "Here's What Happened When the Founders of a $100 Million Company Stopped Using Email Entirely," *Business Insider*, accessed May 31, 2016, http://www.businessinsider.com/founders-of-life-is-good-stopped-using-email -2015-12.

10. Jeff Spencer, e-mail message to author, January 25, 2016.

11. Roman Yako, "The Dollar Shave Club Strategy—Marketing with Relation-ships," Kinshipology, accessed May 31, 2016, http://www.kinshipology.com/ engage/dollar-shave-club-strategy-marketing-with-relationships/.

12. Quoted in Jillian D'Onfro, "Steve Jobs Used to Ask Jony Ive the Same Question Almost Every Day," *Business Insider*, accessed May 31, 2016, http://www.business insider.com/this-is-the-question-steve-jobs-would-ask-jony-ive-every-day-2015-10.

Chapter 6

1. "Elbert Hubbard, Quotes," Goodreads, accessed May 31, 2016, http://www .goodreads.co/quotes/40708-the-sculptor-produces-the-beautiful-statue-by -chipping-away-such.

2. A version of this language appeared in: Lisa Bodell, "Doing Away with Stupid Rules," Wall Street Journal, July 31, 2012, accessed July 28, 2016, http://www.wsj. com/articles/SB10000872396390444860104577559560237866648.

3. Liz Tinkham (Accenture), interview with author, January 2, 2016.

Chapter 7

1. "Hans Hofmann, Quotes," Goodreads, accessed May 31, 2016, http://www .goodreads.com/quotes/70138-the-ability-to-simplify-means-to-eliminate-the -unnecessary-so.

2. Steve Strelsin, "Simplify: The Most Important Leadership Skill," Axiom Consulting Partners, accessed May 31, 2016, http://www.axiomcp.com/simplify-the-most-important-leadership-skill-2/.

3. Please see https://www.iextrading.com/.

4. Brad Katsuyama (IEX), interview with author, August 6, 2015.

5. Andrew McDougall, "P&G to Become a 'Simpler' Business with Beauty Refocus 'Essentially Done,'" IFF Lucas Meyer Cosmetics, accessed May 19, 2016, http://www.cosmeticsdesign-europe.com/Brand-Innovation/P-G-to-become-a-simpler-business-with-beauty-refocus-essentially-done.

6. Ron Ashkenas, interview with author, July 9, 2015.

7. Dmitry, "Steve Jobs: Innovation Is Saying 'No' to 1,000 Things," Zurb Blog, accessed May 31, 2016, http://zurb.com/article/744/steve-jobs-innovation-is-saying-no-to-1-0.

8. Jack Preston, "Richard Branson: Three Rules of Simplicity That Every Business Should Follow," Virgin, accessed May 31, 2016, https://www.virgin.com/entrepreneur/richard-branson-three-rules-of-simplicity-that-every-business-should-follow.

9. Ron Ashkenas, interview with author, July 9, 2015.

10. A version of this article appeared in the May 2014 issue of *Harvard Business Review*.

11. Jeff Spencer, interview with author, November 15, 2015.

12. Unidentified individual, personal communication with the author during the Provocateur Program Conference, August 2011.

13. Jeff Woods (SAP), interview with author, August 6, 2015.

14. Ron Ashkenas e-mail to author, January 26, 2016.

15. Dimple Agarwal, Burt Rea, and Ardie van Berkel, "Simplification of Work: The Coming Revolution," Deloitte University Press, accessed May 31, 2016, http://dupress.com/articles/work-simplification-human-capital-trends-2015/.

16. Michael Bungay-Steiner, interview with author, July 10, 2015.

17. Jim Daly, e-mail message to author, January 25, 2016.

18. Rochael Soper Adranly, interview with author, August 21, 2015.

19. Jeff Spencer, interview with author, November 15, 2015.

20. Jeff Spencer, interview with author, November 15, 2015.

21. Jeff Spencer, interview with author, November 15, 2015.

22. Chetan Chandavarkar, e-mail message to author, February 11, 2016.

23. Liz Tinkham (Accenture), interview with author, January 2, 2016.

24. Agnelo Fernandes, interview with author, December 3, 2015.

25. Kelly Leonard, interview with author, August 5, 2015.

26. Preston, "Richard Branson."

27. Alan Siegel, interview with author, August 4, 2015.

28. Alan M. Siegel and Irene Etzkorn, *Simple: Conquering the Crisis of Complexity* (New York: Twelve, 2013), ix–xi.

29. Lisa Bodell, "Stop Being Nice at Work," strategy+business, accessed May 31, 2016, http://www.strategy-business.com/blog/Stop-Being-Nice-at-Work?gko=ebfce.
30. Please consult https://www.ge.com/products.
31. "Decluttering the Company," *The Economist*, accessed May 31, 2016, http://www.economist.com/news/business/21610237-businesses-must-fight-relentless-battle-against-bureaucracy-decluttering-company.
32. Dimple Agarwal et al., "Simplification of Work."
33. Tom Hodson et al., *The Overwhelmed Employee: Simplify the Work Environment* (Westlake, TX: Deloitte University Press: 2014), 97–104.

Chapter 8

1. "'Quote': Simplicity Is the Final Achievement," Acoustic Guitar Forum, accessed May 31, 2016, http://www.acousticguitarforum.com/forums/showthread.php?t=229179.
2. "Business Profile," TD Bank, accessed May 31, 2016, https://www.tdbank.com/exc/pdf/company_fact_sheet.pdf.
3. "Highlights," Vancity, accessed May 31, 2016, https://www.vancity.com/AboutVancity/VisionAndValues/Glance/Highlights/.
4. "Vancity at a Glance," Vancity, accessed May 31, 2016, https://www.vancity.com/AboutVancity/VisionAndValues/Glance/.
5. Vancity Rapid Cycle Innovation Package.
6. Vancity (P. 8, Rapid Cycle #17: Manage Banking Services workshop mandate).
7. Jay-Ann Gilfoy, telephone interview with the author, April 2016.

Index

A

Abbott, 123

Accenture, 4, 120–121, 124

accessibility, 24–25, 60–61

   questions for determining, 202

   simplifying based on, 104, 107

accountability, 182

   for decision-making, 144–145

   executive disconnect and, 31–32

acronyms, 41

adaptability, xiv

Adranly, Rochael Soper, 156

Affinion Group, 74, 155

Agile methodology, 65–66, xv

"Aircraft" exercise, 130

Aldi, 86–87

Allstate Insurance, 57–58

American Airlines, 71

Apple, 93–94

approval processes, 40, 125, 165

Arpey, Gerard, 71

The Art of Readable Writing (Flesch), 168

Ashkenas, Ron, 143, 146

assessment of complexity, 39–55, 83, 104

Atlantic (magazine), 33

Atlassian, 15

automation, 171–172

awareness of complexity, 100, 101, 159

Axiom, 135–137

B

B-2 "stealth" bomber, 36

B-52 bomber, 35–37

Bain & Company, 3, 5, 6, 144

barriers, 130–131

Barry, Dave, 19

BATS, 27

blackout periods, 129

Blockbuster, 72

Bloomberg, 15

Boston Consulting Group, 13, 15

Box of Crayons, 155

brainstorming, 115–116

brands, simplifying, 142–143

Branson, Richard, 168

Bungay-Stanier, Michael, 155

bureaucracy, 7–8, 129

Burnett, Leo, 57–58

Burt, Ronald, 67

business intelligence group, 63–67

busywork, 2

buy-in, 95–96, 138–141, 184

C
Capital One, 72
Carell, Steve, 168
Chandavarkar, Chetan, 165
change, complexity added from dealing
    with, 9–10
Chopin, Frederic, 175
Citibank, 168–169
Clarizen and Harris, 6
Clayton, Victoria, 33
Cleveland Clinic, 63–67
clutter, 165
Coca-Cola, 127
Codes of Conduct, 152–155
cognitive biases, 22
Colbert, Stephen, 168
Commerce Bank, 145
communication, 187–188. *See also* e-mail
    clarity in, 168–169
    in corporate culture, 136
    diagnostics as conversation starters, 54
    language in, 123
    questions for determining understand-
        ability of, 200–201
    of Simplification Code of Ethics, 155
    technology and overload in, 3–4
competitive advantage, 189–190, xiv
complexity
    assessing your, 39–55
    awareness of, 100, 101
    B-52 replacement and, 35–37
    bureaucracy and, 7–8
    busywork and, 2
    costs of, 9–10
    creation of, 1–18
    diagnostic on, 42–54, 104, 122
    emotional drives behind, 32–35
    facing up to problems in, 54–55
    identification of, 101–102, 110
    identification of, hiring interview ques-
        tions on, 160
    individual, 41–42

    from insider mindset, 29–31
    intentional, 26–29
    Killing Complexity tool for,
        110–116
    leaders in creating, 82–84
    meaningful work and, 57–78
    organizational, 41–42
    from the quest for more, 29, 31–32
    as sabotage, 143
    technology and, 3–4
    unintentional, 5–7
    unintentional creation of, 21–22, xv
    warning signs of, 39–41
Confucius, 1
connectivity, constant, 4
consensus-driven culture, 12
contracts, 125
coordination overload, 40
corporate culture, 135, xiv
    consensus-driven, 12
    definition of, 136
    at GE, 173
    global workforces and, 11–12
    meaningful work and, 60–61
    of simplicity, 137–174
    of simplicity *vs.* complexity, 115
    at Vancity, 179
cortisol, 70
Cosmopolitan, 124
Coty, 142
courage, 86–87, 94
creativity, 13, 67–69
crowd-sourcing, 127
Culbert, Samuel, 8
culture of busy-ness, 2. *See also* corporate
    culture
customers
    benefits of simplicity for, 82, 84
    desire of for simplicity, 73–74
    frustration among, 40
    simplicity premium and, 73
CVS, 62–63

D

Daly, Jim, 31, 74, 155

Daniels, Aubrey, 9

Day, Patrick, 64–67

decision-making

  authority for, 12

  empowering direct reports with, 123

  fear of, 33–34

  questions for simplifying in, 104

  leader decisiveness and, 93–94

  simplifying, 144–145

  too many choices and, 73–74

defensiveness, 166, 185–186

de-layering, 143–144, 173

Deloitte, 9

Deloitte Australia, 10

Destination Hotels, 166–167

Dhanoa, Seema, 182–183, 189

Direct Edge, 27

divesting, 125

Dollar Shave Club, 91

downtime, 4

Dubin, Mike, 91

Dukakis, Michael, 54

E

Einstein, Albert, 26

eliminating, 169

e-mail, 127, xii, xiii

  as complexity barrier, 131

  experiments on, 15

  guidelines for, 152

  number of unimportant, 12–13

  time spent on, 3

  unsubscribing from, 172

Emerson Electric Company, 3

emotional needs, 32–35, 187

employees

  benefits of simplicity for, 84

  desire for meaningful work, 57–78

  engagement of, 13–14, 166–167

  expectations on, 146

  onboarding, 124

  ownership of simplification by, 156–157

  passion in, 9

  performance expectations on, 15

  simplifiers, hiring, 157–164

empowerment, 144–145, 155–156, 189–190

engagement, 13–14, 69–70

  of employees in simplification, 90

  increasing employee, 166–167

  of leaders in simplification, 136–137

  performance evaluations and, 9

  personal, of leaders, 92–93, 94

  of simplifiers, 157

  in vision, 138–141

execution, 102, 175–190

  hiring interview questions on, 162

  Simplification Tactics tool for, 121–129

  at Vancity, 176–190

executive disconnect, 31–32, 81–82

expense reports, 125

F

Fai, Christina, 182–183

Fast Company, 59, 71–72

fear, 33–34, 53, 185–186

feedback, 124, 141, 167, 170

Fernandes, Agnelo, 166–167

Fey, Tina, 168

Fidelity Investment, 79–81

Financial Conduct Authority, 87

fine print, 28–29

Flash Boys (Lewis), 24, 26–27, 138

Flesch, Rudolf, 168

flexibility, 187

focus, 22, 90–92, 94, 164–166, 188

  in Kill a Stupid Rule, 117

  maintaining long-term, 189–190

  Simplicity Versus Value Matrix for, 113–115

  in simplifying, 105–106

  "two today" and, 171

forms, simplifying, 168–169
frustration, 40, 51
Future of Work study, 14
futurethink, 52

G
Gabel, 15
Gallup, 13
General Electric, 16, 173–174
General Motors, 71–72
G.I. Joe cartoon, 97
Gilfoy, Jay-Ann, 177–180, 182, 183–190
Global Brand Simplicity Index, 72,
    73, 126
globalization, 11–12
goals for simplicity, 172
Goethe, Johann Wolfgang von, 39
golden rule, 85–86
Google, 15, 72, 126, 129, 152
Google Docs, 128
Gould, Bob, 80
government, complexity in, 35–37. *See
    also* regulation
government regulation, 10–11
growth, 142–143

H
habit formation, 102, 136, 163
Hagel, John III, 9
HBO, 125, 126, 127
Hearst, Patti, 21, 22
Henderson, Fritz, 71–72
hiring questions, 157–164
Hofmann, Hans, 135
How to Invest Your Time Like Money
    (Saunders), 5
Hubbard, Elbert, 97

I
IBM, 124
IDEO, 156
IEX, 26–27, 138

IKEA, 25–26
Immelt, Jeffrey, 16, 173
improvement *vs.* simplification, 101
initiatives, 40
innovation, 67–69, xiv
    definition of, 22
    encouraging, 126
    rapid cycling method in, 65–67,
        180–190
    at Vancity, 184
insider mindset bias, 29–31
interview questions for hiring simplifiers,
    157–164
Intuit, 15
Investment Company Institute, 80
Ive, Jony, 93–94

J
Jacobs, Bert, 3, 88–89
Jacobs, John, 3, 88–89
jargon, 41, 164
J.D. Power, 74
Jobs, Steve, 93–94, 143
Johnson, Ned, 80
JPMorgan Chase, 127

K
Katsuyama, Brad, 24, 138
Kaufman, Scott Barry, 67
Khazan, Olga, 59
Kill a Stupid Rule tool, 116–121, 125
Killing Complexity tool, 110–116
kindergarten test, 123
Kucharik, Chris, 64

L
Lafley, A.G., 142–143
L.A. Story (movie), 20
"The Laundry Decree," 7–8
leaders/leadership
    benefits of simplification for, 135–137
    buy-in from, 95–96

as chief simplification officers, 135–174
courage in, 86–87, 94
decisiveness in, 93–94
executive disconnect and, 31–32,
    81–82
as facilitators of simplification, 188
focus for, 90–92
mindsets of simplicity for, 86
minimalist sensibility for, 88–89, 94
personal engagement of, 92–93, 94
results orientation of, 89–90, 94
vision of, 138–141
walking the walk by, 170–173
Lean Six Sigma, 190, xv
legalese, 28–29
Leonard, Kelly, 168
Levine, Mark, 91
Lewis, Dave, 86–87, 88
Lewis, Michael, 24, 26–27, 138
Lidl, 86–87
Life is Good, 3, 88–89
LinkedIn, 72

M
managers
    streamlining layers of, 143–144
    time spent in meetings by, 5–7
    value of staff time for, 128–129
Martin, Steve, 20
"The Massachusetts Miracle," 54–55
McKinsey Global Institute, 3, 13
meaningful work, 57–78, xiv
    creativity/innovation and, 67–69
    culture and, 60–61
    employee retention and, 13–14
    impact of simplicity on, 61–67
    regulation and, 11
meetings, xi–xv
    audits on, 165
    as complexity barrier, 131
    emotional needs and, 32–33
    length of, 16

simplifying, 126–127
time taken by, 5–7
Merck Canada, 89–90, 142, 144, 145,
    157, 164–165
metrics, 15, 146–152. *See also* perfor-
    mance evaluations
    evolving, 152
    at Vancity, 182
millennials, 59
mindsets
    insider bias, 29–31
    of meaning, xiv
    of more, 34–35
    of simplicity, 79–96, xiv
    minimal as possible, 24, 60–61
    leadership in, 88–89, 94
    questions for determining, 198–200
    simplifying based on, 104, 106
Molloy, Margaret, 79
Moore, Bob, 3
more, the quest for, 29, 31–32, 34–35
multitasking, 3–4, 70
mutual funds, 79–81

N
NASDAQ, 27
National Association of Manufacturers,
    10
Netflix, 72
New York Stock Exchange, 27
niceness, concern about, 170

O
Office of Strategic Services, 143
organizations, knowledge of, 81–82
organization *vs.* simplification, 100–101
outsourcing, 169
overload, choice, 73–74, 87

P
Parks and Recreation, 69–70
passion, 9

performance
  at GE, 173–174
  impact of complexity on, 13
  increased expectations for, 15
  leadership results orientation and,
    89–90
  simplification and, 70–74
performance evaluations, 8–9, 123–124
Perri, David, 189
P&G, 142–143
phone numbers, keeping, 72–73
Pitney Bowes, 165
PizzaExpress, 125
planning, 6–7
Poehler, Amy, 69–70
policies and procedures
  assessing complexity in, 41
  minimal, understandable, repeatable,
    accessible, 60–61
  at Vancity, 177–190
presentations, 128, 131
presenteeism, 70
prioritization, 102
  focus and, 164–166
  hiring interview questions on, 161
  Killing Complexity tool in, 110–116
  rapid cycling model and, 183–184
  Simplicity Versus Value Matrix for,
    113–115
  of time-consuming tasks, 112–113
privacy policies, 28
problem solving, 7–8
product line simplification, 142–143
Progressive Insurance, 25

Q
questions for simplifying, 103–107
quick wins, 102, 108, 147, 165, 184

R
rapid cycling, 65–67, 180–190
reactive approaches, xii–xiii

redundancies, eliminating, 143–144, 165
regulation, 10–11, 116
repeatability, 24, 60–61
  questions for determining, 201
  simplifying based on, 104, 107
reporting
  as complexity barrier, 131
  excessive complexity in, 32
  executive disconnect and, 31–32,
    81–82
  global workforces and, 11–12
  on simplification metrics, 152
  simplification of, 84–85, 127–128
  time spent on, 13
resilience, 187
resistance, 91–92
results orientation, 89–90, 94
rewards and recognition, 124, 166–167
Richer, Julian, 68
Richer Sounds, 68, 128
risk aversion, 53, 185–186
risk management, 33
Route 128 technology, 54–55

S
SAP, 14, 145
Saunders, Elizabeth Grace, 5
Saxenian, AnnaLee, 55
Scripps Health, 74–76
Seagate, 5
Second City, 168
Serious Fraud Office, 87
Siegel, Alan, 168
Siegel+Gale, 72, 73, 168–169
Siemens, 16
Silicon Valley, 55
simplicity
  benefits of, 62–67
  business results from, 70–74
  creativity/innovation and, 67–69
  definition of, 22–24–25
  driving from the top, 84

ethical imperative for, 82–85
goal statement for, 172
golden rule on, 85–86
imperative for, 14–16
maintenance of, 53–54
meaningful work and, 61–62
as mindset, 79–96, xiv
ongoing assessment of, 53–54
sweet spot in, 25–26
value placed on, 42–48
weaving into strategy, 141–143
simplicity premium, 88
Simplicity Toolkit, 97–133
    50 Questions for Simplifying, 103–107
    Kill a Stupid Rule tool, 116–121
    Killing Complexity tool, 110–116
    Simplification Tactics tool, 121–129
    Simplification Worksheet, 107–110
Simplicity Versus Value Matrix, 113–115
Simplicity Vision Statement, 139–141
simplification
    benefits of, 16
    brainstorming solutions for, 115–116
    buy-in for, 95–96
    Code of Conduct on, 152–155
    defining the challenge in, 105
    employee engagement in, 90
    ethos of, 167
    execution of, 102
    extreme criteria for, 169
    50 questions for, 103–107, 195–202
    focus in, 105–106
    as habit, 102, 136
    improvement vs., 101
    keys to success in, 187–189
    by killing stupid rules, 115–121
    leaders' engagement in, 92–93
    leaders in, 135–174
    making room for the new through, 68
    metrics for, 146–152
    misconceptions about, 99–101
    as operating principle, 101

opportunities created by, 61–62
organization vs., 100–101
perspectives represented in, 156–157
prioritization in, 102
quick wins in, 102, 108, 147, 165
rapid cycling model for, 182–190
resistance to, 91–92
at Scripps, 74–76
small things first in, 100
solution generation for, 106–107
at Staples, 16–17
steps in, 101–103
succeeding at, 175–190
teams for, 155–164, 182–190, 188
toolkit for, 97–133
vision for, 138–141
worksheet for, 107–110
simplification jams, 124
Simplification Tactics tool, 121–129
simplifiers
    identifying, 157
    training new, 169–170
social media, 172
Society for Human Resource Manage-
    ment, 9
Southwest Airlines, 71
Spencer, Jeff, 89–90, 142, 157, 164–165
Sprint, 125
Stanford Program in Law, Science &
    Technology, 28–29
Staples, 16–17
Starbuck, Bill, 6–7
State Street Global Advisors, 59
status quo thinking, 39–40
Stemberg, Tom, 16–17
Stockholm syndrome, 21–22
strategy, 187
    finding time for, xiii–xiv
    metrics related to, 147
    weaving simplicity into, 141–143
streamlining, 169
Strelsin, Steve, 135–137

stress, 69–70
structure, 179–183
systemizing, 171–172

T
Task Worksheet, 111–113
teams, for simplification, 155–164, 167,
    182–190, 188
technology, 3–4, 11, 179. *See also* e-mail
tenacity, 187
Tesco, 86–87, 88
threat management, 33
throwing things out, 172
time, 1
    boundaries in, 85–86
    inventories of, 171
    in the moment, 9–10
    spent on e-mail, 3
Timmons, Jay, 10
Tinkham, Liz, 120–121, 166
Tolstoy, Leo, 57
toxic people, deleting, 171
training new simplifiers, 169–170
transparency, 69
Twohill, Lorraine, 72
"Two Today" practice, 171

U
Uber, 22
understandable, making things, 24,
    60–61
    questions for determining, 200–201
    simplifying based on, 104, 106
University of Pennsylvania's Science of
    Imagination Project, 67

University of Virginia, 6
unnecessary tasks, xi–xv
unsubscribing, 172

V
vacation time, 124
value, 104, 106
    of complexity barriers, 132
    questions for determining, 195–198
    of simplicity for leaders, 135–137
    Simplicity Versus Value Matrix,
        113–115
    of staff time, 128–129
Vancouver City Savings Credit Union
    (Vancity), 176–190
Vanderbilt University, 10–11
Van Gorder, Chris, 75
vendor audits, 125
videoconferences, 3–4
Virgin Group, 168
vision, 138–141
Vogl, Roland, 28–29
voicemail, 127
Volkswagen, 15
VoloMetrix, 5, 84

W
Wahlenmaier, Chris, 71
Welch, Jack, 35, 63, 81
"What if I didn't?," 171
Woods, Jeff, 145
worksheets
    Simplification, 107–110
    Task, 111–113
writing, clarity in, 168–169

About the Author

Lisa Bodell believes in the power of simplification. She is the founder and CEO of futurethink, a company that uses simple techniques to help organizations embrace change and increase their capability for innovation. She brings her compelling message to more than 100,000 people a year, showing them how to eliminate mundane and unnecessary tasks from their everyday routine so that they have more time for work that matters. Bodell has transformed teams within organizations like Google, Novartis, Accenture, and more. Drawing on her practical Midwestern upbringing and entrepreneurial background, she has used the power of simplification to launch three successful businesses, write two books (*Kill the Company* and *Why Simple Wins*), travel to more than forty countries and all fifty states, and sit on boards such as Novartis's Diversity and Inclusion Board and the Global Advisory Council for the World Economic Forum.

Get to the work that matters.
Visit www.futurethink.com to get the entire
Simplification Toolkit and learn about other resources that
can help you start simplifying right now.